Seal of Philadelphia
County, 1683

Seal of Philadelphia
City, 1683

PHILADELPHIA
PORTRAIT OF AN AMERICAN CITY

PHILADELPHIA
PORTRAIT OF AN AMERICAN CITY

a Bicentennial history by

Edwin Wolf 2nd
Librarian

The Library Company of Philadelphia

developed, edited, and produced by
Walton Rawls

designed by
Martin Stephen Moskof

Stackpole Books

Library of Congress Cataloging in Publication Data

Wolf, Edwin, 1911-
    Philadelphia, portrait of an American city.

    Includes index.
    1. Philadelphia—History.   I. Title.
F158.3.W72   974.8'11   75-22182
ISBN 0-8117-1231-1

Printed by The Winchell Company, 1315 Cherry Street, Philadelphia, Pa. 19107
Published by Stackpole Books, Cameron & Kelker Streets, Harrisburg, Pa. 17105

(Frontispiece) Philadelphia, photograph by George Adams Jones

CONTENTS

PREFACE

In the preface to his five-volume *History of the United States,* James Truslow Adams wrote: "It is obviously impossible to compress our whole story into one 'history' which shall tell everything which all readers of different sections and different interests might care to know." Such a statement is appropriate to this volume.

This is not *the* history of Philadelphia, but an overview of more than three centuries of the city's growth, change, and varied life patterns. The introductory essays to the chapters tell a chronological story intended more to give the flavor of successive eras than to provide a complete chronicle. The pictures with their accompanying text are selective and impressionistic. From literally thousands of paintings, drawings, prints, and photographs a choice had to be made. From scores of books and articles kernels of information had to be gathered. Another might have made different choices. It was far more difficult for me to exclude than include from the illustrative and factual wealth available.

No one could attempt to condense Philadelphia's history without the help of the works and research of others. No footnotes and no bibliography have been appended, for this is intended to be a book for the general reader, but to a few works and a few scholars I am particularly indebted. Like a great monument of exhaustive industry, indispensable to any delver into this city's past, stand the three weighty volumes of J. Thomas Scharf and Thompson Westcott's *History of Philadelphia, 1609-1884.* What an incredible number of facts are contained in it! For a survey of the years from 1875 to 1925, and especially for the almost day-by-day chronology of that half century, George Morgan's Sesquicentennial *City of Firsts* proved invaluable. And Joseph Jackson's *Encyclopedia of Philadelphia* was rich in both basic information and fascinating trivia.

I was fortunate, as an associate editor of a still unpublished, far more complete history of Philadelphia, to have had the privilege of reading the finished chapters of that work-of-many-authors. From the sections which covered most of the nineteenth century, by Edgar P. Richardson, Nicholas B. Wainwright, Elizabeth M. Geffen, Russell F. Weigley, and Dorothy D. Gondos, I saw the whole period broadly and ably delineated. In addition, Mr. Wainwright turned over to me the draft of his work on the period 1820-1860, which he had prepared for this history, with permission to use whatever I wished. Margaret B. Tinkcom most kindly read over and edited for the better the chapter 1900-1920. To all these scholars I am most grateful.

The huge task of gathering pictures from which to make a selection was most competently carried out by Sara L. Day, Mary D. Ballen, and Carol McConochie, the last of whom made arrangements with the owners of the originals, listed the illustrations, and saw that they matched the text to which they belonged. I am most appreciative of their enthusiasm, interest, encouragement, and hard work.

The main sources for the illustrations have been the collections of the Historical Society of Pennsylvania and Library Company of Philadelphia from which approximately two-thirds of the pictures were obtained. These have been designated in the credit lines as HSP and LCP respectively. Nicholas B. Wainwright, James E. Mooney, and Peter J. Parker of the Historical Society have been most generous in allowing me and my assistants full access to their superb holdings of prints, drawings, and photographs, unquestionably the richest in existence for the iconography of Philadelphia. In providing material from the Library Company the whole staff has been most helpful, but especially Stefanie A. Munsing, its print curator. The photographs of these in-house items were carefully taken by Joseph Kelly of Photo-Illustrators, Inc., who was always most obliging and patient.

In securing the many other photographs from outside institutions we acknowledge the courtesies extended to us by Robert Looney of the Free Library of Philadelphia, Frank H. Sommer, III, Elizabeth H. Hill, and Karol A. Schiegel of the Henry Francis du Pont Winterthur Museum, Richard J. Boyle and Kathy Zickler of the Pennsylvania Academy of the Fine Arts, Francis James Dallett of the University of Pennsylvania Archives, Eugene Roberts and Francis and Joseph Gradel of the *Philadelphia Inquirer*, Emma N. Papert of the Metropolitan Museum of Art, Alfred J. Wyatt and Landis Garrett of the Philadelphia Museum of Art, Winifred E. Popp and Bruce Henry of the Huntington Library, Arno Jacobson of the Brooklyn Museum, Charles L. Seeburger of the American Swedish Historical Foundation, George E. Hess of Williams & Marcus Company, Raymond V. Shepard, Jr., of Cliveden, Whitfield J. Bell, Jr., of the American Philosophical Society, Robert D. Schwarz of Girard College, Mrs. Joseph McCosker of the Atwater Kent Museum, Roger W. Moss, Jr., of the Athenaeum of Philadelphia, Nicki Thiras of the Addison Gallery of American Art, Andover, Wilson G. Duprey of the New-York Historical Society, Georgia B. Bumgardner of the American Antiquarian Society, Denise D'Avella of Yale University Art Gallery, V. Clain-Stefanelli of the Smithsonian Institution, Edie Seila of the Moore School of Engineering, University of Pennsylvana, Monroe H. Fabian of the National Portrait Gallery, C. S. Laise of the Mariners Museum, Newport News, Warren A. McCullough of Independence National Historical Park, Arlene Cushman of Christ Church, James Kise of the Curtis Publishing Company, George R. Packard of the Evening and Sunday *Bulletin*, Philip A. Pines of the Hall of Fame of the Trotter, Goshen, Barbara L. Curtis of Haverford College Library, Herbert S. Milburn, Jr., of *National Geographic Magazine*, Harrison Mooney of the Philadelphia Electric Company, Frederic Miller of the Urban Archives Center, Temple University, Frances Israel of the *Temple Times*, R. Bruce Inverarity of the Philadelphia Maritime Museum, Al Strobl of the City Planning Commission, George Hatzfield of the Penn Mutual Life Insurance Company, D. Elizabeth Austin of the Philadelphia Redevelopment Authority, John Maass of the Office of the City Representative and other individuals whose names appear in the credit lines.

The William Penn Foundation is responsible for the concept of this volume. Walton Rawls was engaged to develop the idea and supervise the production of the book. I was asked to write the text and choose the illustrations. Martin Stephen Moskof was chosen to design the book and The Winchell Company to print it. The whole project is due to the initiative and generosity of the Foundation, which believed that Philadelphia in the Bicentennial year deserved a publication which would celebrate the city's distinguished history. I am grateful for the support which the members of the board of the Foundation gave me.

Edwin Wolf 2nd, *Library Company of Philadelphia*   *July 4, 1975*

PHILADELPHIA

PORTRAIT OF AN AMERICAN CITY

1609-1730

When Henry Hudson sailed into the mouth of Delaware Bay in 1609, he paid little heed to his discovery beyond noting that the land trended toward the northwest and that a great river emptied into a bay full of shoals. It took three-quarters of a century until this seed of discovery sprouted and blossomed, but the successful growth of Philadelphia was without parallel in British America. However, before the grant of Pennsylvania to William Penn, the flux and reflux of Dutch, Swedish, and English up and down the river had not resulted in even the beginnings of urban life. The deerskins and otter and beaver furs were never of the quality or quantity of those brought to the French at Quebec or to the Dutch at Albany. Tobacco was the main field product for export, but it was inferior to that grown in Maryland and Virginia. Although the nationals of one European country fought with those of another for control of the river over a period of half a century, the spoils were so sparse that the victor permitted the conquered to share in them.

Tolerance already had become customary by the time Quaker tolerance was formally established under Penn's charters of liberty. In spite of occasional shows of force there had been an acceptance by the Dutch of the Swedes, whose expeditions were frequently led and partially manned by Dutchmen. The cost of opposition to the colonial power dominant at a particular time was measured only by individual foolhardiness or stubbornness. It cost the Dutch three dead and ten wounded when Governor D'Hinoyossa at Fort Amstel (now Newcastle, Delaware) ineffectually tried to prevent Sir Robert Carr in 1664 from taking over the territory in the name of the Duke of York, to whom Charles II had granted it. Thereafter peace reigned on the Delaware. Indians in small numbers wandered in and out of the region; Swedish and Dutch settlers remained on their riverside farms; English Quakers established themselves in West New Jersey in 1677, and a few set themselves up on the opposite shore. The most diverse population of any American colony was ready to welcome the laying-out of the city of Philadelphia.

William Penn, seeking his utopia, allowed for the diversity and added to it by selling the tract which became Germantown to Francis Daniel Pastorius and his associates. Unfortunately for Penn's peace of mind, he was not only a utopian governor but also a land speculator who expected a return on his investment. After he received the

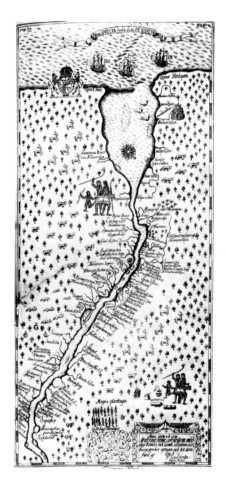

(Facing) *The Swedes and the Indians in New Sweden,* frontispiece engraving from Tomas Campanius Holm, *Kort Beskrifning om Provincien Nya Swerige uti America,* 1702 (HSP)
(Above) Map of New Sweden, engraving from Tomas Campanius Holm, *Kort Beskrifning om Provincien Nya Swerige uti America,* 1702 (HSP)

13

(Above) *The Landing of William Penn from the "Welcome" at Upland*, (detail) etching by Arnold Anderson (HSP)

charter for Pennsylvania from Charles II in March, 1681, in recompense for a loan made to the monarch by his father Admiral Sir William Penn, he set about establishing a government and selling the land. Spelling out a frame of government which was liberal for its day and a code of laws noteworthy for its guarantee of open courts, jury trials, and prompt justice, and for its declaration of religious freedom, Penn commissioned his cousin William Markham to go over and administer the province in his name.

Meanwhile he was offering his land for sale. The standard package included a tract of 5,000 acres somewhere in Pennsylvania, a building lot in the planned city, and a dividend of eighty acres in the so-called liberty lands north and west of the city limits. Amazingly enough, he convinced 750 purchasers to invest in Pennsylvania real estate, chiefly merchants, shopkeepers, and skilled craftsmen from London, Bristol, Dublin, and elsewhere, most of them Quakers. Only about half of the "first purchasers" came to America, but literally thousands of other settlers were attracted by Penn's promotional material to try their luck in what he pictured as the American land of opportunity—not too hot, not too cold, peaceful, fertile, tolerant, and under the governance of a generous and philosophical proprietor. Within the year 1682 twenty-three ships brought immigrants to Pennsylvania.

Faced with a vast unsurveyed area and the problems of divided interests and what turned out to be the unequal value of equal-size lots and tracts, Penn's neat pattern of land distribution did in some measure break down. His original intention had been to lay out the city which would be the capital and kernel of the province at Upland (now Chester). Thomas Holme, the surveyor-general, and Penn's other land commissioners discovered that too many Swedes held title to too much land there to make quick occupation feasible. Consequently, they decided to site Philadelphia—the City of Brotherly Love—as Penn named it, farther up the Delaware, north of the confluence of the Schuylkill, where the brothers Svenson were willing to sell. By the time Penn debarked from the *Welcome* at Newcastle on October 27, 1682, some lots had been laid out and some surveys recorded. He quickly by purchase extended Philadelphia west to the Schuylkill, making the city a 1,200-acre rectangle from river to river.

A remarkable economic growth ensued. Rich arable land surrounded Philadelphia in every direction, and as the fields were cleared, plowed, and harvested a surplus of farm goods was brought to town for export. In spite of the port's situation far up-river, mercantile trade became the mainstay of the city's economy and remained such for almost a century and a half. Flour, meat, and barrel staves were shipped to Quaker connections in the West Indies where sugar was bought for sale in England, the proceeds of which were put out for manufactured goods to be imported into the colony. The Free Society of Traders, over two hundred investors who put up £12,500, was incorporated by Penn in 1682, and hoped to monopolize this trade. The company received a 20,000-acre tract in what became Frankford and a hundred-acre strip inside the city running west uphill from the river between Spruce and Pine streets. There on a hill stood the Society's trading house. Its ambitious plans were frustrated by the individualistic merchants who controlled the government of the province, and the Free Society was forced out of business in 1686.

As the supply of money slowly grew through trade, the demand increased for artisans: coopers, tinkers, shoemakers, weavers, brewers, masons, wheelwrights, tailors, joiners, chandlers, millers, and even silversmiths. It was this combination of businessmen willing to gamble in sea-borne adventures and capable craftsmen who found a steady market for the work of their hands that was responsible for Philadelphia's expansion. The growth in trade was slow at first, but after 1720 it accelerated. New York was overtaken in the 1750s and Boston was passed before the Revolution. By the end of the seventeenth century there were about 2,200 persons living in some four hundred houses within the city, and population increased by fifty percent or more each decade in the early eighteenth century.

The success of Philadelphia as an entrepot created many of the problems with which Penn and his heirs had to struggle. The absentee governor and landlord spent less than two years in Pennsylvania on his first visit. He left behind him controversy between "first purchasers" and others over desirable city lots and a party of Quaker merchants whose interests increasingly diverged from those of the proprietor. The free air of America fostered a desire for less government from afar and more local power. It was during Penn's brief second and last visit to Philadelphia that, on October 25, 1701, he elevated the small town of brick houses by charter into a city. Men

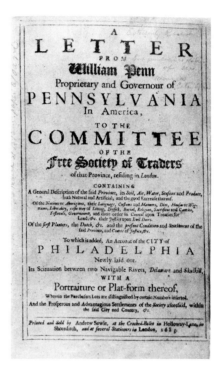

(Above) Title-page of *A Letter from William Penn to the Committee of the Free Society of Traders,* 1683 (HSP)

friendly to him were made the first chief officers—Edward Shippen mayor, Thomas Story recorder, and Thomas Farmer sheriff. Aldermen and common councilmen were, after the proprietor's initial appointments, empowered to choose their own successors and to elect the mayor. There were few municipal powers, and in the early days the mayor-designate not infrequently paid a penalty rather than serve. The city officials were also, as in England, the judges of the lower courts. Freemen were those worth fifty pounds in land or other assets. But most of the political activity was provincial in scope. The city officials were essentially stewards, supervising the wharves, regulating the markets, paving the streets, and keeping law and order.

There was a great deal of squabbling in the City of Brotherly Love. George Keith, the first master of the Quaker school established in 1689 (now William Penn Charter School), became a theological thorn in the side of the established hierarchy of the Yearly Meeting. He sought for the Friends more order, greater formality, and less active participation in government. A split developed with political overtones which set the more successful Quakers, led by the attorney-general Thomas Lloyd, against those of lesser stature. Keith was harassed; he went back to England and in 1700 joined the Church of England; shortly thereafter he returned to America, a violent anti-Quaker and an Anglican missionary.

The sharpest animosities seem to have been internecine. It was Quaker against Quaker in the struggle which continued after Penn's departure in 1701. David Lloyd, the ablest lawyer in the city and the most effective—and abrasive—spokesman for the Assembly, sought more liberal provisions in the charters and clarification of some of its terms. Penn had come to the point where he considered any criticism of his actions ingratitude and was adamant in refusing to make any alterations. James Logan, secretary of the Governor's Council, opposed Lloyd vigorously and remained for decades the chief supporter and agent of Penn, his widow, and his heirs. By 1710 the political situation had become stabilized with the conservative Quaker worthies well in charge of the city and province.

A decade of quiet prosperity ended in 1722 with the bursting of the South Sea Bubble in England and the subsequent economic panic. At about the same time Sir William Keith, the governor who had for five years successfully balanced the interests of all factions in Penn-

(Facing) Wampum Belt given by the Indians to William Penn (HSP)
(Overleaf) *Penn's Treaty with the Indians* (detail) painting by Benjamin West (Pennsylvania Academy of the Fine Arts)

sylvania, threw in his lot with the radicals. Among several issues involved, the principal one was the issuance of paper currency favored by those who owed money and paid rent. Once more political war broke out. In the city during the 1726 elections there was rioting at the polls, and the popular party celebrated its victory by burning the pillory and stocks. The young Boston-born printer Benjamin Franklin and his Junto associates, mostly tradesmen or mechanics, were opprobriously called "leather aprons." It is significant that Franklin's first political pamphlet, written in 1729, was in favor of more paper money. The older conservatives and supporters of the proprietors such as James Logan and Isaac Norris saw the new era as the triumph of the mob and Governor Keith as its demagogic leader.

The new blood included many non-Quakers among whom the most influential were the Anglicans. From a small congregation set up at the end of the seventeenth century, they grew in numbers and importance. The governors who were commissioned by the Penns and Thomas Penn himself were members of the Church of England and subtly their prestige attracted others to their communion. Closer to the pulse of the common people were the Presbyterians. Francis Makemie came to Philadelphia in 1692 and organized a mixed group of English, Welsh, Scots, and French Presbyterians into a congregation. In 1704-5 they built a church, known as the Buttonwood Church, in a fine grove of sycamores on High Street west of Second. Even earlier, in 1688, a Baptist church had been formed on Pennypack Creek. When the Keithian schism took place, some of the dissidents left the Meeting and became Baptists. Many of them were Welsh, and Abel Morgan, their minister from 1711 to 1722, wrote and had printed in Philadelphia a concordance of the Bible in Welsh. A confusion of German sects, including Dunkers and Mennonites, settled in and around Germantown. Penn's belief in the importance of religious freedom even permitted Catholics, who were looked upon most suspiciously after the accession of William and Mary in 1688, to worship openly. Mass was certainly celebrated in the city as early as 1708. However, no priest took up residence until Father Joseph Greaton. He secured the land on which St. Joseph's was to be built in 1729 and began erecting the church two years later. In its diversity lay Philadelphia's strength.

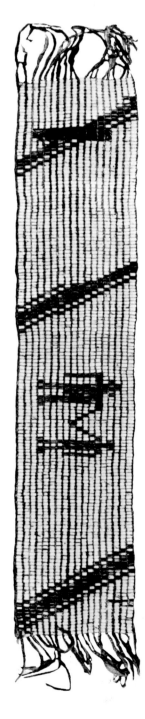

Of all the areas of early European contact with the Indians, Pennsylvania was the most sparsely inhabited by natives. When the Swedes first came with their trade goods and built rude shelters of branches and reeds as the Finns had long done at home, they found only a loose collection of small tribes, the most important being the Lenni Lenapes or Delawares. They lived in scattered villages, hunting, fishing, and raising some crops, and one or two of these villages may have been within the present limits of Philadelphia. Although Indians fought Indians for hunting grounds in the back country, there was no sustained warfare against the European traders. But, as elsewhere on the continent, smallpox and probably measles decimated the Indians who had no resistance to the imported diseases. By the time of Penn's arrival in 1682 the Delawares numbered no more than about four thousand, most of them living north of the newly established city. They were essentially a gentle people; the Iroquois scornfully called them "women." Happily, the Quakers came in peace. Philadelphia was the only town of early settlement where fortifications against the Indians were never constructed.

(Above) *Delaware Indian Family*, engraving from Tomas Campanius Holm, *Kort Beskrifning om Provincien Nya Swerige uti America*, 1702 (LCP)
(Below) Deeds from Queen Christina of Sweden to Sven Schute and Hans Amundsson Besh for Land in Pennsylvania, August 20, 1653 (HSP)

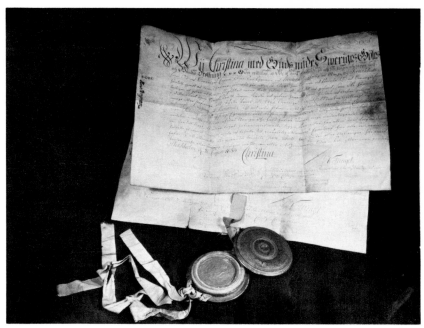

Furs not a settled colony were the goal of the Europeans who first came to the South River, as the Dutch in New Amsterdam called it. Although a Swedish expedition under Pieter Minuet built a fort at Christina (now Wilmington) as early as 1638, the river remained under the control of the Dutch ensconced further north at Fort Nassau. Because of European alliances, the presence of the Swedes was tolerated, but when some English in 1641 built a trading post near present-day Salem, New Jersey, the Dutch expelled them. The establishment of a formal Swedish government came in 1643 with the arrival of Johan Bjornsson Printz, a huge, coarse, impulsive soldier who had been commissioned governor. He promptly built forts at commanding sites along the river which cut off the Dutch from the Indian fur trade. The next move in this game of chess was that of Pieter Stuyvesant, the peg-legged governor of New Amsterdam. He built a stronghold, Fort Casimir (now Newcastle), below Christina. The game was engaged. Printz's successor, Johan Claudius Risingh, took Casimir. Stuyvesant in 1654 took Christina. The colony of New Sweden thereby came to an end, but the Swedes who had settled along the river remained peacefully under the succeeding Dutch and English governments.

(Above) *A Chief of the Lenni Lenapes,* water-color sketch by a member of the Watson family, from the manuscript of John Fanning Watson's *Annals of Philadelphia* (LCP)
(Below) Iron Chest said to have come with the Sinnickson Family to America in 1638 (American Swedish Historical Foundation)

By the banks of the Delaware three-quarters of a mile below Dock Creek an Indian village called Wicaco once stood. There Swedes in 1669 built a log blockhouse as protection for a number of their countrymen who had settled on that land, which had been first patented by Queen Christina to Sven Schute as early as 1653 and was confirmed by the Dutch governor Alexander D'Hinoyossa in 1664 to Schute's heirs the Svensons. Made of sections of tree trunks notched at the end and cross-laid, the log cabin was a common kind of Finnish and Swedish structure, and so the earliest buildings in what is now Philadelphia were thus constructed. When the Swedish settlers were ordered to build a church in 1675, they modified the log fort. Poor they were at first, but as Penn's town flourished so did its pre-Penn inhabitants. It was decided that a more suitable place of worship should be built, and Gloria Dei, the present Old Swedes' Church, was dedicated in 1700.

(Above) *First Swedes' Church and House of Sven Svenson*, pen-and-ink drawing by John Fanning Watson, from the manuscript of his *Annals of Philadelphia* (HSP)
(Below) Gloria Dei, Old Swedes' Church, photograph by Richards & Betts, 1854 (LCP)

William Penn, the founder of Philadelphia, was a very complicated person. His father was a buccaneer admiral who gained his first successes during Cromwell's Commonwealth and so managed his affairs that he was knighted by Charles II at the Restoration. The earliest portrait of young Penn shows him in armor. In 1667 he chose the rebellious and difficult life of a dissenter; he became a Quaker. Most of his writings and most of his theoretical consideration of government, including his liberal-for-the-time charters and laws, were completed before he set foot in his new-founded city. Thereafter, hard financial problems and the attitudes of Philadelphia's influential citizens antagonistic to proprietary control corroded Penn's creativity and his patience. Psychically he disintegrated; it was impossible to be a governor, a landlord, and an idealist.

(Above) William Penn's Desk (LCP)
(Below) *William Penn*, engraving by John Hall after drawing by Du Simitière from a bust by Sylvanus Bevan (HSP)

The South East Prospect of the City of Philadelphia, painting by Peter Cooper, ca. 1720. (detail) (LCP)

The band of settlement that Penn envisaged across the Delaware–Schuylkill peninsula cut through forest land which had to be cleared before streets could be laid out and houses built. The first inhabitants of Philadelphia, strictly defined, sheltered themselves in caves hollowed out of the steep bank along the Delaware. Soon, however, an ample supply of brick-clay was discovered in the southwest quadrant of the planned city. Kilns were built, and the red-brick city began to rise. Among the larger and finer houses constructed before the turn of the century were those of Edward Shippen and Samuel Carpenter, both on South Second Street. Shippen, a merchant originally from Boston, was distinguished for three great things: the biggest person, the biggest house, and the biggest coach in town. James Logan wrote to Penn that when Shippen married for the third time his young wife's apron strings were already high. Penn stayed in his house briefly late in 1699, and later governors occupied it as their residence. Carpenter, one of Philadelphia's richest and most influential citizens until his business failure, came to the city from Barbados. Just as his distinctive slate-roof, H-type house was finished in January, 1700, Penn took it over for the duration of his stay. William Trent, the founder of Trenton, bought it in 1703 and sold it to the elder Isaac Norris six years later.

(Above) *Edward Shippen's House on Second Street,* watercolor by W. L. Breton (HSP)
(Below) *The Slate-Roof House on Second Street,* watercolor by W. L. Breton (HSP)

When Penn first came up the river in the fall of 1682 to inspect the site of his capital city, he landed at the Dock, a tidewater basin at the foot of Spruce Street into which ran a south-easterly flowing creek. A drawbridge crossed the narrow opening at its Delaware mouth through which small vessels could enter the snug harbor. At the very beginning of Philadelphia's existence the Dock seemed destined to be the city's center, but when the steep banks to the north were cut down and wharves built it lost its impor-tance. At Penn's arrival the Blue Anchor on the Dock, the town's first tavern, was nearing completion. With-out other easy means of spreading the news, a focal point was needed for communication; the inn or tavern became that point. So important was it in the life of the city that in 1701 Penn ordained that the landing places at the Blue Anchor and the Penny-Pot House at Front and Vine streets should be available for common use. In a grove of the virgin walnut forest on the north side of Chestnut Street between Fifth and Sixth another inn was established just before the end of the century which became busier after the State House was built across the street. It was a bit to the north at the Pewter Platter Tavern that William Penn, Jr., roistered with his drinking companions to such scandal that the local authorities sent him home— abruptly. Much of the official and unofficial life of the city took place in taverns.

(Above) *The Blue Anchor Tavern and the Dock*, photogravure after Frank H. Taylor (LCP) (Below) *State House Inn*, wash drawing by Edward W. Mumford (LCP)

Every great myth is built upon a foundation of truth. Penn dealt fairly, according to his lights, and peaceably with the Indians; he purchased land instead of taking it by force. His colony became a haven for the remnants of tribes virtually annihilated by the unremitting savagery of the English on the coastal plains to the north and south, for word reached along the forest paths that the Quakers were men of peace. There are records of treaties between Penn and many Indian sachems. As he wrote to the Free Society of Traders in the summer of 1683: "I have had occasion to be in council with them upon treaties for land and to adjust terms of trade." However, it is doubtful that Penn actually met with Chief Tamanend (or Tammany) and his Lenni Lenapes, together with some Susquehannocks, under an elm tree at Shackamaxon early in November, 1682. Nevertheless, the legend of the treaty there was early imbedded in Philadelphia history. Benjamin West painted that legend, but Penn was an athletic thirty-eight-year-old and not a paunchy old man dressed in the clothes worn two generations after the event was supposed to have taken place. Such a meeting somewhere and sometime may have taken place, but West's picture transcends a need for documentation. As the primitive Quaker artist Edward Hicks transmuted Penn's treaty, it has become a symbol of peace.

Penn's Treaty with the Indians, painting by Edward Hicks (Mr. and Mrs. Meyer P. Potamkin)

From the first settlement Quaker Meetings sprang up spontaneously: one at Shackamaxon in Thomas Fairman's house; one in 1684 on the central square where the Quarterly Meeting expected the city would focus; another, the Bank Meeting, facing the river; and several in the outlying counties. It was soon obvious that the center of the town's activity would be elsewhere. In 1695 the Great Meeting House, fifty feet square, was erected at the corner of Second and High (Market) streets. Its centrality was confirmed about 1709 when the handsome, steepled Town Hall and Court House was built as the head of the High Street market whose sheds extended westward. Up the balustrade to the second floor the enfranchised freemen of the county marched to cast their votes. There all the courts in the colony held sessions; and there both the city and provincial governments conducted their affairs. On market days the weavers of Germantown brought in their stockings and cloth. The Conestoga or covered wagon, later to become the symbol of the American West, was a common sight. James Logan had adapted the vehicle, used for army supply trains in Europe, to take Indian trade goods up to the Conestoga country and to bring back furs. It became a standard carrier along the rutted inland trails.

(Above) *Fairman's Mansion & Treaty Tree,* engraving by Serz after Brittan (LCP)
(Below) *The Old Courthouse,* painting by Russell Smith (HSP)
(Facing, above) The First Issue of the *American Weekly Mercury,* December 22, 1719 (LCP)
(Facing, below) Title-page of Samuel Atkins, *Kalendarium Pennsilvaniense,* 1686 (HSP)

Scratch a Quaker and find a pamphleteer. From the time George Fox formed the Society of Friends, tracts explanatory, exhortatory, accusatory, and defensive by its members poured from the presses. Penn himself, no mean writer of strong prose, spoke glowingly in pamphlets of the seductive advantages of the land he had for sale. Unlike other English settlements, Pennsylvania deemed a printing press almost immediately essential. William Bradford, trained by the Quakers' favored London printer Andrew Soule, whose daughter he married, was sent over to Philadelphia in 1685. His first piece of work, the earliest printing in the Middle Colonies, was an almanac. Slim polemical pamphlets and official publications soon followed. However, Bradford printed not only by order of the Meeting, but espoused the cause and published the inflammatory tracts of the schismatic George Keith. Tried by Quaker magistrates—doing unto others as had been done unto them—the printer in 1693 was forced from the province. He moved to New York, but his printing shop returned to Philadelphia in 1718 under the guidance of his son Andrew, who the following year began the city's first newspaper, the American Weekly Mercury.

There was little doctrinal difference between the Quakerism of George Fox and William Penn and the tenets of the Dutch and German Mennonites whom they visited and preached to in 1677. The German sects inclined more to mysticism, but they found a common bond with the Friends in the persecution they also suffered at the hands of an orthodox national church. Penn's colony offered them a haven. The first such group to sail to America came under the auspices of the Frankfurt Land Company which had bought a large tract from Penn. As agent for the company Francis Daniel Pastorius settled the German and Dutch Mennonite colonists in Germantown in 1683, and became its most influential citizen. He was more learned than any other inhabitant of Pennsylvania, owned a substantial library, wrote voluminous works which he never had printed, and taught both in the village German school and in the Friends' School in Philadelphia. In 1688 Pastorius and other Mennonites sent the Friends' Meeting a protest against Negro slavery: "Here is liberty of Conscience wch is right and reasonable; here ought to be likewise liberty of y^{e} body." Not long afterwards a band of German mystics emigrated under the leadership of Johann Kelpius and settled near Germantown in caves along the Wissahickon.

The first Anglican church in Philadelphia was built in 1695 for a congregation of about five hundred persons. That structure was several times enlarged until 1727 when work was begun on Christ Church as it now stands on the same site. A minister was sent by Dr. Thomas Bray, the Bishop of London's energetic emissary in America. And Bray in 1698, to give an intellectual underpinning to the church, sent over a substantial library, the first in the city. William III gave funds to the support of Christ Church; Queen Anne gave it sacramental silver. Soon it numbered among its parishioners some of the wealthiest and most influential citizens.

Most luxury items had to be imported from England. But a number of silversmiths set up in business, among them Johannes de Nys, William Vilant, and Francis Richardson, the first of a famous family of craftsmen. In the absence of banks, it was common practice to turn silver coins into plate in good times and to sell the silver by weight when adversity struck. Sign painters plied their trade; one such, Peter Cooper, limned the first view of the city. However, the earliest artist in a real sense to establish himself in Philadelphia was the Swede Gustavus Hesselius, who came in 1711 and not only painted portraits but also built organs. One of the pioneer clockmakers of the area was Christopher Saur, who constructed clocks in Germantown about 1730 before he set up his printing establishment. As the city expanded, the local production of fine artifacts expanded with it.

(Facing, above) *Johann Kelpius,* watercolor by Christopher Witt, ca. 1705 (HSP)
(Facing, below) Silver sent by Queen Anne to Christ Church (Christ Church)
(Above) Face of Clock made by Christopher Saur (LCP)
(Below) *Tishcohan,* painting by Gustavus Hesselius, 1735 (HSP)
(Right) Silver Tankard made for George and Mary Emlen by Johannes de Nys, 1717 (HSP)

It did not take long before the more successful merchants, modeling their style on that of an English country squire, built themselves country houses on the hills and along the rivers beyond the bounds of the city proper. One of the first was Penn's own estate at Pennsbury on the Delaware above Bristol. Fruit orchards, herb and vegetable gardens, hay fields, and pens and grazing grounds for domestic animals were the essentials. Few colonials had leisure until midcentury for the culture of ornamental shrubs and flowers. The post-and-rail and picket fences were American expedients; there had not been time, and later no inclination, to grow the hedgerows which enclosed English fields. An elegant and typical mansion was Isaac Norris' Fairhill, neatly symmetrical with its two dependencies, erected in 1712, but unfortunately burned by the British in 1777.

Flowing water, of which there was a sufficiency in the country surrounding Penn's "Greene Country Towne," kept mill wheels moving. One of the most unusual was the pioneer papermill, the first in America, of Willem Rittinghuysen (later Rittenhouse) established on a branch of the Wissahickon in 1690. Grist mills for grinding flour sprang up along the Germantown watershed and on Tacony and Darby creeks. In 1720 flour cost nine shillings and sixpence in Philadelphia as compared to as much as fifteen shillings in New York and twenty-eight shillings in Boston. Farther away from town, the Durham Iron Furnace, which began production in 1729, was owned by a Who's Who of prominent Philadelphians, among them Anthony Morris, James Logan, Clement Plumsted, William Allen, Andrew Bradford, Joseph Turner, Griffith Owen, and Samuel Powel. Shipyards began work as early as 1683 on the Delaware from High (Market) Street to Vine; shipbuilding remained for centuries a major Philadelphia industry. With Wilcox's ropewalk, Morris' brewhouse, a glass factory in Kensington, and weavers in Germantown the diversity of the county's industry was set.

Some visitors objected to the precise rectangularity of Philadelphia's streets; nonetheless, hundreds of American cities and towns across the country adopted the gridiron pattern. Whatever the inspiration of Penn's plan—various authors have suggested several models— it works. The streets still exist almost as he had them laid out, and many of them bear their original names: "High, Mulberry, Sassafras, Vine,/Chestnut, Walnut, Spruce, and Pine." There are still four open-spaced squares; City Hall rises on the center square. The town, however, did not grow quite as Penn had intended. It took many years for houses and stores to march west along High (now Market) Street, and residences never, as anticipated, rubbed shoulders along the Schuylkill. Activity, building, and growth moved north and south along the Delaware. Thomas Holme's map, which was used to illustrate Penn's land-sale pamphlets, indicated the lots as they were to be allocated to original purchasers and others, but quickly the most valuable land was subdivided and lesser streets and alleys were cut through. The hoped-for greenery disappeared. The high banks along the river Penn had retained for himself, but gradually he sold them off to the wealthier merchants who leveled them to accommodate shipping. The port of Philadelphia became its heart.

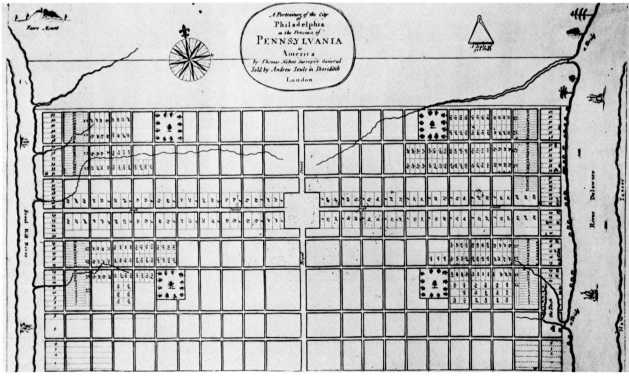

1730-1765

At midcentury the artist George Heap saw a city as he looked across the Delaware from the Jersey shore. Wharves stretched inviting fingers out into the ship-busy harbor. Sturdy warehouses presented a mercantile front beyond and above which rose the steeples of churches and public buildings. Deep-toned bells rang out across the water to welcome prizes taken by the city's privateers as well as visiting dignitaries, to celebrate victories and other special occasions, and to call up the fire companies. Thanks to the products of the fertile land surrounding Philadelphia, it enjoyed a lucrative trade across the Atlantic, down to the West Indies, and up and down the coast. Flour, wheat, bread, pork, and barrel staves were the main exports, but a little walnut wood, a few barrels of whiskey, and even several casks of snakeroot and ginseng formed part of the varied cargoes which were shipped out of the port. Far more was imported, notably manufactured hardware and soft goods from the British Isles, as well as sugar and molasses from the West Indies, and wine, oranges, and lemons from the Canary Islands, the Iberian peninsula, and France.

In spite of the disruption of normal commerce caused by wars between England on the one hand and France and Spain on the other from 1739 to 1748 and from 1754 to 1763, Philadelphia grew in size, population, and wealth at a faster rate than any other city in the British empire. The value of imports from Great Britain rose from £8,592 in 1730 to £238,637 in 1749 after the treaty of Aix-la-Chapelle ended King George's War, and jumped sensationally to £707,998 in 1760 after the capture of Quebec. The sudden glut of goods in the warehouses of Philadelphia's merchants brought on a mercantile depression which lasted almost to the eve of the Revolution. An increase in the number of poor necessitated a public subscription to supplement governmental funds and the erection of a new almshouse.

While trade fluctuated, local tradesmen and artisans found an increasing market. Small industries sprang up whose need for skilled and unskilled labor was a magnet which drew thousands of immigrants from Ireland and Germany and for a while encouraged the slave trade. In 1749 alone twenty-two ships brought 7,000 Germans into the port. Ship captains became rich selling the services of indentured servants. Self-help societies came into being to protect the welfare of fellow immigrants: the St. Andrew's Society for Scots, the

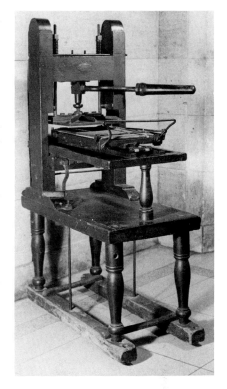

(Facing) *Christ Church*, painting by William Strickland (HSP)
(Above) Printing Press of Franklin's time (Williams & Marcus Company, on indefinite loan to the Franklin Institute)
(Overleaf) *An East Prospect of the City of Philadelphia*, detail of engraving after George Heap and Nicholas Scull, 1754 (HSP)

To the Honourable Thomas Penn and Richard Penn, true
and Counties of NEWCASTLE, KENT *and* SUSSEX *on* DELAWARE,

German Society, a group of Irish which became the Friendly Sons of St. Patrick, the Society of the Sons of St. George for Englishmen, and the St. David's Society for Welshmen. There were so many Germans in and around Philadelphia that German newspapers were established, several successful German printing shops were set up, and many important news broadsides and political pamphlets were issued in that language.

There seemed to be a continuing demand for shoemakers and tailors, for coopers and tinsmiths, for maltsters and bakers, but it was the building trade which enjoyed the greatest boom. Private houses, country mansions, and public buildings were begun and finished to create an urban and suburban complex of considerable scope for a provincial city. Elegant Christ Church, an expression of the richest and most socially elevated personages in town, begun in 1729, was completed in 1754 when its tuneful bells were installed in the steeple, the highest on the skyline. The old Town Hall at the foot of the market facing Second Street, which also housed the courts and provincial offices, could no longer provide adequate space for its manifold use. The construction of the new State House, on Chestnut Street between Fifth and Sixth—almost at the westernmost apex of the city's built-up sprawl—was begun in 1732.

A new market on Second Street between Pine and Cedar (South) was opened in 1745, and in 1759 the High Street market, as the increased population's demand for food grew proportionately, was extended from Front to Third Street. And as the Irish Catholic community grew, Father Robert Harding tore down an old church and built the larger St. Joseph's on Willing's Alley. During the French and Indian War the need to house Colonel Henry Bouquet's Royal American Regiment created dissension when the Assembly ordered them quartered in the local inns. As a result army barracks were built in the Northern Liberties. Samuel Rhoads, to whom Franklin entrusted the building of his house in Franklin Court, elsewhere in the city was putting up houses as a developer. Carpenter, architect, and builder, he was the first to build speculatively for sale on more than a limited scale.

By the time the city's bells rang out for the Peace of Paris in 1763 there were more than a hundred taverns in Philadelphia to lodge travelers and provide food and drink for all. Some were tiny holes-in-

(Above) *The British Barracks*, wash drawing by Edward W. Mumford (LCP)

the-wall in Southwark where sailors could get noggins of rum. Others, chiefly along High Street, were places of important, if unofficial, assembly, like John Biddle's Indian King where the food was good, and William Bradford's London Coffee-House which became an informal commercial exchange and political rendezvous. Regular communication with New York from some inns was established by wagon and boat, and after Franklin became deputy postmaster-general in 1753 a mail network was organized which linked all the colonies.

For many years Philadelphia was more closely tied to England than to New England or the South. The first Philadelphian to gain an international reputation, James Logan, had connections in New York but none elsewhere in the colonies. As a weighty member of the governor's council, the Penn family's personal agent, negotiator with the Indians whom he entertained at his Germantown estate, chief justice of the supreme court, and for a year and a half in 1736-37 acting governor of the province, the Quaker merchant was until the late 1740s the most important, if controversial, individual in town. Learned letters and published essays on mathematics, the germination of corn, and optics made him known to such European cognoscenti as the astronomer Halley, the great Swedish naturalist Linnaeus, the Hamburg polymath Fabricius, and the amateur scientist and friend of many Americans Peter Collinson. Logan formed the finest library in British America and left it to the public. Through his backing and with his encouragement Thomas Godfrey invented an improved mariner's quadrant and won grudging recognition from the Royal Society; John Bartram was taught botanical taxonomy and introduced to patrons abroad; and Benjamin Franklin was lauded and supported in his political and scientific endeavors.

The growing city found a catalyst in Benjamin Franklin, the hardworking tradesman, shrewd politician, effective propagandist, and wide-ranging experimentalist, who took the lead in many ventures. Within comparatively few years he founded an impressive number of Philadelphia institutions: the Library Company, the Union Fire Company, the American Philosophical Society, the Academy and College, the Pennsylvania Hospital, and the Contributionship for the Insurance of Houses from Loss by Fire. If the litany seems long, it merely underlines the Franklinian influence on the development of the city. It was, however, his electrical experiments—the recognition

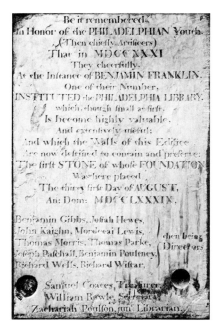

(Above) *Stenton, the Country Home of James Logan,* wood engraving by Walter M. Aikman (HSP)
(Below) The Cornerstone of Library Hall, 1789 (LCP)

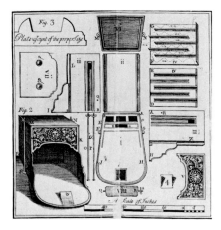

of the positive and negative flow of electricity, more significantly than his flying a kite in a thunderstorm—which made him internationally famous. His improved stove, too, was widely hailed. Several universities at home and abroad honored him with the title of "Doctor," and as Dr. Franklin he became the most famous of all Philadelphians.

It was really all part of an urban maturing process. As the century passed the halfway mark, paving was extended further out from a central hub; the city provided whale-oil street lamps; a night-watch paid for by taxes was established; and several fire companies offered improved protection. Social and sporting clubs came into being, such as the City Assembly for dancers and the Colony in Schuylkill for fishermen. Horse races were held on a course around Centre Square. Skating was a favorite winter recreation. William Allen, James Hamilton, Isaac Norris, Benjamin Chew, and other men of wealth owned coaches, and well-made, weighty silver tankards and coffee pots and cans graced their cupboards as evidences of their financial status. There was even a literary salon, the blue-stocking Elizabeth Graeme surrounding herself with a coterie of young writers such as the versatile Francis Hopkinson, Thomas Godfrey whose play, *The Prince of Parthia,* was the first by an American author to be staged, the poet Nathaniel Evans, and the genteel preacher Jacob Duché.

While politics were principally at the provincial level, the sharpening of the division between contesting interests was played out in and affected the city. The Assembly, controlled by Quakers, was frequently hostile to the proprietary governors and their supporters. The election in October, 1742, was hotly contested and resulted in violence. Voters had to climb the narrow Town Hall steps to cast their ballots, hence control of the steps was to a certain extent control of the votes. The Quakers stationed themselves there; a mob of sailors recruited by the opposition tried to take over; a melee ensued. Aided by German allies, the Quaker partisans counterattacked and drove the sailors back to their ships. Some of the most prominent citizens of Philadelphia were actively embroiled in the affair. Unfortunately, the hiring of mobs for partisan purposes became more frequent, and may have created a precedent for the stormy public protests at the time of the Stamp Act and thereafter.

The absolute necessity of protecting the frontier during the French and Indian War, the presence of soldiery in the city after the construction of the barracks, and the appeal of Anglican "fancy" to the sons and grandsons of members of the Society of Friends did much to diminish the pacifistic and political influence of the Quakers. Idealism moved them to form the Friendly Association to make peace with the Indians and to join with antiproprietary forces to undercut and oppose the interests of the governor and his council. But after the Peace of Paris in 1763, gradually the Anglican and Presbyterian elements of the city took over most of the political offices. The scions of Quaker families who joined the Church of England from Thomas and John Penn to Samuel Powel and John Cadwalader merged into the élite which provided both reactionary and radical leadership on the eve of the Revolution.

(Above) *Francis Hopkinson and Elizabeth Graeme*, pencil sketch by Benjamin West, ca. 1758 (HSP)

In 1729 Benjamin Franklin opened the New Printing Office on High Street near the market. Almost from the beginning the business flourished. Legal forms, well printed and accurately phrased, were perennial bread-and-butter items for sale. Franklin gained colony-wide influence after he took over The Pennsylvania Gazette, enlivened it, and increased its circulation. Even more financially rewarding was the contract for the official printing of the province, including its paper money which Franklin ingeniously protected against counterfeiting by also printing on it the impression of a singular tree leaf. But his greatest success and lasting reputation came from the series of Poor Richard Almanacks. Spiced with wit and maxims of good common sense, they made his name—or, rather, pseudonym—a household word. A long, distinguished and varied career behind him, Franklin began his will: "I, Benjamin Franklin, Printer."

(Facing) Benjamin Franklin Drawing Electricity from the Sky, painting by Benjamin West (Philadelphia Museum of Art: The Mr. and Mrs. Wharton Sinkler Collection)
(Above) The First Issue of *The Pennsylvania Gazette* Published and Printed by Franklin, October 2, 1729 (LCP)
(Below) Title-page of the First *Poor Richard Almanac* for 1733 (HSP)

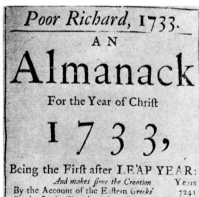

Poor Richard, 1733.

AN

Almanack

For the Year of Christ

1733,

Being the First after LEAP YEAR:

And makes since the Creation Years
By the Account of the Eastern Greeks   7241
By the Latin Church, when ☉ ent. ♈   6932
By the Computation of W.W.   5742
By the Roman Chronology   5682
By the Jewish Rabbies   5494

Wherein is contained

The Lunations, Eclipses, Judgment of the Weather, Spring Tides, Planets Motions & mutual Aspects, Sun and Moon's Rising and Setting, Length of Days, Time of High Water, Fairs, Courts, and observable Days.

Fitted to the Latitude of Forty Degrees, and a Meridian of Five Hours West from London, but may without sensible Error, serve all the adjacent Places, even from Newfoundland to South-Carolina.

By RICHARD SAUNDERS, Philom.

PHILADELPHIA:
Printed and sold by B. FRANKLIN, at the New Printing-Office near the Market.

Numb. XL.

THE
Pennsylvania GAZETTE.

Containing the freshest Advices Foreign and Domestick.

From Thursday, September 25. to Thursday, October 2. 1729.

THE Pennsylvania Gazette *being now to be carry'd on by other Hands, the Reader may expect some Account of the Method we design to proceed in.*

Upon a View of Chambers's *great Dictionaries, from whence were taken the Materials of the* Universal Instructor *in all* Arts *and* Sciences, *which usually made the First Part of this Paper, we find that besides their containing many Things abstruse or insignificant to us, it will probably be fifty Years before the Whole can be gone thro' in this Manner of Publication. There are likewise in those Books continual References from Things under one Letter of the Alphabet to those under another, which relate to the same Subject, and are necessary to explain and compleat it; these taken in their Turn may perhaps be Ten Years distant; and since it is likely that they who desire to acquaint themselves with any particular Art or Science, would gladly have the whole before them in a much less Time, we believe our Readers will not think such a Method of communicating Knowledge to be a proper One.*

However, tho' we do not intend to continue the Publication of those Dictionaries in a regular Alphabetical Method, as has hitherto been done; yet as several Things exhibited from them in the Course of these Papers, have been entertaining to such of the Curious, who never had and cannot have the Advantage of good Libraries; and as there are many Things still behind, which being in this Manner made generally known, may perhaps become of considerable Use, by giving such Hints to the excellent natural Genius's of our Country, as may contribute either to the Improvement of our present Manufactures, or towards the Invention of new Ones; we propose from Time to Time to communicate such particular Parts as appear to be of the most general Consequence.

As to the Religious Courtship, *Part of which has been retal'd to the Publick in these Papers,, the Reader may be inform'd, that the whole Book will probably in a little Time be printed and bound up by it self; and those who approve of it, will doubtless be better pleas'd to have it entire, than in this broken interrupted Manner.*

There are many who have long desired to see a good News-Paper in Pennsylvania; *and we hope those Gentlemen who are able, will contribute towards the making This such. We ask Assistance, because we are fully sensible, that to publish a good News-Paper is not so easy an Undertaking as many People imagine it to be. The Author of a Gazette (in the Opinion of the Learned) ought to be qualified with an extensive Acquaintance with Languages, a great Easiness and Command of Writing and Relating Things cleanly and intelligibly, and in few Words; he should be able to speak of War both by Land and Sea; be well acquainted with Geography, with the History of the Time, with the several Interests of Princes and States, the Secrets of Courts, and the Manners and Customs of all Nations. Men thus accomplish'd are very rare in this remote Part of the World; and it would be well if the Writer of these Papers could make up among his Friends what is wanting in himself.*

Upon the Whole, we may assure the Publick, that as far as the Encouragement we meet with will enable us, no Care and Pains shall be omitted, that may make the Pennsylvania Gazette *as agreeable and useful an Entertainment as the Nature of the Thing will allow.*

The Following is the last Message sent by his Excellency Governour *Burnet,* to the House of Representatives in *Boston.*

Gentlemen of the House of Representatives,

IT is not with so vain a Hope as to convince you, that I take the Trouble to answer your Messages, but, if possible, to open the Eyes of the deluded People whom you represent, and whom you are at so much Pains to keep in Ignorance of the true State of their Affairs. I need not go further for an undeniable Proof of this Endeavour to blind them, than your ordering the Letter of Messieurs *Wilks* and *Belcher* of the 7th of *June* last to your Speaker to be published. This Letter is said (in *Page* 1. of your Votes) to inclose a Copy of the Report of the Lords of the Committee of His Majesty's Privy Council, with his Majesty's Approbation and Order thereon in Council; Yet these Gentlemen had at the same time the unparallell'd Presumption to write to the Speaker in this Manner; *You'll observe by the Conclusion, what is proposed to be the Consequence of your not complying with His Majesty's Instruction (the whole Matter to be laid*

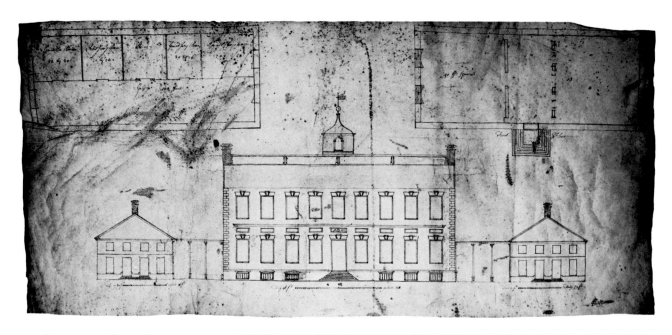

The Town Hall was becoming too crowded for its multiple uses. In 1729 the Assembly authorized the construction of a State House. Either the lawyer Andrew Hamilton or the master carpenter Edmund Woolley drew the plans. Although the Assembly met in the new building in 1735, it remained unfinished for quite a while. The tower and belfry were not completed until 1753. The Library Company moved into the upper floor of the west wing in 1740; Indians in town on official business were sometimes lodged in the east wing. Meanwhile a bell had been ordered from England to celebrate the fiftieth anniversary of Penn's 1701 Charter of Privileges. When it was tried out, it cracked. Two local "Ingenious Work-Men," Pass and Stow, recast it, and the bell was hung in June, 1753. The tower deteriorated over the years to such an extent that by 1774 a contemporary account could state that "they are afraid to ring the bell, lest by doing so the steeple should fall down." The Liberty Bell may not have rung out on July 8, 1776, the day the Declaration was publicly proclaimed, although the other city bells did.

(Above) *Elevation of the State House,* ink drawing attributed to Andrew Hamilton, 1732 (HSP)
(Below) Edmund Woolley's Bill for Plans for the State House, 1735 (HSP)
(Facing) *The Liberty Bell* (Independence National Historical Park)

BIBLIA,

Das ist:

Die

Heilige Schrift

Altes und Neues

Testaments,

Nach der Deutschen Uebersetzung

D. Martin Luthers,

Mit jedes Capitels kurtzen Summarien, auch
beygefügten vielen und richtigen Parlleien;

Nebst einem Anhang

Des dritten und vierten Buchs Esrä und des
dritten Buchs der Maccabäer.

Germantown:

Gedruckt bey Christoph Saur, 1743.

The little village of Germantown, founded by Francis Daniel Pastorius northwest of the city proper, was fast growing into a flourishing town. It consisted basically of a market square, a single main street, outlying mills, and the country estates of gentry such as James Logan's Stenton. Although many of the Germans who immigrated into the province during the first half of the century pushed on to the frontier in what is now Pennsylvania–Dutch country, significant numbers settled in Philadelphia county. Churches of various sects, a school, and Christopher Saur's books and newspaper catered to their needs so successfully that there was concern that the Germans would remain unassimilated and possibly hostile to the British majority. Most frequently allied to the Quakers because of their pacifistic and pietistic beliefs, they were a political force to be reckoned with, as Franklin, who had once called them "Palatine boors," learned to his sorrow when he needed their support.

(Facing) Title-page of Saur's First German Bible, 1743 (LCP)
(Above) *Market Square, Germantown,* painting by William Britton (Philadelphia Museum of Art: The Edgar William and Bernice Chrysler Garbisch Collection)
(Below) Germantown Academy, photograph by Richards, 1859 (LCP)

The city's privateers, among them the incongruously named but very successful Le Trembleur (Quaker), at first held their own after the outbreak of war with Spain in 1740. Rich prizes were hailed with joy. Four years later France joined against the English. By 1747 American losses increased. Philadelphia was thrown into a panic when French vessels boldly marauded up the Delaware. Franklin, in a well-argued pamphlet, Plain Truth, convinced the citizens to protect themselves. Militia companies, the Associators, were promptly organized as volunteers joined up. A small fortification was constructed at the foot of Society Hill and a major battery built south of Old Swedes' Church dominating the river. A lottery was held to purchase cannon; the independent-minded Quaker James Logan was the largest buyer of tickets. In 1748 peace permitted the concerned inhabitants to relax their defenses.

The Battery.

G. Vandergucht Sculp

Although the Treaty of Paris ended
the war between the French and the
British, hostility seethed in the wilder-
ness between the Pennsylvania fron-
tiersmen and the Indians. Neither
party was especially merciful. In December, 1763, a group of Scotch-Irish
settlers known as the Paxton Boys
massacred a score of friendly Conestoga
Indians at Lancaster. John Penn ordered their arrest. Full of resentment,
a mob of the Paxton Boys and their
supporters marched on Philadelphia
in February to force the Assembly
to adopt an Indian extermination
policy. A strong body of regular soldiers and militiamen was mustered
to defend the city. To avoid an armed
confrontation Franklin, at the request
of the governor, went out to Germantown and succeeded in persuading
the Lancaster County protestants to
go home. The affair produced an outpouring of virulent pamphlets and
cartoons, and left a faction-ridden city.

(Facing, above) *Hercules and the Waggoner*,
woodcut cartoon by Franklin from *Plain Truth*,
1747 (LCP)
(Facing, below) *The Association Battery*, engraving from Scull and Heap's *East Prospect*,
1754 (HSP)
(Above) Town Hall from *The Paxton Expedition*, cartoon by Henry Dawkins, 1764 (LCP)
(Below) Title-page of an Anonymous Paxton
Boy Pamphlet, 1764 (LCP)

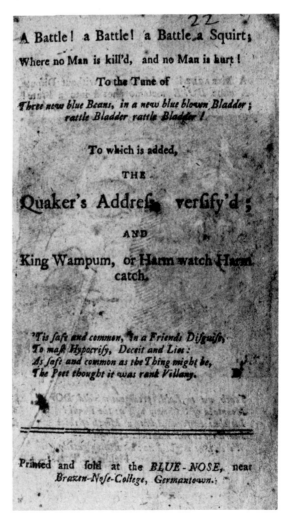

A Battle! a Battle! a Battle a Squirt;

Where no Man is kill'd, and no Man is hurt!

To the Tune of

Three new blue Beans, in a new blue blown Bladder;
rattle Bladder rattle Bladder!

To which is added,

THE

Quaker's Address versify'd;

AND

King Wampum, or Harm watch Harm
catch.

'Tis safe and common, in a Friends Disguise,
To mask Hypocrisy, Deceit and Lies:
As safe and common as the Thing might be,
The Poet thought it was rank Villany.

Printed and sold at the BLUE-NOSE, near
Brazen-Nose-College, Germantown.

The uneasy state of the province was reflected on the urban political scene. The Assembly in the spring of 1764 adopted a petition to the king asking him to take over the government from the proprietors. Franklin was a proponent of royal government, as were the Quakers and Moravians. On the side of the Penns ranged the Anglicans and Presbyterians. A violent debate ensued, marked by unparalleled printed and graphic slander and scurrility; no public figure was spared. In the fall election Franklin and his political aide Joseph Galloway ran for the Assembly from the county of Philadelphia on the "Old Ticket." Aging Isaac Norris, the long-time speaker of the Assembly, and the silversmith Joseph Richardson were supported by both factions. Young John Dickinson led the Proprietary Party, the "New Ticket," to a sweeping victory in Philadelphia.

(Above) *The German bleeds & bears ye Furs* and *An Indian Squaw King Wampum spies,* cartoons against Franklin and the Quakers, engravings, 1764 (LCP)
(Below) Returns of the October, 1764, Election (HSP)

Norris	3874
Richardson	3842
Dickinson	2039
Pawlin	1972
Fox	1963
Strettell	1951
Kepele	1932
Hughes	1925
Harrison	1921
Galloway	1918
Antes	1914
Evans	1911
Franklin	1906
Fleeson	1884

Philadelphia's prosperity depended on conflicting forces, the extension of the frontier—hence farm products and lumber—and trade with the Indians—whence furs. As the settlements pushed westward, additional land was peaceably purchased. But when the French and Indian War broke out, the long quiet was ended as the Indians took the opportunity to thrust back the English. The Quakers, opposed to war and the proprietary government, fished in troubled waters by forming a Friendly Association to seek peace and trade. With the end of the war in 1763, two major firms—Baynton, Wharton and Morgan, and Simon, Trent, Levy and Franks—pushed their trading posts across the Alleghenies. Pontiac, chief of the Ottawas, threatened by the pressure, attacked the traders. The uprising was suppressed. A treaty was agreed to at Fort Stanwix in 1768 by which additional land was sold to the Penns and the hope of recompense was held out to the "Suffering Traders." For years the convoluted accounting of undeveloped real estate, trading losses, debts, transfers of interests, bankruptcies, and pyramiding land companies kept Philadelphia businessmen and lawyers in turmoil.

(Above) Receipt by the Indian Chiefs of Land Sold to the Penns at the Fort Stanwix Peace Treaty, 1759 (HSP)
(Below) Silver Indian Peace Gorget made for the Friendly Association by Joseph Richardson, 1757 (HSP)

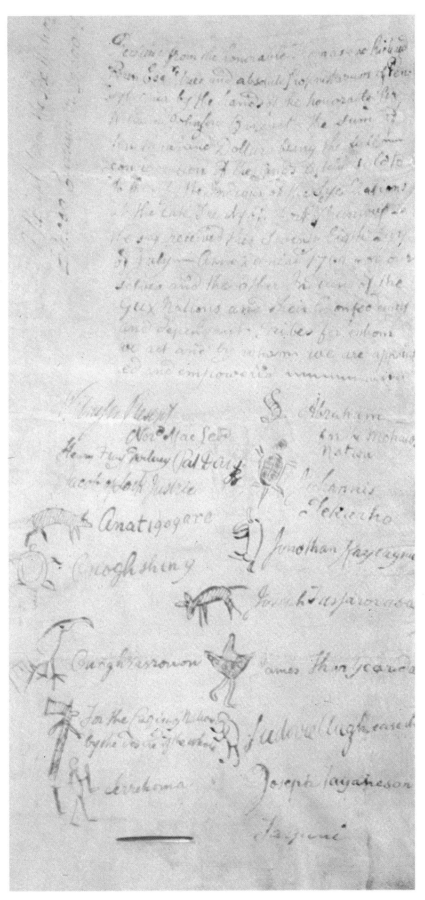

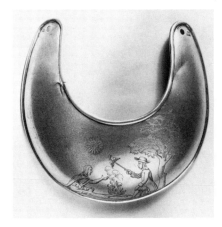

There were provincial panjandrums who though in primitive circumstances —as Europe erroneously regarded the New World for years—succeeded in building country seats of distinction. It is true that they were not palaces, but they were residences of charm and beauty. Bush Hill of the Hamiltons and more dramatically Mount Pleasant of the quasi-pirate, privateer Captain John MacPherson represented an attempt by Americans to match an English squire's, not a nobleman's, establishment. Even so humble a gatherer of botanical specimens for the gentry as John Bartram, having built his house himself, laid out a garden of exotics. Along the Schuylkill, residences and mansions arose which were as distinguished as any country houses in America.

(Facing) *James Hamilton,* painting by Benjamin West (HSP)
(Above) *Mount Pleasant,* watercolor by David J. Kennedy (HSP)
(Right) *Bush Hill,* engraving by Tiebout after J. Hoffman, from the *New York Magazine,* 1793 (LCP)
(Below) *Plan of John Bartram's House and Garden,* ink drawing, 1758 (Earl of Derby; photograph HSP)

BUSH-HILL,
The Seat of William Hamilton Esq.ʳ near Philadelphia

A rising community of competent physicians—unique on the fringes of the British empire—became concerned with the lack of professional care available to the poor in the growing city. Dr. Thomas Bond had the idea that a community hospital was needed. He got the interest of Franklin, who thereupon promoted the Pennsylvania Hospital. In a pioneer example of matching funds, the Pennsylvania Assembly agreed to put up £2,000 if those interested in the hospital could raise an equal sum. Three doctors, Thomas and Phineas Bond and Lloyd Zachary, promised to contribute their services gratis for three years. Franklin within a month and a half secured cash and pledges amounting to £2,751.16.8. "I do not remember any of my political Manoeuvres, the Success of which gave me at the time more Pleasure," he later reminisced.

A South-East Prospect of the Pennsylvania Hospital with the Elevation of the intended ...

(Above) *A South-East Prospect of the Pennsylvania Hospital,* by J. Steeper and H. Dawkins after Montgomery and Winter, 1761 (LCP)
(Below) Title-page of Franklin's *Some Account of the Pennsylvania Hospital,* 1754 (LCP)

SOME

ACCOUNT

OF THE

Pennsylvania Hospital;

From its firft RISE, to the Beginning of the *Fifth Month,* called *May,* 1754.

PHILADELPHIA:

Printed by B. FRANKLIN, and D. HALL. MDCCLIV.

Although the Quakers early in the city's history saw to it that education in the form of the three R's was available, they did not feel that higher education was necessary. Advanced teaching for those who could afford it was on a private basis by tutors. An institution of higher learning was first promoted by Franklin in 1749. It came into being when subscriptions raised by a board of trustees enabled the new school to take over a building used by the revivalist preacher George Whitefield on Fourth Street near Mulberry (Arch), combining it with a charity school already located there. Under the direction of the first provost, the Reverend William Smith, the academy soon became a college. In 1757 it graduated its first class, which included such talented young men as Jacob Duché, Francis Hopkinson, Samuel Magaw, and John Morgan.

(Above) *The Academy Buildings on Fourth Street*, watercolor by W. L. Breton (HSP)
(Right) *Provost William Smith*, painting by Gilbert Stuart (University of Pennsylvania)
(Below) Title-page of Franklin's *Proposals for the Education of Youth in Pensilvania*, 1749 (LCP)

PROPOSALS

Relating to the

EDUCATION

OF

YOUTH

IN

PENSILVANIA.

PHILADELPHIA:
Printed in the Year, M.DCC.XLIX.

W Williams Pinx.ᵗ   HD, Fecit.

BENJAMIN LAY.

Lived to the Age of 80, in the Latter Part of Which, he Observ'd extreem Temperance, in his Eating, and Drinking, his Fondness, for a Particularity, in Dress, and Customs, at times, Subjected him, to the Redicule of the Ignorant, but his Life who were Intimate with Him, thought Him, an Honest Religious man.

The Quakers had early condemned slavery. The eccentric Benjamin Lay and the erstwhile planter Ralph Sandiford wrote strongly against it; later Anthony Benezet became colonial America's most prolific antislavery pamphleteer. Few Quakers did, indeed, carry on the trade after the first decades of the century. Nonetheless, after the duty on slaves was lowered in 1729, the importation of Africans rose markedly for a few years. However, as a flood of German and Scotch-Irish redemptioners began to pour into the city in the 1730s—a flow which continued until the outbreak of the French and Indian War—the demand for slaves lessened. But once again the trade picked up when bond servants were able to cancel their indentures by joining the British army. By the time the war was over, between one and two hundred Negroes were arriving each year. At its peak in 1767 the slave population in Philadelphia may have been almost 1,400 persons. Precipitously, as antislavery propaganda intensified, the importation of slaves decreased. At the same time the number of free blacks increased.

(Facing) *Benjamin Lay*, engraving by H. Dawkins after W. Williams, ca. 1760 (Quaker Collection, Haverford College Library)
(Above) Title-page of Anthony Benezet's *Short Account Of that Part of Africa Inhabited by the Negroes*, 1762 (LCP)

A SHORT
ACCOUNT
Of that PART of
A F R I C A,
Inhabited by the
N E G R O E S.

With Respect to the *Fertility* of the Country; the *good Disposition* of many of the *Natives*, and the *Manner* by which the SLAVE TRADE is carried on.
Extracted from divers Authors, in order to shew the *Iniquity* of that TRADE, and the *Falsity* of the ARGUMENTS usually advanced in its *Vindication*.
With Quotations from the Writings of several Persons of Note, *viz.* GEORGE WALLIS, FRANCIS HUTCHESON, and JAMES FOSTER, and a large Extract from a Pamphlet, lately published in *London*, on the Subject of the SLAVE TRADE.

The Second EDITION, with large Additions and Amendments.

Do you the neighb'ring, blameless *Indian* aid;
Culture what he neglects, not his invade,
Dare not, Oh! dare not, with ambitious View
Force or demand Subjection, never due.
* * * * * * * * * * * *
* * * * * * * * * * * *
Why must I *Africk*'s sable Children see
Vended for Slaves, tho' formed by Nature free?
The nameless Tortures cruel Minds invent,
Those to subject whom Nature equal meant?
If these you dare, altho' unjust Success
Impow'rs you now, unpunish'd, to oppress
Revolving EMPIRE you and yours may doom;
Rome all subdued, yet *Vandals* vanquish'd *Rome*.
RICHARD SAVAGE, *on publick Spirit.*

P H I L A D E L P H I A:
Printed by W. DUNLAP, in the YEAR MDCCLXII.

Robert Smith was the best-known architect of colonial America. A carpenter who was a builder and at the same time his own designer, he constructed many buildings in the city as well as college halls in Princeton and Providence and an insane asylum in Williamsburg. His first major work was the steeple of Christ Church in 1752-54, but his masterpiece was St. Peter's on Pine Street, which he undertook in 1758. Smith's style was comparatively plain: brick with white trim, neatly proportioned and balanced, embellished with Palladian doors and windows. The pre-Revolutionary town took some of its neat appearance so frequently commented on from Smith's buildings, for also his were the Third Presbyterian Church on Pine Street (1766), the large Zion Lutheran Church at Fourth and Cherry streets (1767), and the Walnut Street Prison (1773-74). If Smith himself was not the architect for Carpenters' Hall, he was a leading participant in its planning and execution. The plainness of his architectural design, called severity by some, echoed the underlying Quaker influence.

The Jail. Philad.

Malcom del At fc

(Above) *The Jail, on Walnut Street,* engraving by Malcolm (HSP)
(Below) *North-East View of St. Peter's Church,* lithograph by Kennedy & Lucas after W. L. Breton, 1829 (LCP)
(Facing) *Zion Lutheran Church,* engraving by William Birch, 1799 (HSP)

It is impossible to compare eighteenth-century Philadelphia, a provincial town on the fringes of the British empire, with the metropolis of London. Wealth and its effects in the arts both fine and useful in one city and the other were, literally and figuratively, an ocean apart. While merchants of the American city were happy to see themselves even recognizably portrayed, it was after his transplantation to a more demanding London that the small native artistic talent of Benjamin West blossomed. Those Americans who could bank their profits in silver on a sideboard were satisfied to have it heavy, if plain, and in somewhat old-fashioned taste. Their chairs and tables, well-made in walnut wood which was handily available, were in a conservative transitional Queen Anne mode. Most families, however, bought simpler fare, and Philadelphia makers of Windsor chairs met a great demand.

(Above) *Jane Galloway,* painting by Benjamin West (HSP)
(Below) Windsor Chairs, by Francis Trumble (Independence National Historical Park)
(Facing, above) Bedroom in the Philadelphia Queen Anne Style (Henry Francis du Pont Winterthur Museum)
(Below) *Colonial Costumes,* pen-and-ink sketches from John Fanning Watson's *Annals of Philadelphia* (LCP)

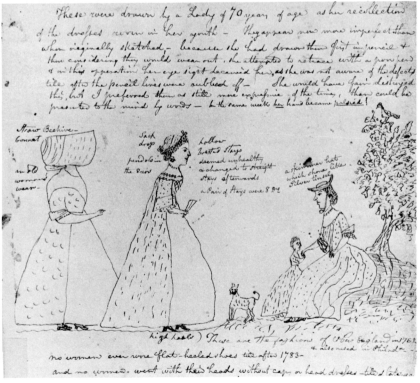

These were drawn by a Lady of 70 years of age, as her recollection of the dresses worn in her youth — they appear now more imperfect than when originally sketched — because she had drawn them first in pencil & then considering they would wear out, she attempted to retrace with a grown pen & in this operation her eye sight deceived her, as she was not aware of the defect till after the pencil lines were rubbed off — She would have fain destroyed this, but I preferred them as still more expressive of the times, than could be presented to the mind by words — In the same week her hand became palsied!

Straw Beehive bonnet

in 50 women wear.

Sack drop pendula in the sun

Hollow Breasted Stays deemed unhealthy & changed to straight Stays afterwards — a Pair of Stays were 8 D⁢

a skimmer hat which shone like Silver Tinsel

high heels) These are the fashions of New England in 1762 & also used in Philad⁢

no women ever wore flat-heeled shoes till after 1783 —

and no women went with their heads without caps or head dresses till of late —

SCHUYLKILL

Frivolous amusements, as most entertainment was classed by the town's sobersides, were indulged in by both the wealthy and the poor. Theater began tentatively. The Quakers, supported by other rectitudinous sects, were able to bar dramatic performances from the city proper, but in 1754 Lewis Hallam's company of players gave a performance in William Plumsted's warehouse in Southwark, over the city line. "Vice" for many years flourished beyond the technical reach of the city fathers. A new Southwark Theatre in 1759 became a permanent place of theatrical production. To it, as less restrictive influences became predominant, the Hallam company regularly returned, making Philadelphia an American theatrical center.

Unlike most of the colonies, Pennsylvania from the beginning promised freedom of worship. No other provincial capital in British America, therefore, enjoyed a greater diversity of religious sects than Philadelphia. The predominance of the Society of Friends quite early gave way to the strong establishment of the fashionable Anglican Church, an influx of Scotch-Irish Presbyterians, and a variety of German groups. Small minorities, too, found they could exist peaceably. Catholics, Baptists, Methodists, and Jews settled and formed congregations in the city.

For the BENEFIT of

Mr. Lewis Hallam,

By a Company of COMEDIANS from L O N D O N,

At the NEW THEATRE, *in* Water-street,

This present Evening (being the Twenty-seventh of *May*, 1754) will be presented a C O M E D Y, called,

TUNBRIDGE WALKS;

O R,

The Yeoman of Kent.

The Part of *Woodcock* (the Yeoman of *Kent*) by Mr. *Malone.*

| Reynard, | | Mr. *Rigby.* |
| Loveworth, | } by { | Mr. *Miller.* |

Captain *Squib*, by Mr. *Lewis Hallam.*
The Part of Mr. *Maiden*, by Mr. *Singleton.*

The Part of *Belinda*, by Mrs. *Becceley.*

Penelope,		Mrs. *Clarkson.*
Lucy,	} by {	Miss *Hallam.*
Mrs. *Goodfellow*,		Mrs. *Rigby.*

And the Part of *Hillaria*, to be perform'd by Mrs. *Hallam.*

To which will be added, a BALLAD OPERA, called,

The C O U N T R Y W A K E;

O R,

H O B *in the* W E L L.

The Part of *Flora*, to be perform'd by Mrs. *Becceley.*

Sir *Thomas Testy*,		Mr. *Clarkson.*
Friendly,	} by {	Mr. *Adcock.*
Old *Hob*,		Mr. *Miller.*
Dick,		Master *L. Hallam.*

| Hob's Mother, | | Mrs. *Clarkson.* |
| Betty, | } by { | Miss *Hallam.* |

And the Part of *Young Hob*, to be perform'd by Mr. *Hallam.*

Tickets to be had at Mrs. *Bridges's*, *in* Front-street, and of Mr. *Hallam.*

BOX 6s.   PIT 4s.   GALLERY 2s. 6d.

N. B. The Doors will be open'd at Five, and the Play to begin at Seven a Clock. *V I V A T R E X.*

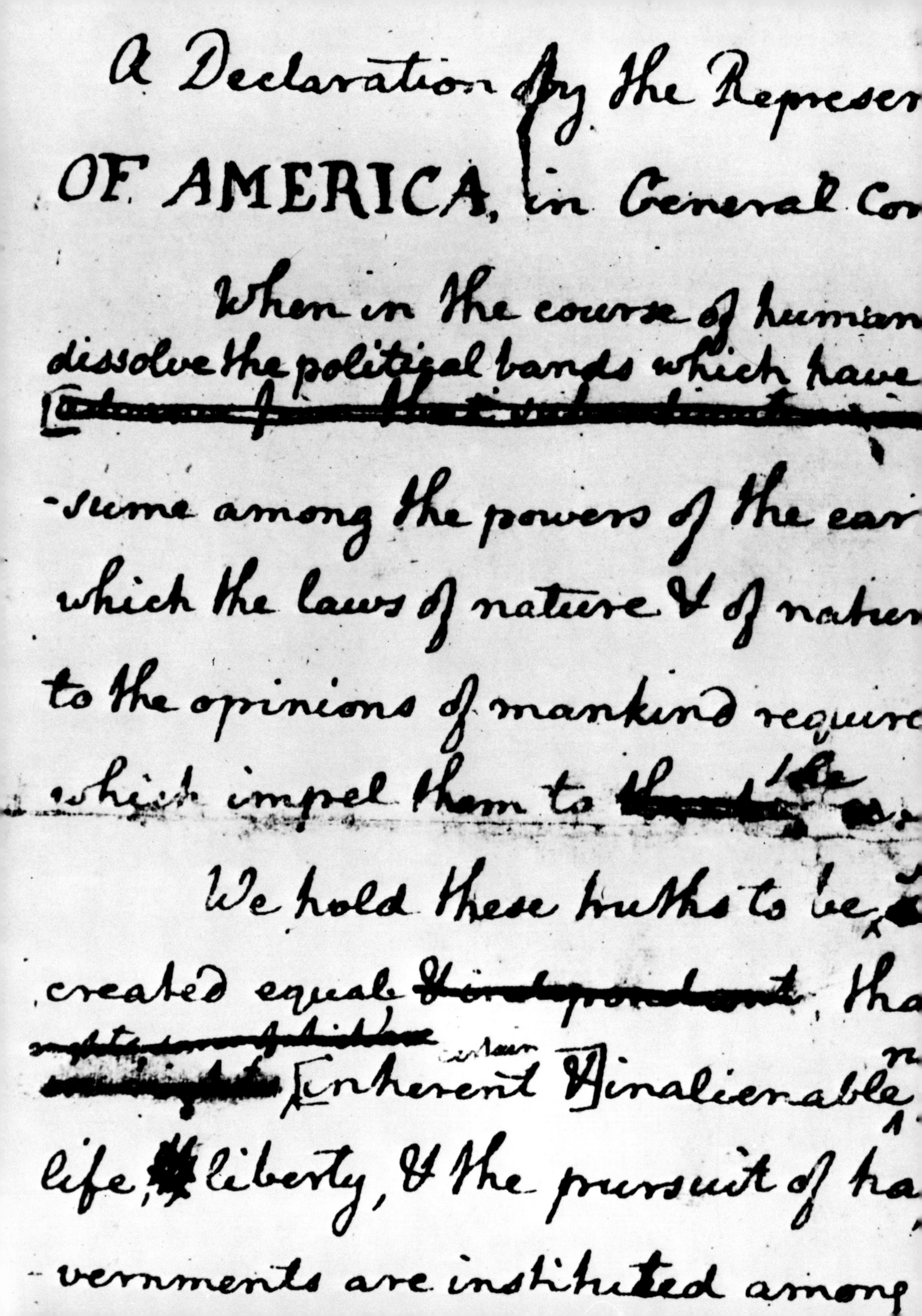

A Declaration by the Represe

OF AMERICA, in General Con

When in the course of human

~~dissolve the political bands which have~~

-sume among the powers of the ear

which the laws of nature & of natur

to the opinions of mankind require

which impel them to ~~the~~

We hold these truths to be,

created equal ~~& independent~~, tha

~~inherent~~ & inalienable

life, liberty, & the pursuit of ha

-vernments are instituted among

...es of the UNITED STATES

...s assembled.

...ts it becomes necessary for ~~the~~ one people

...~~eted~~ them with ~~another~~, and to

~~————————————————————~~ as

separate and equal

~~————————————~~ station to

...od entitle them, a decent respect

...at they should declare the causes

...tion.

~~————~~;

~~abandon——~~ that all men are

~~they are~~ endowed by their creator with ~~eq~~

~~that equal creation they derive~~

...at

...ong [~~which~~] ^these^ are ~~————————————~~

...ss; that to secure these ^rights^ ~~ends~~, ge

..., deriving their just powers from

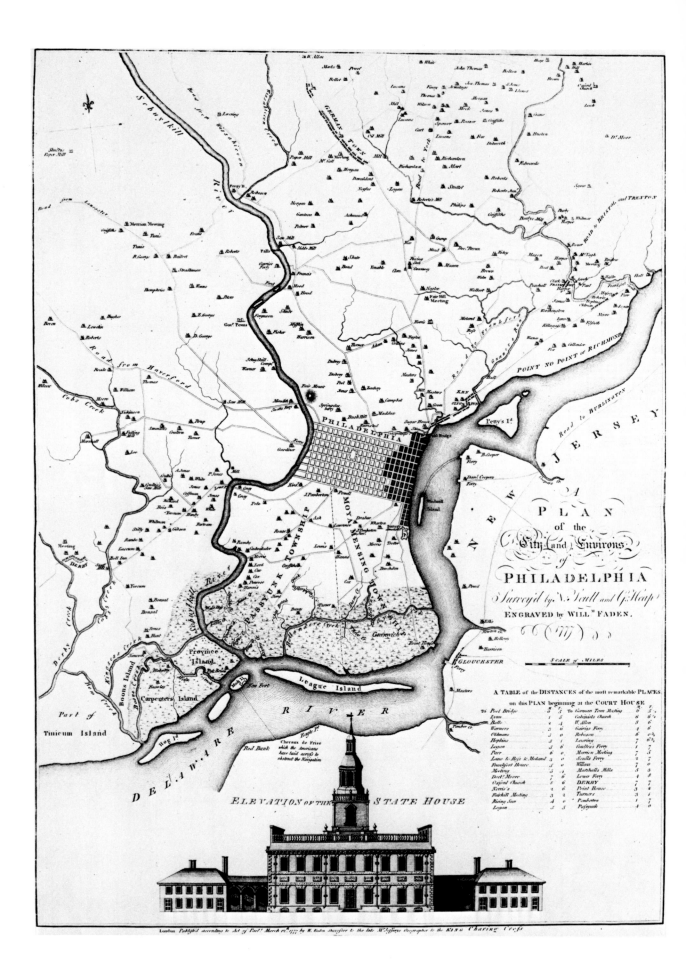

A
PLAN
of the
City and Environs
of
PHILADELPHIA
Survey'd by N. Scull and G. Heap
ENGRAVED by WILLᴹ FADEN.
1777

SCALE of MILES

A TABLE of the DISTANCES of the most remarkable PLACES
on this PLAN beginning at the COURT HOUSE.

ELEVATION OF THE STATE HOUSE

London, Publish'd according to Act of Parl.ᵗ March 12ᵗʰ 1777 by W. Faden Surveyor to the late Mʳ Jefferys Geographer to the KING Charing Cross.

1765-1785

The French and Indian War having ended, the seas were once more pacific in the Atlantic. Philadelphia's merchants with overseas and coastal trade, the basis of the city's prosperity, were again able to export the natural products of the province and bring back freely the manufactured and exotic goods of Europe and the West Indies. So freely did imports flow in that a glut of drygoods caused a decade-long depression in that area of commerce. In other respects the province flourished to such an extent that Chief Justice William Allen in 1766 called it the "wonder of the world." This was paradoxically the era of grandeur and of rebellion.

Benjamin Franklin, the agent of Pennsylvania in London, made one of his few errors of political judgment when in 1765 he underestimated the hostile reception of the Stamp Act in the colonies. When William Hughes, Franklin's friend, was appointed collector of the tax in Philadelphia, the absent agent's innocent wife was subjected to the threat of an unfriendly mob which might have stormed the new house in Franklin Court had not armed protection come to her aid.

Similar reactions throughout the colonies culminated in the Stamp Act Congress in New York at which a Declaration of Rights and Grievances was drafted by the Philadelphia lawyer John Dickinson. Franklin quickly changed his tack and became the most effective advocate of the act's repeal. In support of his new role, articles which Franklin had published in England and a mordant cartoon he designed to push repeal were reprinted in Philadelphia. The success in 1766 of his and chiefly the colonies' opposition was widely and enthusiastically hailed.

Politically there were problems, but, except in certain sectors, the town was doing well economically. It was doing so well that the demand for immigrants, indentured servants, and free agents, be they sailor or cabinetmaker, attracted a spectrum of skilled and unskilled workers. So the years before the Revolution were ones of growth, the population increasing from 17,063 in 1760 to 23,436 in 1769. Houses for artisans and workers spread south into Southwark and northward in the Northern Liberties. Mansions for the rich, interspersed with alley houses, were built or rebuilt on the city streets.

The times were propitious, too, for the expansion of cultural activities. Dr. John Morgan in 1765 was responsible for the founding of the medical school of the College of Philadelphia. It grew

(Facing) *A Plan of the City and Environs of Philadelphia*, engraving by William Faden after N. Scull and G. Heap, 1777 (HSP)
(Above) *Magna Britannia her Colonies Reduc'd*, Franklin's Stamp Act cartoon, etching, 1766 (LCP)
(Below) Advertisement for Emigrants from Ireland, 1773 (Free Library of Philadelphia)

(Above) Orrery Constructed by David Rittenhouse for the Academy of Philadelphia, 1772 (University of Pennsylvania)
(Below) *Charles Thomson*, bust by William Rush (American Philosophical Society)
(Facing) John Dickinson's First Draft of the Stamp Act Resolutions, 1765 (LCP)

and flourished and was not only the first but for years the best in the country. The American Philosophical Society, long dormant, came alive. In 1768 it united with a newer, similar group to emerge as a stimulating force in the quest after knowledge in scientific and recondite fields. When the transit of Venus across the sun occurred in 1769, the Society organized observations as part of an international network. David Rittenhouse watched from Norristown; a platform was erected in the State House yard for another telescope; and Clement Biddle peered through the Library Company's instrument at Cape Henlopen, where an important lighthouse had been erected four years earlier. Although excitement brought tears to Rittenhouse's eyes at the critical moment, his competence created two orreries—mechanical devices run by clockwork to demonstrate the movement of the solar system—the most sophisticated astronomical mechanisms the colonies had produced up to that time. In this burst of civic enthusiasm, the Union Library Company in 1769 merged into the Library Company of Philadelphia, increasing the latter's already large book resources.

All shades of political opinion helped build the physical and intellectual structure of the city. While adherence to the proprietors may have given an aura of distinction to the supporters of the Penn family—the Allens, Chews, and Willings (some of them later loyalists)—these were not the only men of means in the city. If wealth be equated with conspicuous spending, it was such unequivocal patriots as John Dickinson, Samuel Powel, John Cadwalader, and Robert Morris who should be counted wealthy. Dickinson, the widely hailed author of *Letters from a Farmer in Pennsylvania*, married a Norris heiress and had a substantial law practice. Powel, the last colonial and first Revolutionary mayor, was the chief beneficiary of his grandfather's estate. Cadwalader inherited, wed, and earned his fortune. And Robert Morris was said to have been the most successful merchant in town. Yet, all of these men played roles of importance in the Revolution, as did Charles Thomson, although a merchant one of the most radical of radicals, and his ally William Bradford, the city's premier printer and publisher.

It was the elegance of Whig and Tory alike which John Adams enjoyed and wrote Abigail about, when he came to town in the early autumn of 1774 to attend the First Continental Congress. Philadel-

We the ~~Committees~~ Deputies from the Colonies of Massachusetts Bay, Rhode Island, Connecticut, New York, New Jersey, Pennsylvania, the Lower Counties on Delaware, Maryland and South Carolina, in General Congress assembled, ~~for vindicating & asserting the Rights & Liberties~~ ~~the Inhabitants of~~ ~~the said Colonies~~ declare,

I. 1st That his Majesty's Subjects in these Colonies owe ~~bear~~ the same Allegiance to the Crown of Great Britain, that is due from ~~bought the~~ his ~~Majesty's natural born Subjects born within~~ ~~within~~ that the Realm

2ly That all Acts of Parliament not inconsistent with the ~~Rights & Liberties~~ Principles of freedom are obligatory upon the Colonists—

3ly That his Majesty's Liege Subjects in these Colonies are as free as his Majesty's Subjects in Great Britain

Dele /// Insert A

phia was not only geographically the central city of the British colonies, it was politically in the middle. Hesitantly its merchants joined in a non-importation agreement in 1769, but they maintained it longer and stronger than did those of other American ports. There was not as much truculence in Philadelphia as in Virginia nor as much violence as in Massachusetts. The city was big enough, varied enough in political opinion, and tolerant enough to house, welcome, and support the colonial delegates, with their diverse backgrounds, who came to create and administer a new, independent nation. Samuel Curwen, who unhappily left for England, stated: "Philadelphia is wholly American, strong friends to congressional measures; at least, no man is hardy enough to express a doubt of the feasibility of their projects."

The Revolution brought the city to the peak of its historical fame and, for a brief period of British occupation, humiliated it. With the activities of the rebellious colonies and, after July 4, 1776, of the new nation centered in Philadelphia, there developed a two-tiered life. On a national level the conduct of the war, the foreign relations, and the economy of the United States created a flux and reflux of officials and excitement. It was in Philadelphia that the Declaration of Independence was adopted, printed, and first read publicly to the people. But on the local scene there was also ferment.

The province of Pennsylvania declared itself an independent state in Carpenters' Hall in June, 1776. Elections took place, a new state constitution was adopted, and the Pennsylvania Assembly continued to meet in town. The municipal government gave up its powers, and a Committee of Safety took over the supervision of law and order according to the resolutions of Congress and the state. Militia companies were raised from the citizens. Outright Tories, Quaker pacifists, and others who exhibited no revolutionary fervor became increasingly subject to antagonism, arrest, and attack. A group of these, chiefly Quakers, was arrested and exiled to Virginia. Prices came under strict control as shortages grew; the production of arms and ammunition was encouraged; and blankets were requisitioned. The capital of the newly formed United States had little opportunity to enjoy its status.

With British General Howe's successful assault on and occupation of Philadelphia, there was a change for the worse. Congress

(Above) *One of the Belles of the Meschianza,* wash drawing by John André, from the manuscript of John Fanning Watson, *Annals of Philadelphia* (LCP)

moved to York, and the State House bell was carted to Allentown. Thousands of British and Hessian troops were quartered wherever houses or public buildings were available. Officers, of course, commandeered the finer homes. Loyalist followers of the army moved into shops abandoned by those who fled. And many Philadelphians, sympathetic to the British cause, apathetic, or simply unable to leave, stayed on. Balls, plays, drinking, gambling, and, it was claimed, debauchery enabled the wealthy Tories, preferred civilians, and senior officers to pass their time without undue discomfort or boredom. While military discipline during most of the occupation held down harm to persons and property, damage was done. The long unoccupied soldiers, as with all occupying troops, were hard on their forced hosts. It was the shortage of fuel which triggered most of the damage; furniture, paneling, sheds, and floors were broken up to feed warming fires. North of the British fortifications, which crossed the peninsula at Bush Hill, destruction created a no man's land; Dickinson's mansion at Fair Hill, Jonathan Mifflin's house, and two dozen others were burned. During the final stage of the occupation, the city figuratively and literally took on the stench of abandonment.

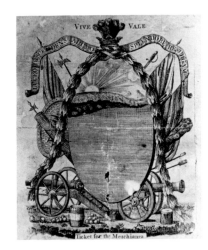

It was amazing how quickly after the American soldiers returned that things were restored to normal, if indeed there ever was normalcy during the war. Congress moved back from York; the Pennsylvania Assembly reconvened. A good many of the most notorious Tories decamped with the British; others were hailed before courts, attainted and stripped of their property; and a few were hanged as traitors. A radical mob, suffering from severe inflation and the shortage of goods, kept looking for victims on whom to wreak vengeance. Even a group of merely moderate patriots was forced to hole up in James Wilson's house and was rescued only by the intervention of the governor at the head of troops. Benedict Arnold, the military commander of the re-occupied city, fell into disfavor for his friendship with wealthy dissidents. In the eyes of the general public there was no sharp dividing line between wealth and treachery. When American officers organized a dance, even some of the belles of the Meschianza, the final grand ball of the departing British officers, were invited. However, with scarcities increasing, the continual demand for more soldiers and military supplies, inflation and speculation rampant, and the war's inconclusive continua-

(Above) Ticket for the Meschianza, engraving by James Smither, 1778 (LCP)

Illumination.

COLONEL TILGHMAN, Aid de Camp to his Excellency General WASHINGTON, having brought official acounts of the SURRENDER of Lord Cornwallis, and the Garrisons of York and Gloucester, those Citizens who chuse to ILLUMINATE on the GLORIOUS OCCASION, will do it this evening at Six, and extinguish their lights at Nine o'clock.

Decorum and harmony are earnestly recommended to every Citizen, and a general difcountenance to the leaft appearance of riot.

October 24, 1781.

tion, occasions for joy and celebration were few and all the more cherished.

There was joy when one of the many Philadelphia privateers brought in a prize. The ever-popular Washington was resoundingly hailed on his official visits to his superior authority, the Congress. However, it was the French who gave the citizens the most to be pleased with. The alliance between the two countries was celebrated early in 1779, and the new French minister, the Chevalier de la Luzerne, was greeted with cannon salutes, ringing of bells, and a military escort. There were few American victories to cheer Philadelphians, but the passage of the splendidly uniformed French troops through the city in 1781 and word that another French loan had been obtained did hearten them.

Even as the war was being won, financial disaster loomed. Continental paper money, which Congress had had no choice but to keep issuing for the purchase of supplies, had depreciated in value to such an extent that it was fast becoming worthless. To enable the government to maintain its credit, Congress appointed the Philadelphia entrepreneur Robert Morris superintendent of finance. The business acumen which had enabled him to prosper during the war was brought to bear on his country's problems. The French and Dutch loans, turned into viable currency by the foreign exchange specialist Hyam Salomon, broker to the Office of Finance, helped alleviate the situation. The hard money used by the French to buy supplies for their troops, which also passed through Salomon's hands, helped too. Morris' principal plan for stabilizing currency and credit was, however, the Bank of North America. This marked the beginning of the city's role as the financial, as well as the political, capital of the country, a role it maintained until the Second Bank of the United States lost its charter in 1836.

Woes were temporarily forgotten when news arrived of the surrender of Cornwallis at Yorktown. And then the city, struggling with economic problems, looked forward to better times.

(Above) Broadside Announcing the Victory at Yorktown, 1781, facsimile (HSP)
(Facing) *Robert Morris,* painting by Charles Willson Peale (Pennsylvania Academy of the Fine Arts)

The Stamp Act provoked the first open and unified protest against what had been a series of restrictive measures and added taxes imposed by Parliament upon the colonies. From 1765 on hundreds of Philadelphians gathered publicly to hear news, express indignation, and plan counteraction. The stamp tax on newspapers, almanacs, documents, playing cards, and other papers was to go into effect November 1, 1765. Newspapers clamorously ceased publication rather than submit. Trade, already stagnant as the result of a depression, almost ceased. Under the circumstances, it was not surprising that a majority of conservative merchants would join with political radicals in a non-importation agreement. The unexpected violent American reaction resulted in the repeal of the Stamp Act in 1766. Its demise was jubilantly hailed in Philadelphia.

The Townshend Acts which went into effect in 1767 annoyed but did not incense Philadelphia's merchants. The selective duties were, however, burdensome. When Boston and New York urged a joint boycott in the spring of 1768, the local merchants at first refused to go along. But then everybody was talking about John Dickinson's Letters from a Farmer in Pennsylvania, which maintained the position that Parliament had no right to tax the colonies without their consent; he urged immediate adoption of non-importation agreements. His essays, published serially in newspapers up and down the seaboard and in many pamphlet editions, made him the first national hero of American discontent. His was the most effective statement of the pre-Revolutionary propaganda war. On March 10, 1769, the merchants of Philadelphia signed a non-importation agreement. Exports from England to Philadelphia dropped from £371,830 in 1768 to £134,881 in 1770. Gradually, commercial competitiveness overcame principles, and the agreement was rescinded in the fall of 1770.

"I once heard you say," Benjamin Rush wrote John Adams, "the active business of the American Revolution began in Philadelphia in the act of her citizens in sending back the tea ship, and that Massachusetts would have received her portion of the tea had not our example encouraged her to expect union and support in destroying it."

News arrived that the tea ship Polly had sailed from London late in September, 1773, for Philadelphia, and on October 18th a crowd assembled to protest the ship's arrival. As this became imminent, handbills signed by a "Committee for Tarring and Feathering" warned any Delaware pilot and Captain Ayres of the Polly what to expect if the ship were brought up the river. James and Drinker, the consignees of the tea, were told not to accept it. On Christmas Day the ship came up to Chester, and a committee was sent to inform the captain of the state of affairs. At a meeting in the State House yard two days later, attended by thousands of Philadelphians and witnessed by Captain Ayres, it was resolved that the tea "shall not be landed." The Polly turned back and returned home.

(Facing) Last Issue before the Stamp Act of William Bradford's *Pennsylvania Journal*, October 31, 1765 (LCP)
(Above) *To the Delaware Pilots*, Broadside warning against the Tea Ship *Polly*, 1773 (LCP)
(Below) *The Patriotic American Farmer, J[oh]n D[ic]k[i]ns[o]n Esqr. Barrister at Law*, engraving by James Smith, 1768 (LCP)
(Overleaf) *The Repeal or the Funeral of Miss Ame-Stamp*, English cartoon, 1766 (LCP)

THE PATRIOTIC AMERICAN FARMER.
J-N D-K-NS--N Esqr BARRISTER at LAW.

TO THE
DELAWARE PILOTS.

THE Regard we have for your Characters, and our Defire to promote your future Peace and Safety, are the Occafion of this Third Addrefs to you.

In our fecond Letter we acquainted you, that the Tea Ship was a Three Decker; We are now informed by good Authority, fhe is not a Three Decker, but an *old black Ship, without a Head*, or *any Ornaments*.

THE *Captain* is a *fhort fat* Fellow, and a little *obftinate* withal.----So much the worfe for him.----For, fo fure as he *rides rufty*, We fhall heave him Keel out, and fee that his Bottom be well fired, fcrubb'd and paid.----His Upper-Works too, will have an Overhawling----and as it is faid, he has a good deal of *Quick Work* about him, We will take particular Care that fuch Part of him undergoes a thorough Rummaging.

WE have a ftill *worfe Account* of *his Owner*;----for it is faid, the Ship POLLY was bought by him on Purpofe, to make a Penny of us; and that *he* and Captain *Ayres* were well advifed of the Rifque they would run, in thus daring to infult and abufe us.

Captain Ayres was here in the Time of the Stamp-Act, and ought to have known our People better, than to have expected we would be fo mean as to fuffer his *rotten* TEA to be funnel'd down our Throats, with the *Parliament's Duty* mixed with it.

WE know him well, and have calculated to a Gill and a Feather, how much it will require to fit him for an *American Exhibition*. And we hope, not one of your Body will behave fo ill, as to oblige us to clap him in the Cart along Side of the *Captain*.

WE muft repeat, that the SHIP POLLY is an *old black Ship*, of about Two Hundred and Fifty Tons burthen, *without a Head*, and *without Ornaments*,----and, that CAPTAIN AYRES is a *thick chunky Fellow*.----------As fuch, TAKE CARE to AVOID THEM.

YOUR OLD FRIENDS,

THE COMMITTEE FOR TARRING AND FEATHERING.

Philadelphia, December 7, 1773.

1715

1745

Within this Family Vault lie (it is to be hop'd never to rise again) the Remains of
Hearth mon — ship
mon — Excise B
Jew B — Gen.
Warrants &c

CONWA

ROCKINGHAM

GRAFT

Manchester

Burial Serv

Funeral Sermon by Anti Sejanus

Brief The G: Deft

M: American papers 1766

As the colonial period drew to a close, the richness and elegance of the fine town houses of the city impressed all who saw them. Nowhere in America were there skilled artisans more capable of embellishing a room in the high Georgian style, men such as the carpenter John Nevell, the carver Hercules Courtenay, and the plasterer James Clow. The finest surviving examples of interiors are those created for two men, both merchants and mayors, John Stamper and Samuel Powel. John Dickinson's house on Chestnut Street between Sixth and Seventh must have been equally grand, for the owner spent the huge sum of £3,929 improving and decorating it shortly before the Revolution. Although exteriors of the red brick houses were plain except for the pillared doorways, the interiors were decorated with elaborate paneling and intricate plasterwork. Such a one was that refurbished by the newly wed John Cadwalader, "whose furniture and house," wrote Silas Deane in 1774, "exceeds anything I have seen in this city or elsewhere."

(Above) *John Cadwalader and his Family,* painting by Charles Willson Peale (Capt. John Cadwalader)
(Below, left) Red Morocco Binding, by Robert Aitken, on Hugh Blair, *Lectures on Rhetoric and Belles Lettres,* 1784 (Michael Papantonio; *Antiques*)
(Middle) The Powel House, 244 South 3rd Street (HSP)
(Right) Trade Card of Benjamin Randolph, engraving by James Smither, ca. 1767 (LCP)

It was in Philadelphia that the useful arts received their most elaborate colonial American interpretation. The combination of available wealth and a series of non-importation agreements encouraged local craftsmen to execute pieces in competition with imports. The Philadelphia highboy with its ornate broken pediment and sculptured front drawer was characteristic of this period's high-style workmanship, while the chairs and tables of Thomas Affleck, Benjamin Randolph, and Jonathan Gostelowe also carried out the rococo motifs illustrated in Chippendale's The Gentleman and Cabinet-Maker's Director. At the same time, on the site of an older factory in Kensington, the Philadelphia Glass Works made ware similar to the popular Bristol glass. The first china made in America, "good porcelain as any heretofore manufactured at the famous factory in Bow near London," came from Bonnin and Morris' short-lived local manufactory in 1769. The master silversmith Joseph Richardson, Sr., was capable of engraving and ornamenting his tea sets in the most intricate fashionable manner.

(Above) The Stamper-Blackwell Parlor, with Philadelphia Chippendale Furniture (Henry Francis du Pont Winterthur Museum)
(Below) Teakettle and Stand, by Joseph Richardson, Sr. (The Mabel Brady Garvan Collection, Yale University Art Gallery)
(Right) China Basket, by Bonnin and Morris (Henry Francis du Pont Winterthur Museum)

The Carpenters' Company, modeled on an English trade guild, was founded in Philadelphia in 1724. The master carpenters decided to build their own meeting place in 1770, and it was finished three years later. The structure, in a court off Chestnut Street, proved more expensive than expected, but its brick cruciform shape with white Palladian doors and windows was an ornament to the city. The Library Company, having outgrown its quarters in the State House wing, rented and moved into the second floor in 1773, where its books and museum remained for seventeen years. It was, however, when the First Continental Congress convened in Carpenters' Hall on September 5, 1774, that the building was endowed with the golden aura of history. In a real sense, the elegant building could be considered the seed pod of the United States. Less nationally pertinent, but locally significant, was the meeting there of the Provincial Convention of Pennsylvania in June, 1776, which declared the province no longer a colony but an independent state.

It was the pamphleteer Tom Paine's clarion call for immediate independence which nudged public opinion and the Congress toward that irrevocable step. In January, 1776, he anonymously issued Common Sense, a reasoned but rhetorical attack on British tyranny and a firm advocacy of American liberty. The times were receptive. Common Sense became an instantaneous success; it was reprinted up and down the Atlantic seaboard and even overseas. It is said that 120,000 copies were sold within three months. Although Common Sense is Paine's best-known work, few today can quote even a sentence from it. Many, however, remember: "These are the times that try men's souls," the beginning of The American Crisis, published in December, 1776, the first of a series of hortatory essays to bolster American courage in the face of adversity.

Anticipating a favorable vote for independence, Congress on June 11, 1776, appointed John Adams, Benjamin Franklin, Thomas Jefferson, Robert R. Livingston, and Roger Sherman a committee to prepare a declaration. Among them Jefferson was chosen to work up a draft. He had found lodgings on the second floor of the modest house of Jacob Graff, Jr., on the southwest corner of Seventh and High (Market) streets. It was there—the building and its neighbor were turned into a store by Simon and Hyman Gratz about 1798 and torn down in 1883—that the thirty-three-year-old Virginian wrote the "original rough draft" of the Declaration of Independence which Adams and Franklin amended only slightly. However, the wording as agreed to by the committee was not adopted until after considerable excision and revision by Congress.

(Left) Carpenters' Hall (HSP)
(Middle) *Thomas Paine*, engraving by W. Sharp after Romney, 1793 (HSP)
(Below) The Graff House at the Southwest Corner of 7th and Market Streets (LCP)
(Facing) Thomas Jefferson's Draft of the Declaration of Independence with corrections by Benjamin Franklin and John Adams, 1776 (Library of Congress)

A Declaration by the Representatives of the UNITED STATES OF AMERICA, in General Congress assembled.

When in the course of human events it becomes necessary for one people to dissolve the political bands which have connected them with another, and to assume among the powers of the earth the separate and equal station to which the laws of nature & of nature's god entitle them, a decent respect to the opinions of mankind requires that they should declare the causes which impel them to the separation.

We hold these truths to be self-evident; that all men are created equal, that they are endowed by their creator with equal inherent & inalienable rights; that among these are life, liberty, & the pursuit of happiness; that to secure these rights, governments are instituted among men, deriving their just powers from the consent of the governed; that whenever any form of government becomes destructive of these ends, it is the right of the people to alter or to abolish it, & to institute new government, laying it's foundation on such principles & organising it's powers in such form, as to them shall seem most likely to effect their safety & happiness. prudence indeed will dictate that governments long established should not be changed for light & transient causes: and accordingly all experience hath shewn that mankind are more disposed to suffer while evils are sufferable, than to right themselves by abolishing the forms to which they are accustomed. but when a long train of abuses & usurpations [begun at a distinguished period, &] pursuing invariably the same object, evinces a design to reduce them under absolute Despotism, it is their right, it is their duty, to throw off such government, & to provide new guards for their future security. such has been the patient sufferance of these colonies; & such is now the necessity which constrains them to expunge their former systems of government. the history of the present king of Great Britain is a history of unremitting injuries and usurpations, [among which appears no solitary fact to contradict the uniform tenor of the rest, but all have] in direct object the establishment of an absolute tyranny over these states. to prove this, let facts be submitted to a candid world, [for the truth of which we pledge a faith yet unsullied by falsehood.]

When the Second Continental Congress convened on May 10, 1775, the members came together around green-baize-covered tables in the Assembly Room of the State House. The Pennsylvania Assembly had moved to the second floor. The two buildings on the corners of Fifth and Sixth streets had not yet been built; the steeple, removed in 1781, was still in the shape to which it was later restored by Strickland. In the paneled east room on July 2, 1776—the date John Adams thought future generations should celebrate—Congress resolved, "That these United Colonies are, and of right ought to be, free and independent States." On the 4th of July the Declaration of Independence was adopted. John Nixon, sheriff of Philadelphia, read the Declaration to the crowds in the State House Square. Nevertheless, the engrossed parchment document was not signed until over a month later, at which time men who were not present on the critical day were able to sign while some who had actually voted for independence missed their chance.

After the Battle of Germantown the long room upstairs in the State House was used as a temporary hospital for the wounded. During the occupation British troops were quartered there, and, in disdain, they left it "in a most filthy condition & the inside torn to pieces." Congress returned to the city in July, 1778, and met regularly in the State House until June, 1783, when army mutineers demanding back pay made it expedient to move to Princeton.

(Above) *Committee Submitting the Draft of the Declaration to Congress*, painting by John Trumbull (Yale University Art Gallery)
(Middle) *A N.W. View of the State House taken in 1778*, engraving by J. Trenchard after C. W. Peale, from the *Columbian Magazine*, 1787 (HSP)
(Below, left) Original Flag of the Philadelphia Light Horse Troop made in 1775, from William P. Clarke, *Official History of the Militia and National Guard of Pennsylvania* (LCP)
(Below, right) *The Manner in which the American Colonies Declared themselves Independent of the King of England*, engraving by Noble after Hamilton, from Edward Barnard, *New, Comprehensive and Complete History of England*, 1782 (LCP)
(Facing, above) *George Washington*, from the painting by Charles Willson Peale (Pennsylvania Academy of the Fine Arts)
(Below) *American General and American Rifleman*, engraving from Edward Barnard, *New, Comprehensive and Complete History of England*, 1782 (LCP)

George Washington, over six feet tall, towered above his fellows and had about him a mien of dignity and authority. Seeking a soldier upon whom the still somewhat separatist colonials could look with respect, Congress, at the instance of John Adams, had on June 16, 1775, chosen Washington to be commander-in-chief of the American army. At once he was off to Boston where the fighting was. In the summer of 1777 Washington came back to Philadelphia on his way to meet the British under Howe, and the citizens saw him riding at the head of his troops accompanied by Henry Knox, Tench Tilghman, and the newly arrived French volunteer the Marquis de Lafayette. In January, 1779, during a visit of several weeks in the city, at the request of the Supreme Executive Council he sat for his portrait to Charles Willson Peale. On their way to Yorktown in 1781 large elements of the French and American armies passed through Philadelphia, and Washington was colorfully escorted into town by the City Light Horse. Periodically throughout the war, Philadelphians saw and hailed the man who was first in war and first in the hearts of his countrymen.

There were no Continental troops regularly responsible for the defense of the city. The voluntary Light Horse (later First City) Troop, organized late in 1774, and the Associator battalions made themselves available, but they had little to do but drill and parade until the early winter of 1776. Then a false rumor spread that Howe's British army had sailed from New York on its way to Philadelphia. Thomas Wharton, Jr., president of the Council of Safety, and David Rittenhouse, its vice-president, exhorted the volunteers and called for additional recruits. Civilians began fleeing the city. Fortunately, Washington, in Bucks County, remained calm and calculating. His surprise crossing of the Delaware and his victory at Trenton on December 26th assured Philadelphia that it was safe for the time being.

After several false alarms, Howe landed with his troops at the end of August, 1777, at the head of Chesapeake Bay and came north. Washington moved down to block him. The two armies met along the Brandywine, which the British crossed at several fords to surprise the American upstream flank under Sullivan. The reserve under Washington prevented a catastrophe, and the American general was able to effect an orderly withdrawal. The city mobilized for defense as Howe continued north, slowly enough, fortunately, for Washington to regroup his forces and pull out toward the northwest. Congress taking no chances moved to Lancaster on September 18th, and then farther on to York. A bold stroke by "Mad Anthony" Wayne to get at the British rear ended in a disaster at Paoli on September 20th. After considerable marching and countermarching, Howe entered undefended Philadelphia on September 25th.

The British occupation of Philadelphia was pleasant for the officers and wealthy Tories, uncomfortable for the troops, and bitter for the citizenry as a whole. Perhaps eight to ten thousand fled before the redcoats marched in. With supercilious exaggeration one officer recorded that only Quakers and canaille remained. In fact, some solid citizens stayed, although many did, indeed, leave. Passivity rather than enthusiasm or resistance was the attitude of most Philadelphians. The Americans made it difficult for the enemy to revictual and refuel from the outlying areas. Foraging parties did, however, break through from time to time, but the winter was cruel for most everyone, and mortally so for many American prisoners of war in the Walnut Street jail. But with houses and barracks to live in the British were better off than Washington's inadequately clothed Continentals who kept an occasionally breached but resilient collar across the peninsula of the Schuylkill and Delaware rivers.

By his EXCELLENCY
Sir WILLIAM HOWE, K. B.

General and Commander in Chief, &c. &c. &c.

PROCLAMATION.

WHEREAS It is expedient for the Security of the Inhabitants, the Suppression of Vice and Licentiousness, the Preservation of the Peace, the Support of the Poor, the Maintenance of the nightly Watch and Lamps, and the Regulation of the Markets and Ferries, with other Matters in which the Oeconomy, Peace, and good Order of the City of Philadelphia and its Environs are concerned, that a Police be established; I do therefore constitute and appoint JOSEPH GALLOWAY, Esq; SUPERINTENDENT GENERAL, assisted by three Magistrates of the Police, to be hereafter appointed, with Powers and Authority to make such Orders and Regulations from Time to Time, as may most effectually promote the salutary Ends above proposed, and to nominate and appoint such a Number of inferior Officers under them as may be found necessary to carry the said Orders and Regulations into Effect: And that their Authority shall extend in and over the Country lying between the Rivers Delaware and Schuylkill, and within the Chain of Redoubts from River to River: And I do hereby enjoin and require all Persons whatever, to pay due Obedience to the SUPERINTENDENT GENERAL, Chief Magistrates, and all others acting in Authority under them, in the Execution of their Duty, and all military Officers commanding Guards, to aid and assist them where it shall be found necessary.

Given under my Hand at Head-Quarters in Philadelphia, this 4th Day of December, 1777.

W. HOWE.

By his Excellency's Command,
ROBERT MACKENZIE, Secretary.

PHILADELPHIA, PRINTED BY JAMES HUMPHREYS, JUNR. in Market-street, between Front and Second-streets.

General Sir William Howe was frustrated because his brother, Admiral Lord Richard Howe, could not bring his ships up the Delaware and supply the city by sea. Chevaux-de-frise protected by a few small American fortifications and a minuscule navy prevented free access. Pounding away with superior naval forces on the river and sending troops across to Jersey to attack fortifications from the rear, the British fought to clear the way. Still, it was not easy sailing: the Augusta was spectacularly blown up and the Merlin burned. Fort Mercer at Red Bank on the Jersey shore resisted. Then a major effort was centered on Fort Mifflin on Mud Island, which dominated the channel. The defense was heroic but to no avail; ship and shore batteries poured shells into the fort. On November 16, 1777, the survivors of the bombardment made their way to Fort Mercer, which soon thereafter also fell. The Delaware lay open to the British.

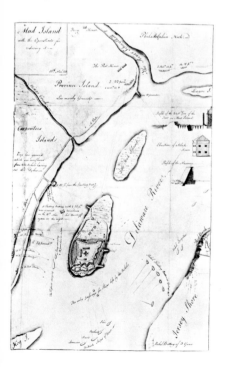

In COUNCIL of SAFETY,

Philadelphia, November 14th 1776,
12 o'Clock, Thursday.

SIR,

WE have certain Intelligence that the Enemy has actually sailed from New York Five Hundred Ships for this City, and that great Numbers had got out of the Hook on 12 o'Clock Yesterday and were steering towards our Capes: As you value the Safety of your Country, and all that is dear and valuable to Men, we most earnestly solicit your immediate Assistance, and that you will march all your Battalion to this City without the least Delay.

As nothing but the most hasty Marching of the Militia will enable us to make a Stand, it is hoped that your Battalion will manifest their usual Spirit, and come forth on this trying Occasion with the Alacrity that will do them Honour. If you can collect any Shovels, Spades, Grubbing Hoes and Pitching Axes, beg you will bring them forward and the People shall be paid for them a full Price.

By Order of Council,

THOMAS WHARTON, Jun. President

The British were established solidly in Germantown on the line of Schoolhouse Lane from the Wissahickon in a northeasterly direction through what is now Logan to Old York Road. After diversionary maneuvers Washington moved down Skippack Pike toward Germantown on the night of October 3, 1777, hoping to surprise Howe and break through his lines. An autumn fog, bad communications, and the stubborn British defense of Cliveden, the Chew Mansion, turned the Americans' expectations into a military defeat. However, the direct attack against the regulars of the king's army by provincials was bold and unprecedented; in Europe it was looked upon with respect. Cautiously, Washington withdrew to the north and eventually to Valley Forge.

(Below) *Cliveden during the Battle of Germantown,* painting by Edward L. Henry (The National Trust for Historic Preservation, Cliveden) (Right) *State House on the Day of the Battle of Germantown,* painting by Peter Rothermel (Pennsylvania Academy of the Fine Arts)

The winter of 1777-78 at Valley Forge marked the lowest point in American fortunes during the Revolution. To that plateau above the Schuylkill Washington had drawn back his troops from Whitemarsh where they were more exposed. Lacking shoes, blankets, overcoats, food, and proper shelter, they suffered bitterly. Cold, aggravated by snow, made the encampment an icy hell. In February the Prussian volunteer Baron Von Steuben joined Washington's army. Patiently, painstakingly, and methodically he taught the motley, ill-equipped troops the elements of drill and military discipline. Out of the winter's misery came an American army which had been taught not only to survive but to maneuver. Spring brought an unprecedented run of shad up the Schuylkill to feed the starving troops, news of the French alliance, and Clinton's replacement of Howe. On June 18, 1778, fearful of being blockaded, the British evacuated Philadelphia.

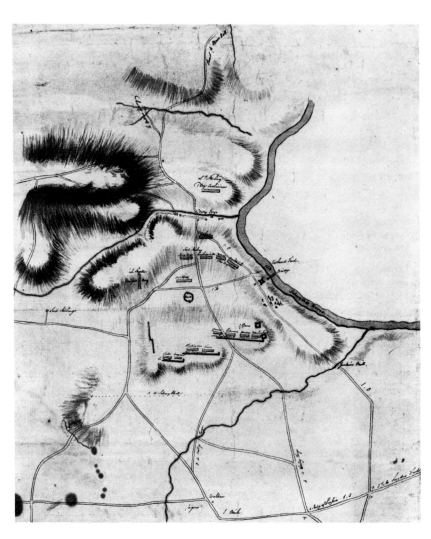

(Above) *Map of Encampment at Valley Forge,* pen-and-ink drawing by a French engineer, 1777-78 (HSP)
(Below) *Washington Reviewing the Troops at Valley Forge,* painting by William T. Trego (Valley Forge Historical Society)

When Sir Henry Clinton pulled the British troops out of Philadelphia, Major General Benedict Arnold entered as the American military commander. A hero of Montgomery's disastrous expedition against Quebec, wounded at the triumph of Saratoga, the dashing officer was welcomed in the liberated city. The welcome cooled, however, as profits from goods under his control flowed into his personal purse. Friendship with known Tories did nothing to encourage a favorable opinion of his governance. He did succeed, nonetheless, in wooing and winning pretty Peggy Shippen and bought Captain John MacPherson's splendid country house. No honest man, the president of the Supreme Executive Council of Pennsylvania believed, could live quite so luxuriously, so a court-martial was instituted. Arnold was acquitted of major crimes but found guilty of a minor one. He was ripe for treason. After contacting Major John André in the summer of 1780, he sold out. In Philadelphia the news of Arnold's treachery stimulated a public demonstration. The patriot-artist Charles Willson Peale designed a float on which an effigy of the two-faced traitor was mechanically prodded by the devil as the wagon moved through the streets. Peggy Shippen, who, Arnold told Washington, was ignorant of his plot, was quickly hustled out of the city to join her husband in British exile.

(Below) *Self-Portrait*, pen-and-ink sketch by John André (Yale University Art Gallery)
(Above) *Margaret Shippen and her Son*, painting by Daniel Gardner (HSP)
(Right) *Arnold in Effigy Drawn through the Streets*, woodcut after Charles Willson Peale, 1780 (HSP)

1785-1800

The postwar period, the Federal era, was a bittersweet one for Philadelphia. The excitement of being the seat of government and the site of the Constitutional Convention was leavened by political turmoil and yellow fever epidemics. Prosperous growth alternated with inflationary depression. Peace was followed by undeclared naval warfare. Yet, by the end of the century, the city was well established as a center of culture, finance, and mercantile trade.

The Founding Fathers of the nation, the victorious generals of the Revolution, and the framers of the Constitution walked its streets. When the venerable Franklin returned home in the autumn of 1785, visitors from all over came to pay him homage. Philadelphia once more saw him, striding no more, but nodding genially as, lamed by gout, he went past familiar landmarks and new buildings on his way to the State House where he presided over the Supreme Executive Council of Pennsylvania. The city rubbed shoulders, some times literally, always figuratively, with the national great.

To meet the demands made by its position as capital and commercial entrepot, the city grew physically and politically. Dock Creek, which wound its way erratically in a northeasterly direction from the Delaware, had become an open sewer and was arched over to create a new street. The old British barracks in the Northern Liberties were torn down and the land given over to the development of houses and stores. The main market behind City Hall was extended another block to the west, and from 1792 the busy corner at Third and Market (formerly High) street was dominated by Cooke's Building, a jeweler's misguided extravagance, too large and too fine to be economically viable. William Hamilton greatly enhanced his gardens at The Woodlands with exotic trees and shrubs, and Robert Morris' The Hills, also overlooking the Schuylkill, was repaired and then remodeled at the end of the century. The impressive center section of the Pennsylvania Hospital, designed by David Evans, Jr., was added to connect the original east wing with the new west extension. Public buildings were erected on either side of the State House, in the vicinity of which structures in the revived classical mode gave architectural distinction to the nerve center of the city.

After its exile in Princeton, Annapolis, and New York, Congress eventually moved back to Philadelphia. Added crowds and added importance came when the Constitutional Convention met in town

(Facing) Silver Peace Medal given to the Indians by President Washington, by Joseph Richardson, Jr., 1793 (HSP)
(Above and following) The Earliest Coins in the Dollar Decimal System of the United States, 1792-94 (Smithsonian Institution)
1793 Half Cent

97

during the summer of 1787. The sessions were confidential, so no popular discussion of or arguments pro and con about the new frame of government took place until the document was published. Then the city and the nation were split between the instrument's defenders and its attackers. In Philadelphia it was the moderates who supported the federal plan embedded in the Constitution; the radicals opposed it. The city at this time was Federalist, with the growing county population far less so. When Philadelphia was reincorporated in 1789, although such erstwhile patriots as John Nixon, Gunning Bedford, Francis Hopkinson, Matthew Clarkson, and Samuel Powel were elected aldermen and Powel chosen mayor, former loyalists, in fact or in public opinion, such as Jared Ingersoll, Benjamin Chew, James Pemberton, Miers Fisher, and Henry Drinker were voted onto the Common Council. The "City of Brotherly Love" within but a few years of the end of the Revolution was counting all men brothers. For a while, in the flush of federalism, there was a conservative trend. After a hard fight, the moderates who had wanted a change in the radical state constitution of 1776 won a new one in 1790.

Robert Morris in the Senate of the United States, Thomas Fitz-Simons in the House, and Tench Coxe as lobbyist extraordinary argued, coaxed, wheedled, and even promised preferred housing to get the votes to bring the government back from New York, if only for a decade. With national actors on the local stage from 1790 on, the affairs of the country overshadowed all else in the taverns, the offices, and the streets of town. The French Revolution and the outbreak of the recurrent war between England and France crystallized a new alignment of political parties, one which resulted in the American two-party system. The administrations of Washington and Adams were pro-English and their local Federalist supporters counted among them government appointees, ministers of the newly organized Protestant Episcopal Church, former army officers, members of the Society of the Sons of St. George, the militiamen of MacPherson's Blues, and many of the wealthiest merchants. For them it was "Huzza for Washington" and the rousing words of Joseph Hopkinson's "Hail Columbia."

On the other side of the political fence were the Francophiles. They included a number of native American liberals such as Benjamin Rush, Clement Biddle, David Rittenhouse, Benjamin Franklin Bache,

Thomas McKean, and Thomas Mifflin. Joining forces with an influx of Irish republican exiles led by Mathew Carey and William Duane, a majority of the free blacks, most of the few Jews in town, and Stephen Girard and other Frenchmen, they called themselves Democratic–Republicans. The white cockade became their badge. Their strength derived from organizations like the Hibernian Society, the Friendly Sons of St. Patrick, the Society of the Sons of St. Tammany, the Democratic Society, and the French Society of the Friends of Liberty and Equality. These anti-Federalists were antagonistic to the haughty tone of the Federal administrations, bitterly condemned Jay's Treaty, and were ready to fight another war against Britain. Demonstrations for or against one course of action, dinners in celebration of victories, and processions to accompany a favorite became regular events in the city.

Peace in 1783 was the opening of a floodgate of imported goods for which the city was at first grateful. With nationhood, however, came national pride, and native industries were promoted more and more. The Pennsylvania Society for the Encouragement of Manufactures and the Useful Arts was founded in 1787 and, significant for the future of Philadelphia as a textile center, imported machines for carding and spinning cotton. Tench Coxe urged the South to make cotton its major crop to supply mills in the North. Alexander Hamilton's report on manufactures further emphasized the need to be self-sufficient. In 1791 the Bank of North America patriotically and practically adopted dollars and cents as standard currency instead of the colonial shillings and pence. A permanent asset to the city was added the following year when the first mint of the United States was established there, a tribute to the technical skill of local engravers and mechanics. Philadelphia then saw an efflorescence of locally made products. John Biddis produced white lead "equal to any imported from Europe"; James Juhan advertised an American piano-forte; Mason & Gibbs manufactured fire engines; William Shepherd built a mill to saw and polish marble; and John Hewson printed calico.

To create industry capital was needed. Another of Hamilton's reforms was the establishment of the Bank of the United States to control currency and credit. It was so successful that, in an era of speculation, the stock of the bank was immediately subscribed to and within four days doubled in price before it gradually subsided again

(Above) 1793 Wreath Cent

Liberty Displaying the Arts and Sciences, painting by Samuel Jennings, 1792 (LCP)

(Above) 1792 Half Disme

to par. Speculative fever infected the city. The purchase of land, with limitless unpopulated acres west of the seaboard states, was the chief form of gambling. But when western migration and settlement could not keep pace with real estate acquisition and taxes became due, the inevitable collapse occurred. Some prominent Philadelphians, Robert Morris, John Nicholson, and James Wilson among them, were ruined.

At the same time, more successfully, merchants expanded their trade. Morris was part owner of the *Empress of China*, the American ship which, sailing from New York, first opened trade to the Far East. In 1786 the *Canton*, Thomas Truxtun captain, began the Philadelphia–China trade which rivaled that of New England. While tea, nankeens, and porcelains were the regular imports from the east, Philadelphia got a taste of Chinese elegance when the Dutch diplomat Braam von Hoogheest settled for a few years in a mansion on the Delaware near Bristol, bringing with him from China servants, pictures, and objects of art.

Shipping subject to loss from storms and hostile men-of-war was a sometimes hazardous, if frequently rewarding, investment. However, marine insurance could moderate possible loss. In 1792 a stock company, the Insurance Company of North America, was formed, the first of its kind. Within six years it was writing virtually the entire marine business of the country. In addition, the company did issue a few term life insurance policies. The first of them in the United States was upon the life of the Philadelphia merchant John Holker in 1796.

Symbolic of the era was the painting, *Liberty Displaying the Arts and Sciences,* which the expatriate local artist Samuel Jennings sent from London to the Library Company for its new building in 1792. While there was an antislavery motif to the whole, the instruments of art and science proclaimed a promise for all. In 1795 the short-lived Columbianum in Philadelphia held the first artists' exhibition of paintings in America. It was fitting, for Charles Willson Peale, its initiator, was at the height of his career as a portrait painter. At the same time many of the famous and the wealthy were sitting for the flattering brush of Gilbert Stuart, then resident in the city. Engravers by the dozen were practicing their trade, making plates for the well-illustrated *Columbian Magazine* and Dobson's *Encyclopaedia.*

In the field of science, the debate over the cause and cure of yellow fever dominated all else. Benjamin Rush, right or wrong, was the leader of the medical profession and the first American physician to gain international recognition. It was his reputation, buttressed by his distinguished colleagues on the faculty of the medical school of the University of Pennsylvania, which attracted students from all over, and particularly from the South. With the American Philosophical Society issuing *Proceedings* on a more frequent basis, the nation looked to Philadelphia for the latest reports on scientific and technological developments. On the eve of the industrial revolution the city was poised to move ahead.

1794 Silver Dollar

For months during the hot summer of 1787 delegates from the thirteen states met in the State House to frame an instrument which would create an effective federal government. After much debate and a good deal of compromising the Constitution of the United States was adopted on September 17, 1787. All the delegates from Pennsylvania were resident Philadelphians, a matter which caused trouble when the state assembly met to consider its action. In December a state convention ratified the Constitution by a vote of two to one, an occasion celebrated with cannons and bells. It was, however, on July 4, 1788, after the ratification by the tenth state had assured the national acceptance of the Constitution, that the city paid its most glorious tribute to the formation of the Union. A grand federal procession wound through the streets all day. Officials, splendidly uniformed troops, symbolic floats, members of various societies, representatives of the trades with emblematic flags and their work instruments, students of the university, Christian clergy arm-in-arm with the Jewish rabbi, and many others paraded circuitously from Third and South streets to Bush Hill where refreshments were provided. It was the most colorful spectacle up to that time held in Philadelphia.

John Dickinson's

7 August 1787

WE the People of the States of New-Hampſhire, Maſſachuſetts, Rhode-Iſland and Providence Plantations, Connecticut, New-York, New-Jerſey, Pennſylvania, Delaware, Maryland, Virginia, North-Carolina, South-Carolina, and Georgia, do ordain, declare and eſtabliſh the following Conſtitution for the Government of Ourſelves and our Poſterity.

ARTICLE I.

The ſtile of this Government ſhall be, " The United States of America."

II.

The Government ſhall conſiſt of ſupreme legiſlative, executive and judicial powers.

III.

The legiſlative power ſhall be veſted in a Congreſs, to conſiſt of two ſeparate and diſtinct bodies of men, a Houſe of Repreſentatives, and a Senate; each of which ſhall, in all caſes, have a negative on the other. The Legiſlature ſhall meet on the firſt Monday in December in every year, unleſs a different day ſhall all be appointed by law.

IV.

Sect. 1. The Members of the Houſe of Repreſentatives ſhall be choſen every ſecond year, by the people of the ſeveral States comprehended within this Union. The qualifications of the electors ſhall be the ſame, from time to time, as thoſe of the electors in the ſeveral States, of the moſt numerous branch of their own legiſlatures.

Sect. 2. Every Member of the Houſe of Repreſentatives ſhall be of the age of twenty-five years at leaſt; ſhall have been a citizen in the United States for at leaſt three years before his election; and ſhall be, at the time of his election, a reſident of the State in which he ſhall be choſen.

Sect. 3. The Houſe of Repreſentatives ſhall, at its firſt formation, and until the number of citizens and inhabitants ſhall be taken in the manner herein after deſcribed, conſiſt of ſixty-five Members, of whom three ſhall be choſen in New-Hampſhire, eight in Maſſachuſetts, one in Rhode-Iſland and Providence Plantations, five in Connecticut, ſix in New-York, four in New-Jerſey, eight in Pennſylvania, one in Delaware, ſix in Maryland, ten in Virginia, five in North-Carolina, five in South-Carolina, and three in Georgia.

Sect. 4. As the proportions of numbers in the different States will alter from time to time; as ſome of the States may hereafter be divided; as others may be enlarged by addition of territory; as two or more States may be united; as new States will be erected within the limits of the United States, the Legiſlature ſhall, in each of theſe caſes, regulate the number of repreſentatives by the number of inhabitants, according to the provisions herein after made, at the rate of one for every forty thouſand, provided that such Holethanuat count one Perſon within the

Sect. 5. All bills for raiſing or appropriating money, and for fixing the ſalaries of the officers of government, ſhall originate in the Houſe of Repreſentatives, and ſhall not be altered or amended by the Senate. No money ſhall be drawn from the public Treaſury, but in purſuance of appropriations that ſhall originate in the Houſe of Repreſentatives.

Sect. 6. The Houſe of Repreſentatives ſhall have the ſole power of impeachment. It ſhall chooſe its Speaker and other officers.

Sect. 7. Vacancies in the Houſe of Repreſentatives ſhall be ſupplied by writs of election from the executive authority of the State, in the repreſentation from which they ſhall happen. V.

(Above) The First Preliminary Draft of the Constitution with Changes in the Hand of John Dickinson, 1787 (LCP)
(Below) An Imaginary Representation of the Constitutional Convention, engraving (photograph, HSP)

The Constitution and a federal government did not come into being by acclamation. There were deals which had to be made. One of them was where the capital of the United States eventually would be located. Sectionalism played its prejudicial part. It took considerable backstage politicking to arrive at the compromise whereby the initial brief convocation of the new government was held in New York in 1789 followed by a move to Philadelphia the following year. That city was to be the seat of government until a federal enclave was established in the undeveloped mud flats on the Potomac. Robert Morris, financier, entrepreneur, and senator from Pennsylvania, played a leading role in making Philadelphia the temporary capital.

Several times during the decade while Philadelphia was the nation's capital, delegations of Indians visited the city to pay their respects to the new government and to negotiate treaties securing their lands. In 1793 forty-seven Senecas, Onondagas, Oneidas, Tuscaroras, and Stockbridges came to town. They admired and were admired. President Washington gave each of them a peace medal made by the local silversmith Joseph Richardson, Jr. They were shown the sights by Frederick Augustus Muhlenberg, Speaker of the House of Representatives, and they were received at the State House by Governor Mifflin. In return they gave an exhibition of war dances and the Seneca chief Red Jacket delivered a formal oration of thanks.

(Above) *View of Con[gre]ss on the Road to Philadelphia*, etched cartoon, 1790 (LCP)
(Below) *Indians being shown the City by Frederick Augustus Muhlenberg*, water color by William Birch (LCP)

American political life—the typical knock-down and drag-out kind of election—began in the last decade of the eighteenth century. Philadelphia as the nation's capital was the center of the arena. There spitting venom were the Irish-born Jeffersonian Mathew Carey and the Anglophile Federalist William Cobbett, whose pseudonym Peter Porcupine became synonymous with mudslinging. Fenno's Gazette of the United States vituperated on behalf of the Washington and Adams faction, while equally scurrilous on the side of the Democratic–Republicans was Bache's General Advertiser, better known in later years as the Aurora. When Bache died in the fever epidemic of 1798, William Duane married his widow and carried on his partisanship. Pamphlets poured from the presses. Demonstrations took place with the Federalists invoking the newly apotheosized Washington, and their liberty-capped, cockade-wearing opponents puffing the new republicanism. The reaction to the intolerance of the Alien and Sedition Acts won Jefferson the presidency. Amazingly enough, in Philadelphia the thunder of words and politicized mass meetings never provoked other than minor incidents of violence.

See Porcupine, in Colours just Portray'd, Anti-Cobbett cartoon, etching and aquatint, ca. 1799 (HSP)

Enjoying the prestige of being the capital of the United States, Philadelphia burgeoned architecturally as did no other American city. It was fortunate in having experienced builders, wide streets, and a unique urban portraitist, William Birch, who lovingly recorded the city's brick and marble elegance, its busy streets and commodious houses. The classical columnar dignity of the façades of many buildings gave the town an appearance of attractive order. Banks, churches, the library, and private mansions in city and country stood proud, red and white, along the rectilinear streets and on hills overlooking the rivers. But there was bustle too, the hoof-clopping, cart-creaking activity of a flourishing city.

(Above) *Library Company of Philadelphia*, detail of etching by W. Birch, 1799 (HSP)
(Below) *Bank of the United States*, etching by W. Birch, 1799 (HSP)

From shortly after the city's founding shipbuilding was a thriving Philadelphia industry. An ample supply of wood from upcountry and skilled mechanics enabled the local yards to meet the demand for merchant ships and men-of-war. During the Revolution and a decade later when neutral American shipping was harassed by Barbary pirates in the Mediterranean and European belligerents in the West Indies, armed government vessels were needed for the protection of trade. There was a busy shipyard in Kensington and a larger one near Old Swedes' Church in Southwark. In the latter Joshua Humphreys in 1796 built the United States, which was placed under the command of Commodore John Barry, the father of the American Navy. Humphreys also built the frigate Philadelphia, which ran aground and was seized in the Tripolitan War. Stephen Decatur won national fame in 1804 by boldly destroying that captured vessel under the noses of the enemy in the harbor of Tripoli.

(Above) *The Burning of the Frigate* Philadelphia *in the Harbor of Tripoli,* painting by an unknown artist (Mariners Museum, Newport News, Va.)
(Right) *Preparations for War, Building the Frigate* Philadelphia *in Southwark,* etching by William Birch, 1799 (HSP)
(Below) *John Barry,* engraving after Alonzo Chappel (LCP)

The first steamboat ever built splashed up the Delaware before the eyes of the members of the Constitutional Convention. John Fitch had begun working on such a project, a boat to be propelled by steam, in 1785. The following year he formed a company in Philadelphia and got the capital to build such a craft. In July, 1786, a curious boat with six paddles on each side worked by cranks connected to a steam engine did indeed go up the Delaware. An improved, but still erratic, version was demonstrated publicly a year later. Fitch was before his time, but within a comparatively few years steamboat service from Philadelphia to Trenton was an advertised reality.

The prison, built at Sixth and Walnut streets in 1774, and its administration were internationally famous. As in prisons everywhere at that time, conditions had been execrable—so bad, in fact, that in 1781 the Society for the Alleviation of the Miseries of Public Prisons was established to reform the whole penal system. At its urging the Pennsylvania Assembly in 1790 created a board of prison inspectors who instituted many changes for the better, including the encouragement of convicts to work for pay. When the legislature in 1794 abolished capital punishment except for first-degree murder, it seemed to many a liberal model had been created. One of the praised reforms was the institution of solitary confinement. Although the yard was used for occasional public events such as Blanchard's balloon ascension in 1793, the first in America, the Walnut Street prison was cold, crowded, and gloomy.

Plan of Mr Fitch's Steam Boat.

SIC ITUR AD ASTRA.

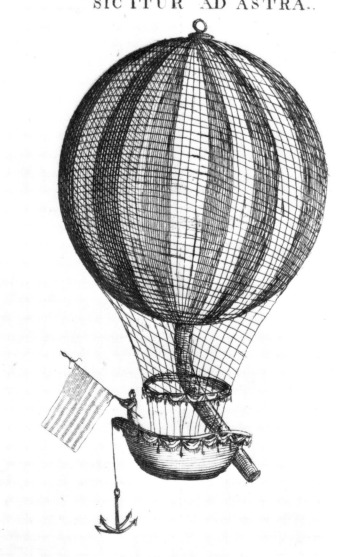

(Above) *John Fitch's Steam Boat*, engraving, from the *Columbian Magazine*, 1786 (LCP)
(Below) *Blanchard's Balloon*, engraving, from his *Journal of my Forty-fifth Ascension, being the first performed in America*, 1793 (LCP)
(Facing, above) *Philadelphia Tavern Scene*, Tobacco Advertisement of Isaac Jones, engraving (LCP)
(Facing, middle) *An East View of Gray's Ferry, near Philadelphia with the Triumphal Arches, &c. erected for the Reception of General Washington*, engraving by J. Trenchard after C. W. Peale, from the *Columbian Magazine*, 1789 (LCP)
(Facing, below left) *John Bill Ricketts, the Trick Rider*, stipple engraving (HSP)
(Facing, below right) *The late Theatre in Chestnut Street*, etching by Gilbert Fox after W. Birch, 1804 (LCP)

Taverns provided the chief places of relaxation—or exhilaration—for every class of citizen from merchant to hostler. There were many inns in town; some were frequented by the best society, others were mere brothels. In addition, the large circus amphitheater, erected by the trick rider John Bill Ricketts in 1787-89, across Sixth Street from Congress Hall, offered equestrian spectacles and housed banquets. Another popular place of resort was Gray's Garden by the floating bridge over the Schuylkill which Washington crossed—exuberantly greeted—on the way to his inauguration in New York in 1789. With the Quaker and Presbyterian influence on the wane and wartime restrictions removed, the theater came to Philadelphia on a permanent basis. From 1785 irregularly until 1790 Lewis Hallam's American Company and its successors played the old Southwark. It was, however, with the opening of the Chestnut Street Theatre in 1794 that the city could boast an adequate structure for plays and operas. Reinagle and Wignell raised the money for the building and brought from England a professional company including an orchestra. From that time, Philadelphia played a major role in the American theatrical scene.

An East View of GRAY'S FERRY, near Philadelphia, with the TRIUMPHAL ARCHES, &c. erected for the Reception of General Washington, April 20th 1789.

In the decorative arts florid curves and elaborate ornamentation became old-fashioned. Simpler, more delicate motifs popularized in England by Hepplewhite and Sheraton became the models for the Federal period. Contrasting colored inlays decorated the straighter lines of the furniture which the Philadelphia cabinetmakers supplied for their customers, and bright paint was sometimes substituted for carving to create a light feeling. Windsor chairs for less formal use and humbler homes continued to be produced locally by many competent craftsmen. Urn-shaped silver tea sets took on a new kind of elegance which bright-cut engraving, beading, and fluting gave them. More and more the American eagle appeared in both wood and metal pieces, a proud affirmation of the quality of native workmanship.

(Above) Painted Philadelphia Hepplewhite Chair made for Elias Hasket Derby of Salem, ca. 1796 (Henry Francis du Pont Winterthur Museum) (Below) Silver Tea and Coffee Service, attributed to Christian Wiltberger, ca. 1799 (Metropolitan Museum of Art; lent by H. H. Walker Lewis)

The concentration of political and financial power in the city created a ferment in the publishing world. Philadelphia was for half a century the book center of the country. First, the well-illustrated Columbian Magazine, then Mathew Carey's American Museum, *paved the way for later successful periodicals. Thomas Dobson's* Encyclopaedia, *the continent's most ambitious printing venture up to that time, proved that American presses and American engravers could produce eighteen quarto volumes of text with over five hundred illustrations. Sheet music, much of local composition or arrangement, came from the establishments of George Willig and Benjamin Carr. The first native American professional novelist, Charles Brockden Brown, made the city the scene of some of his tales and his regular place of publication. The creative intellect was bubbling.*

(Above) Frontispiece and Title-page of *The Columbian Magazine,* 1787 (LCP)
(Right) Frontispiece and Title-page of Dobson's *Encyclopaedia,* 1798 (LCP)
(Below) *The favorite new Federal song adapted to the President's march,* "Hail! Columbia," by Joseph Hopkinson, engraved sheet music, 1798 (HSP)

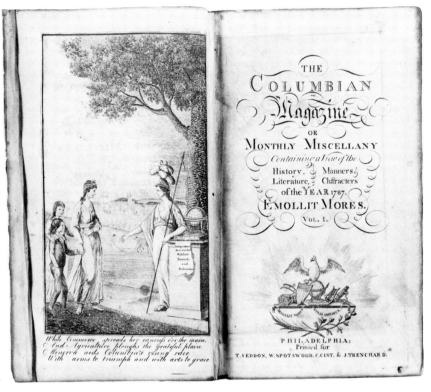

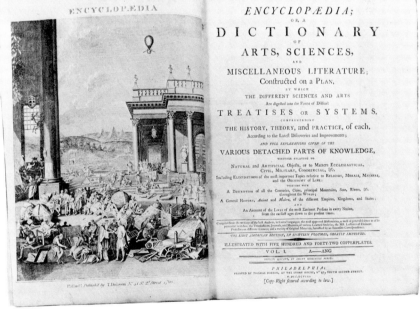

Parties, dinners, and balls enlivened the life of the capital city. So splendid and aristocratic in tone were these that the rising anti-Federalist party spoke bitterly of the "Federal Court" and "Lady" Washington. Indeed, the Washingtons settled down quite luxuriously in the house on Market Street between Fifth and Sixth which Mary Masters had conveyed to her daughter upon her marriage to Thomas Penn. At the apex of the rich social life were Senator William Bingham and his beautiful wife Anne. One of the richest men in the country, Bingham built a palatial mansion on Third Street above Spruce, modeled on the residence of the Duke of Manchester. There the Binghams entertained government officials, foreign visitors, and well-connected Philadelphians. High fashion, elegant furnishings, the clipped, cultured accents of the London banker Alexander Baring, who married a Bingham daughter in 1798, and the melodious French of the Vicomte de Noailles, a refugee from the Reign of Terror—these formed the mixture of cosmopolitan sophistication which the well-to-do enjoyed.

Tobias Hirte of Philadelphia should be better known. He was the first man to advertise American petroleum, the real founder of the oil industry. "If you're off to Philadelphia in the morning," Rudyard Kipling wrote in Rewards and Fairies, "You mustn't take my stories for a guide." He told of the city in the 1790s, and his fictional young hero worked for the real apothecary Hirte at 118 North Second Street. There he sold Indian-French-Creek-Seneca-Spring-Oil which was reputed to cure just about everything. The oil came from a spring a hundred miles north of Pittsburgh, where Edwin L. Drake later pushed down his well. The viscous substance had long been skimmed off the top of the creek and used medicinally by the Indians, from whom Moravian missionaries first learned of it.

(Preceding) An Idealized Representation of an Evening Reception at President Washington's Mansion, painting by Daniel B. Huntington (Brooklyn Museum of Art)
(Right) Advertisement of Hirte's Indian-French-Creek-Seneca-Spring-Oil, 1792 (LCP)

Indianisch=French=Crieck=Seneca=Spring=Oel.

Ein vortrefliches und bewährtes Medicament,

Ist zu haben, zu Philadelphia, bey Tobias Hirte, Num. 118. in der Zweyten-straße die nächste Thür zur Wittwe Käser, Wirthin.

Kurtze Nachricht von diesem Oel, dessen Nutzen und Gebrauch.

Dieses Oel ist auch vor die gegenwärtige Zeit bey folgenden Herren zu haben.

In Philadelphia bey Jacob Ritter, in der Frontstraße die dritte Thür unterhalb der Archstraß, Frantz Löscher, Gast-Wirth an dem obern End der zweyten Straß; in Germantaun bey Peter Leibert, und Justus Fuchs; auf Chesnuthill, bey Samuel Saur; in Schippach bey Henrich Hunsiker; u. s. w. in Bethlehem bey Docter Freytag; in Easton bey William Raab; in Reading bey Ehrhard Roos; in Libanon bey Henrich Pohler; in Friederichstaun bey Jacob Steiner; in Baltimore bey Nicolaus Tschudy. u. s. w.

Chesnuthill, Gedruckt bey Samuel Saur, 1792.

In the middle of August, 1793, people started dying in unusual numbers. The doctors were quick to recognize the plague as yellow fever, but they had no idea what caused it. Miasma, the refugees from Santo Domingo, and filth were among the causes suggested. As the disease spread, at first dozens, then hundreds, died; all who could fled. President Washington and most of the government officials administered the affairs of the nation from Germantown. A committee headed by Mayor Matthew Clarkson and including the merchant Stephen Girard, the publisher Mathew Carey, and others stayed in town and managed civic affairs. They established a hospital at the Hamilton estate of Bush Hill and tried to maintain order in chaos. The Negro community provided the manpower to do what others were frightened of doing. Dr. Benjamin Rush stayed on and treated hundreds with his unvarying regimen of bleeding and purging. His treatment may have been ill-advised, but the presence in town of the country's most famous doctor was heartening, and he was heroic in his attendance on the sick. Those physicians who favored a milder treatment—fresh air, a mild diet, and rest—seemed more successful and no less heroic. With cold weather the fever abated. But in 1797 and 1798 it returned and took its heavy toll.

(Above) The Deshler-Franks-Morris House on the Germantown Pike where Washington stayed during the yellow fever epidemic (HSP)
(Below) Dr. Benjamin Rush, engraving by Edwin from painting by Thomas Sully (LCP)
(Right) Broadside Bill of Mortality during the epidemic, 1793 (LCP)

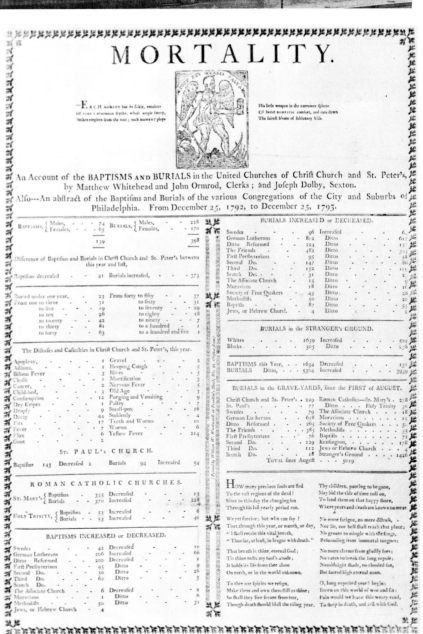

The Anglican church in America immediately after the Revolution was faced with the problem of separating from the Church of England and yet maintaining the apostolic succession of its ministers through traditional consecration. Under the leadership of the Reverend Dr. William White, since 1777 chaplain of Congress and since 1779 rector of the United Churches of Christ Church, St. Peter's, and St. James's, a convention was held in Philadelphia in the autumn of 1785. At that meeting the church christened itself the Protestant Episcopal Church in the United States. An American revision of the Book of Common Prayer was made. Agreement was reached with the Church of England that after three American bishops were consecrated the Protestant Episcopal Church would be on its own. Dr. White, among the first, was consecrated Bishop of Pennsylvania in 1787. He was, and remained until his death in 1836, a moving force in the American episcopate.

The first antislavery organization in America was founded in Philadelphia by a small group of Quakers in 1775, but initially it had little impact on the total community. In 1787 the Pennsylvania Society for Promoting the Abolition of Slavery, and the Relief of Free Negroes was reorganized with the venerable Franklin as president. Many prominent citizens joined the society and its influence grew. Associated groups were encouraged to organize in other states. Congress was memorialized. The society's practical work consisted of aid to free blacks who were continually harassed by kidnappers and of keeping manumission records so that proof of freedom was available.

(Above) *Bishop William White,* mezzotint by Sartain and Thomas Sully (HSP)
(Below) Page from the Minute Book of the Pennsylvania Society for Promoting the Abolition of Slavery, March 5, 1787 (HSP)
(Facing, above) *Absalom Jones,* painting by Rembrandt Peale (National Portrait Gallery, Smithsonian Institution, on loan from the Wilmington Society of Fine Arts, Delaware Art Museum)
(Facing, below) Strip of Road Map out of Philadelphia toward New York, etching, from Christopher Colles, *A Survey of the Roads of the United States of America,* 1789
(Facing, right) Stock Certificate of the Philadelphia and Lancaster Turnpike Road Company, 1795 (HSP)

Discrimination in seating led a number of Negroes in 1787 to withdraw from St. George's Methodist Church and found the Free African Society. Shortly afterward this group split, some under the leadership of Absalom Jones breaking away to establish St. Thomas's African Episcopal Church, while others worked with Richard Allen to form the African Methodist Church, familiarly known as "Mother Bethel." During the yellow fever epidemics at the end of the century, the ministers Allen and Jones and their congregants stayed in the city when others fled. Heroically they nursed the sick and buried the dead, performing those unpleasant and dangerous services voluntarily or for but little monetary reward.

There was no part of the United States which had a richer hinterland than Philadelphia. It lay like a crescent around the city, pulled out of symmetry to the west by the fertility centered at Lancaster. The nation's thrust was in that direction, and the first practical pathway thither was the Lancaster Turnpike, an all-weather road built by a private Philadelphia company. Begun in 1792 and finished two years later, it was long the most traveled westerly highway in the entire country. Soon other companies built additional toll roads to provide the city with links in all directions.

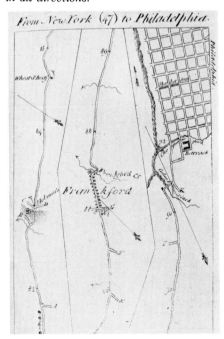

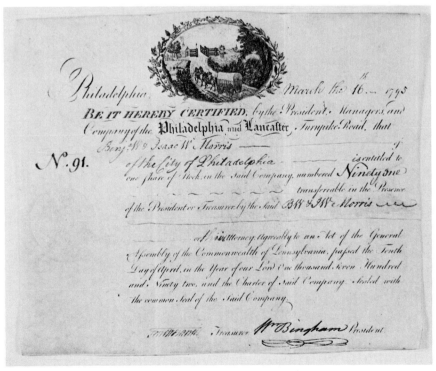

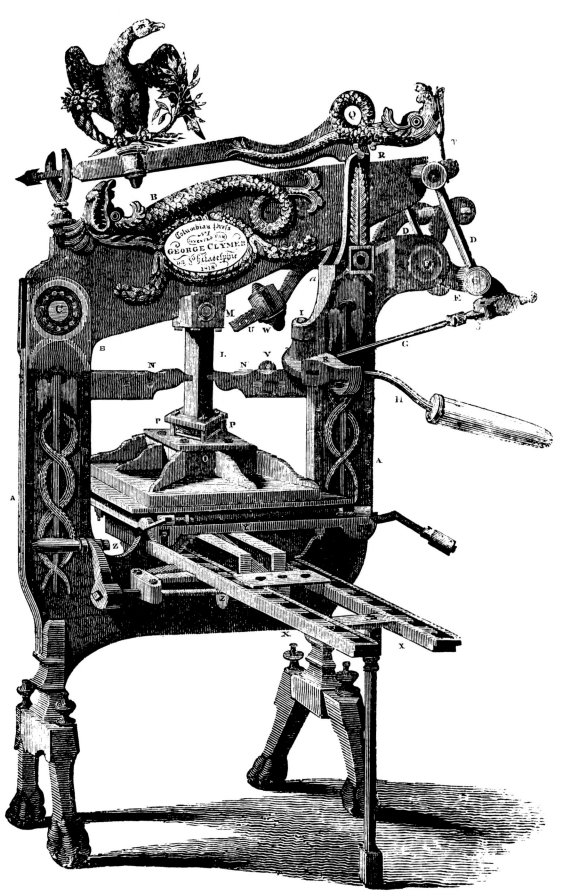

COLUMBIAN PRESS.

1800-1820

Part of the glory had departed; Philadelphia was no longer capital of either Pennsylvania or the United States. Nevertheless, some of the glory did remain. Philadelphia was the largest, richest, and most culturally exciting city in the country.

Although the Napoleonic war in Europe had limited immigration into the country, Philadelphia County's population, which still included parts of present-day Montgomery and Delaware counties, grew from 81,009 in 1800 to 135,637 in 1820. Houses and shops continued to spread in a half-moon pattern with an ever-increasing diameter along the Delaware. In 1799 Frankford, a cluster of mills and small houses up-river, became a borough. Northern Liberties, the fastest growing county area contiguous to the city, was incorporated as a district in 1803, Moyamensing to the south in 1812, and Kensington, just south of Frankford, in 1820. To the west the built-up section crept on toward Broad Street, but the numbered streets on the Schuylkill side were at best paths or unpaved roads which ran past farms and through fields. Although Varlé's 1802 map shows a well-designed town centered on Market Street across the river in West Philadelphia, it was not until William Hamilton sold off much of his land south of Market Street in 1804-6 and the Powels broke up their holding north of there in 1836 that the area consisted of other than large estates, such as The Woodlands, Powelton, and Lansdowne.

Like spokes, turnpikes radiated out from Penn's gridiron to bring more and more of the products of the hinterland fields and forests to the city. Wood was still the only fuel for heating houses and feeding steam engines. The mud and ruts of the old Germantown road, said by many to be the worst in the country, made it impassable at some times of the year and always perilous. A turnpike company was incorporated in 1801 to build a toll road from Third and Vine streets to Germantown. In quick succession other pikes were extended, north along Old York Road, through Frankford to Bucks County, south by way of Chadd's Ford, and up Ridge Road to Norristown.

Philadelphia's ships went to ports all over the world carrying beef, pork, wheat, flour, apples, and lard, and bringing back a large and strange vocabulary of foreign produce and goods. For some of the early years of the century the merchants benefited from England's preoccupation with her war with France, but neutral trade began to be increasingly harassed by the warring powers. Jefferson, outraged

(Facing) George Clymer's Cast-Iron Columbian Press, from William Savage, *Practical Hints on Decorative Printing*, 1822 (LCP)
(Above) Advertisement of the New York Stage Coach, from the *United States Gazette*, April 22, 1819 (LCP)

at this interference with American shipping, declared an embargo in 1808. A serious depression ensued, and unemployment in the city was high. Although the embargo was lifted the following year, commerce once again suffered when war broke out. What had once been the solid foundation of the city's economy now seemed shaky. Philadelphians did not abandon mercantile trade, but they increasingly looked elsewhere for the investment of capital, to turnpikes and later canals, to factories and real estate.

Fortunately, within the boundaries of the county there were many streams to provide water power. Only Baltimore of the major coastal cities had similar resources. Creeks ran down to the Delaware or the Schuylkill from a fall line which followed a serpentine course from Centre Square to Germantown. Mills were established everywhere the flow was strong enough to turn wheels. Machines were an integral part of the area's economic life. With the development of more flexible steam power a need for and the means of making heavier machinery came into being. Competent engineers and ingenious mechanics in a sympathetic climate brought the industrial revolution to Philadelphia.

Politics followed an almost predictable pattern. When Jefferson was elected President over Aaron Burr by the House of Representatives in 1801, the Democratic–Republicans gloated with parades, dinners, and orations. In the city proper a hard core of Federalist merchants and lawyers retained a respectable political following, but in outlying districts of the county laborers, factory workers, the foreign-born, and Negroes turned in majorities for the so-called party of the people year after year. Governor Thomas McKean used patronage, William Duane, the editor of the *Aurora,* used his own brand of rhetoric and invective, and Dr. Michael Leib used the ward level organization to hold the Democratic voters in line. McKean eventually alienated the other two. It was only when the frequent internal squabbles split the Democrats that the Federalists were able to elect their candidates. Sometimes, holding the balance of power, they chose to throw their strength to one or another of the factions—the anti-Leib group was dubbed "Tertium Quids" by Duane. Elections were bitterly contested, but the only major physical confrontation took place when the Federalists, led by Commodore Thomas Truxtun and George Clymer and given muscle by a mob of internally fortified sailors, demonstrated against the embargo early in 1808.

(Facing) *Plan of the City and its Environs,* engraving by P. C. Varlé, 1802 (HSP)

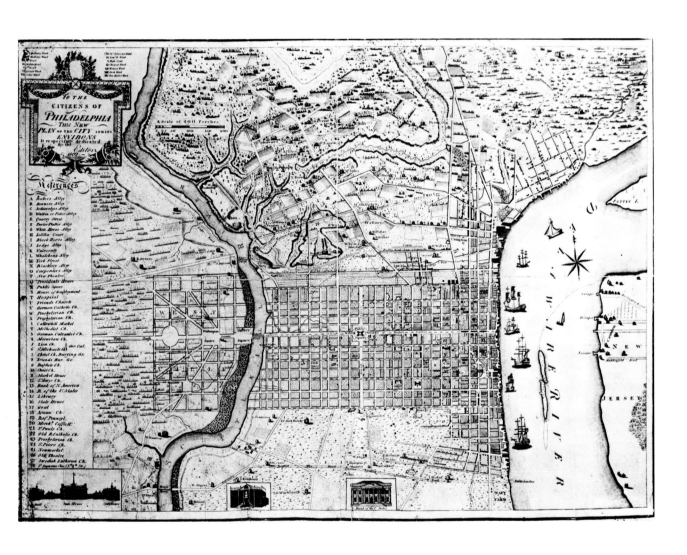

This era was one of the peaks of do-goodism. Philanthropic organizations cropped up like dandelions in the spring. The Pennsylvania Society for the Abolition of Slavery grew in importance. There were founded orphan asylums, schools for the indigent, homes for the pitied and harried Magdalens (the State House Square was their beat), dispensaries which served as outpatient clinics, a Jewish society for visiting the sick and burying the dead, a Protestant society for converting Jews, and mutual aid associations for Englishmen, Frenchmen, Irishmen, and Negroes. Most of the charities were church-stimulated and many of them were started by Quakers who switched energies from matters political to matters humanitarian.

Philadelphia's centrality in the cultural life of the nation remained long after the capital moved to Washington. In 1808 a bill advocating a move back from the dull, uncomfortable, and muddy Federal City won a majority vote in Congress, but a crisis with Great Britain intervened and the resolution was tabled. The luster of the American Philosophical Society with Rittenhouse and Jefferson as successive presidents reached far beyond the shores of the ocean. The expedition of Lewis and Clark was outfitted in the city and there given its scientific guidance. The publishing firm of Mathew Carey became the leading one in the country, and innovations in book production—the fine paper of Amies and the Gilpin Brandywine mills, the type foundry of Binny and Ronaldson, and the iron printing press of George Clymer—were introduced in the Philadelphia area.

Other innovations were welcomed. The new art academy received support from both patrons and artists, and its annual exhibitions were looked-forward-to events. The latest and best in theatrical productions, still predominately British in origin but beginning to include such all-American pieces as James N. Barker's musical drama *Pocahontas,* played to good houses at the Chestnut Street and newly reorganized Walnut Street theaters. Although the classical style in architecture still won the greatest favor, William Strickland, early in America, experimented in the Gothic taste with the striking Masonic Hall which unfortunately burned down—spectacularly—in 1819. John Dorsey, auctioneer and architect on the side, after having designed the Pennsylvania Academy of the Fine Arts building in a neoclassical style, erected an unusual Gothic mansion on Chestnut Street between Eleventh and Twelfth.

The prime movers of much of what went on in the city were members of the three most highly esteemed professions, law, medicine, and the ministry. The Philadelphia bar was outstanding in the quality of its members as jurists and as civic and political leaders. Joseph Hopkinson, Federalist congressman and federal judge; Alexander J. Dallas, compiler of the laws of Pennsylvania, Madison's secretary of the treasury and secretary of war; William Tilghman, chief justice of the Supreme Court of Pennsylvania; and Richard Rush, attorney-general of the United States from 1814 to 1817, were among its luminaries. And in the early years of the century John Sergeant, Charles Jared Ingersoll, and Horace Binney were beginning their long and distinguished careers.

The international reputation of Benjamin Rush, the outstanding professors of the medical school of the University of Pennsylvania, and the recognized excellence of the Pennsylvania Hospital made the city the national center of medical education, research, and publication. Playing active roles as teachers and practicing physicians were Benjamin Smith Barton, botanist; Caspar Wistar, anatomist, successor to Jefferson as president of the American Philosophical Society, and originator of the intellectual gathering known as the Wistar Party; John Redman Coxe, editor of the *American Medical Museum* and the first American pharmacopoeia; Philip Syng Physick, surgeon; William P. Dewees, pioneer obstetrician; and Nathaniel Chapman, litterateur, editor, and teacher of the theory and practice of medicine. The most unusual medical advance of the period was the establishment near Frankford of the Friends' Asylum, a forward-looking institution for the care of the insane.

Early in its history Philadelphia had dreamed of becoming the Athens of America. In the early decades of the nineteenth century it came close to that hope, mixed in good American fashion with Quaker prudence, Calvinist respect for earned wealth, and Yankee ingenuity. It was a pleasant place to live.

(Above) *J. Dorsey's Gothic Mansion,* engraving by B. Tanner after Mills, from the *Port Folio,* 1811 (LCP)

The Pennsylvania legislature authorized the construction of a presidential mansion at Ninth and Market streets in 1791. Unfortunately it was not well thought out. An English visitor noted that the position of the upper and lower stories was reversed so that the pilasters appeared suspended in air. Almost $100,000 was spent before the house was finished in 1797. John Adams refused to live in it. Finally, it was bought by the University of Pennsylvania at public sale in 1800 for $41,650. The small domed building to the east was added in 1805 by Latrobe for the Medical School. The land was cleared in 1829, when two simpler and more practical structures were built facing one another on the lot.

As the city became more densely populated, water from the shallow wells became polluted. Hoping that a supply of pure water would prevent future yellow fever epidemics, hundreds of Philadelphians petitioned the City Councils to do something about it. In 1799 Benjamin Henry Latrobe was selected as engineer by a new municipal Watering Committee. His system brought water from the Schuylkill at Chestnut Street through tunnels and wooden pipes with the aid of two steam-engine pumps to the built-up section of the city. Latrobe designed a circular domed white marble building in Centre Square to house the upper pump. Although the engine was not as reliable as had been hoped, the city's water system was long the best in the nation. Centre Square, where City Hall now stands, but then still in the fields, became a popular park. In 1809 William Rush was commissioned to carve a figure for a fountain to symbolize the source of the water, and he created "The Nymph of the Schuylkill," a classically draped girl holding a bittern from whose mouth the water flowed.

(Above) *The University of Pennsylvania at 9th and Market Streets*, wash drawing by William Strickland, ca. 1820 (HSP)
(Middle) *View of the Water Works at Centre Square*, stipple engraving by C. Tiebout after J. J. Barralet (LCP)
(Below) *Plan of the Engine House of the Water Works at Centre Square*, watercolor drawing by Frederick Graff (HSP)

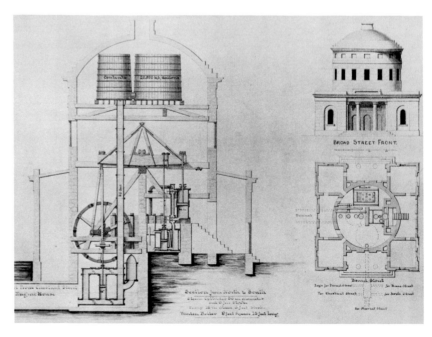

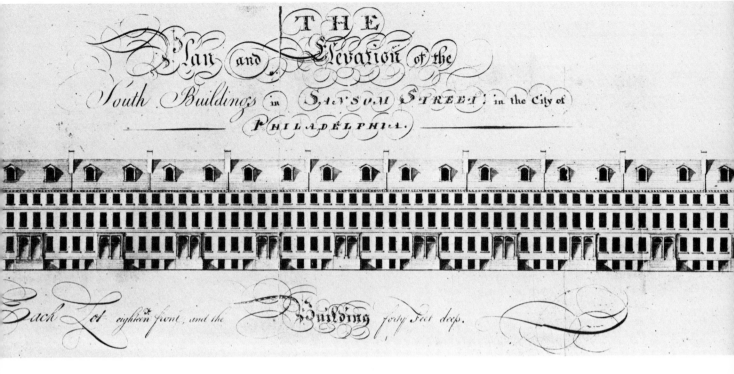

THE Plan and Elevation of the South Buildings in Sansom Street in the City of Philadelphia.

Each Lot eighteen feet front, and the Building forty feet deep.

Row-house development on a large scale began just after the turn of the century, although much earlier small uniform houses had been built in courts and alleys. Joseph Sansom bought the bankrupt Robert Morris' property with its unfinished house, "Morris' Folly," on Walnut Street between Seventh and Eighth at sheriff's sale. After putting through an east–west street named for him, he sold half the land to Thomas Carstairs who built a row on the south side of Sansom Street. Back to back on Walnut Street rose Sansom Row. It was reported that of five hundred houses built annually forty percent of them were put up by Sansom, the city's chief real-estate developer. There were some objections to the uniformity, but row houses, novel early in the 1800s, became commonplace in the city.

(Above) *Elevation of Carstairs' Row on Sansom Street*, ink and wash drawing (LCP)

When Bordeaux-born Stephen Girard died in 1831 he left the largest fortune up to that time accumulated by an American. In the heyday of Philadelphia's mercantile prosperity, he was its most prosperous shipowner, and his vessels traded all over the world—from Smyrna to China. When Congress in 1811 refused to renew the charter of the Bank of the United States, the merchant-turned-banker bought its building and other assets. He used Girard's Bank to build up a remarkable system of credit at home and abroad. The government having failed to sell its loan to finance the War of 1812, Girard and John Jacob Astor took over the unsubscribed portion. Again, when the Second Bank of the United States was talked of and no purchasers could be found for $3,000,000 of its stock, Girard took the whole amount. As the country turned increasingly inward to its own resources, the farsighted banker invested large sums in real estate, amassing huge tracts of land in the undeveloped coal regions.

(Above) *Stephen Girard's Dwelling and Counting House on Water Street*, watercolor by an unknown artist (LCP)
(Below) *Stephen Girard*, engraving by E. G. Williams & Bro. after Bass Otis (LCP)

Mathew Carey was not only the most important Irish Catholic in the United States, but one of the most influential advocates of a protective tariff and the founder of the country's most successful publishing firm. He developed a network of booksellers, particularly in the expanding South and West, which enabled him to sell popular books—school texts, Bibles, and catchpenny items—to a wide audience. He printed the first Catholic Bible in America, but a long-term bestseller was the quarto King James version, the type for which the firm kept standing for many years. As one of the founders of the Philadelphia Society for the Promotion of National Industry and a tireless pamphleteer, he did much to advance American manufactures, establishing continuity between Hamilton's report of 1791 and Clay's "American system."

The nation's first successful literary magazine, The Port Folio, appeared early in 1801. Its editor was Joseph Dennie, a New Hampshire man who had gained some fame as a rural essayist. A vehement Federalist who dressed like a dandy, Dennie succeeded in charming and getting as contributors to his periodical many of the bright young men of Philadelphia, including Joseph Hopkinson, Richard Rush, Nicholas Biddle, Horace Binney, Robert Walsh, Charles Brockden Brown, and others. These men coming together as the Tuesday Club enlivened and graced the social and intellectual life of the town. The magazine, at first a weekly, became a monthly in 1809 and a quarterly in 1820. It ceased publication in 1829. Well printed, with quality illustrations, offering excellent book reviews and feature articles, The Port Folio made the city a center of literary good taste. Although its circulation was modest, it was the first magazine in the country to survive for over a quarter of a century.

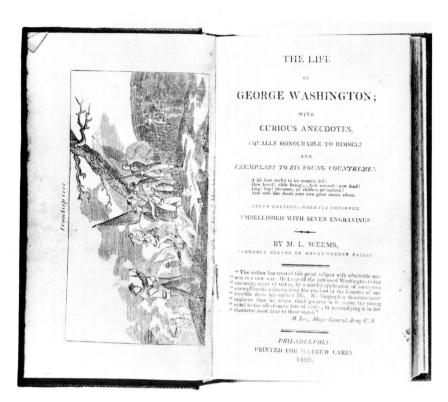

(Above) Frontispiece and Title-page of Parson Weems's *Life of George Washington*, published by Mathew Carey, 1809 (LCP)
(Below) Frontispiece and Title-page of *The Port Folio*, 1815 (LCP)
(Facing) *Mathew Carey*, engraving by Samuel Sartain after John Neagle (HSP)

Machinery and other iron and steel products were among the city's major contributions to the industrial revolution. A pioneer inventor, machinist, and promoter of engines was Oliver Evans, who had developed in Delaware a water-power flour mill which performed every necessary movement without manual labor, a kind of early automation. After he settled in Philadelphia in 1803 Evans became a successful builder of high-pressure engines. He fascinated the town the following year by taking his amphibious steam dredge, the "Orukter Amphibolis," around Centre Square before he chugged it into the river. His Mars Iron Works at Ninth and Race streets was one of the nation's leading steam-engine manufactories.

The War of 1812 threatened Philadelphia, but did not harm it. In the spring of 1813 a blockading British fleet off the capes of the Delaware frightened the defenseless city, and newly formed companies of volunteers and the militia manned Fort Mifflin. When news came late in August, 1814, that Washington had fallen and that the British were marching on Baltimore, an influential Committee of Defense was organized. The First City Troop and other military companies were called up; camps were established far south of the city; fortifications were constructed. Thousands of citizens gave their services to dig breastworks on the west bank of the Schuylkill, at the junction of Gray's Ferry and Darby roads, on the Lancaster Pike, and on the north side of Fairmount. A Negro company was said to have been formed. The troops, resplendent in colorful uniforms, engaged in considerably more ceremony than shooting that summer in Delaware, but when they came home in December they were hailed as heroes.

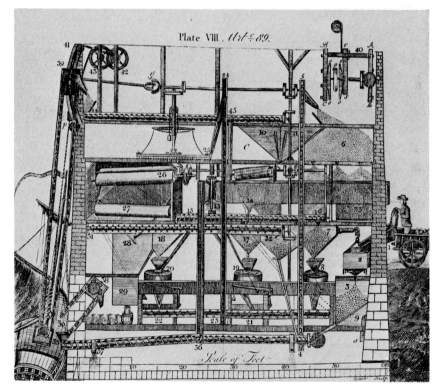

(Above) *The "Orukter Amphibolis,"* woodcut (HSP)
(Below) *Oliver Evans's Automated Mill,* engraving by James Poupard, from Evans, *The Young Mill-wright & Miller's Guide,* 1795 (LCP)
(Facing) *Members of the City Troop and other Philadelphia Soldiery,* watercolor by Pavel Petrovich Svinin, 1814 (Rogers Fund, Metropolitan Museum of Art)

The shortest way to the west was across the Schuylkill. For years passengers and wagons had crossed on ferries and floating bridges, both subject to destruction by floods. By the end of the eighteenth century work was begun at Market Street on a permanent bridge which was opened in 1804. It was the first of several bridges which laced together the two sides of the river. One of the most famous of these was that constructed at Fairmount Avenue in 1812 by a company whose principal shareholder was Jacob Ridgway. The single wooden arch with two carriageways and two footways, 340 feet long, was then the greatest span ever achieved in wood or stone. The engineer and builder was German-born Lewis Wernwag, and the architect of the cover was Robert Mills of South Carolina. The Colossus, as it was called, was "as elegant in appearance as it was bold in structure." It burned in 1838.

(Above) *Upper Ferry Bridge at Fairmount Avenue*, painting by Thomas Birch (HSP)
(Below) *Market Street Permanent Bridge*, etching by Thomas Birch (LCP)

The port of Philadelphia was a
great market basket into which the
wealth of the city flowed. Ships and
sailors, bales and boxes, ropes and tar
were everyday sights and smells. With
the opening of the China and East
India trade, local shipowners, among
them Joseph Sims, Stephen Girard,
Thomas P. Cope, James Large Mifflin,
Willing and Francis, and Jesse and
Robert Waln, sought a share of it.
In 1800 there were forty Philadelphia
vessels engaged in trade with the Far
East. Blue and white Canton china
became readily available; tea and
ginger, nankeen and silk were offered
for sale in quantity by the wholesale
merchants on Water Street. When the
War of 1812 broke out, familiarity
with the sea stood the country in
good stead. Men-of-war from local shipyards and such Philadelphia naval
officers as Stephen Decatur of the
United States and James Biddle of the
Wasp defeated and captured British
men-of-war and merchantmen. The
successful running of the coastal
blockade and the captured prizes were
hailed with delight by the seamen's
fellow-citizens.

(Above) China Clipper *Montesquieu*, painting
by unknown artist (Girard College)
(Below) Ship's Figurehead Bust of Stephen Decatur (Atwater Kent Museum)
(Right) Selection of Export China (Henry Francis du Pont Winterthur Museum)
(Overleaf) *Election Day at the State House*,
painting by John Lewis Krimmel, 1815 (Henry
Francis du Pont Winterthur Museum)

Flowers, birds, shells, and the other wonders of nature excited Philadelphians to such an extent that they became the pundits in the field. Although early travelers had described native birds, it remained for Alexander Wilson to create the first illustrated American ornithology, which appeared in nine volumes from 1808 to 1814. Benjamin Smith Barton, the "father of American botany," was also the father of William P. C. Barton who produced one of the earliest herbals with colored plates in the country. Both Bartons were professors at the University of Pennsylvania. In 1812 a group of nature lovers formed the Academy of Natural Sciences. Within comparatively few years the institution attracted to it the city's professional scientists, the entomologist Thomas Say, the physician Isaac Hays, the anthropologist Samuel G. Morton, the conchologist Isaac Lea, the wealthy natural historian George Ord, and—most important of all—the geologist William Maclure, who was president from 1817 to 1840.

There were more practicing artists in Philadelphia at the beginning of the century than anywhere else in America. Outstanding were young Thomas Sully, portrait painter; John Lewis Krimmel, "the American Hogarth," delineator of genre scenes; Thomas Birch, landscapist and seascapist; William Rush, sculptor in wood; William Charles, etcher and cartoonist; and—outstandingly—the Peale family. Early in 1805, with the help of the prominent lawyer Joseph Hopkinson, Charles Willson Peale's earlier unsuccessful attempts were brought to fruition with the founding of the Pennsylvania Academy of the Fine Arts.

(Above) *Liliodendron Tulipefera*, watercolor by W. P. C. Barton, for Barton's *Flora of North America*, 1821-23 (LCP)
(Below) *Pennsylvania Academy of the Fine Arts, on Chestnut Street between 10th and 11th*, engraving by C. G. Childs after Geo. Strickland, 1828 (LCP)
(Facing) *Herons and Bitterns*, etching by J. G. Warnicke after Alexander Wilson, from Wilson's *American Ornithology*, 1808-14 (LCP)

French was fashionable in Philadelphia. Early emigrés from the Reign of Terror, fugitives from the black revolution in Santo Domingo, and, later, exile Bonapartists all found a friendly home in the city. A host of French craftsmen and professors of various arts were able to profit from the taste of the times. Simon Chaudron and Antony Rasch made outstandingly fine silver in the latest Empire style. The Mouniers were hairdressers who puffed their wigs and chignons; they also sold perfume. Monsieur Poutingham opened a riding school at Tenth and Arch streets, and Monsieur Tessier a fencing academy on South Sixth. A long-time favorite of Philadelphians was Sicard, the dancing master. Private dances and subscription cotillions à la mode Française filled the social season.

(Above) *The Cotillion Party*, etching, from Robert Waln, *The Hermit in America on a Visit to Philadelphia*, 1819 (LCP)
(Below) Advertisement of Mounier's Hairdressing Establishment from the *Aurora*, October 28, 1816 (LCP)
(Right) Mahogany Desk in the Empire Style, by Michael Bouvier (Athenaeum of Philadelphia)

I. P. MOUNIER,
LADIES AND GENTLEMEN'S HAIR DRESSER
· NO. 41—CHESNUT STEET,

TAKES this opportunity of returning his most sincere thanks to his friends and the Ladies of this city, for the liberal encouragement he has met with ; which induced him to go to Paris, where he made a stay of nine months, in order to get a collection of the newest and most fashionable articles in his line—He has likewise made it his particular study to make himself thoroughly acquainted with all the newest and most tasty fashions

He continues to make those famous *implanted Wigs*, of which he is the inventor, and which are fitted so close to the skin, as perfectly to imitate the growth of natural hair, and deceive the most scrutinizing eye.

The large assortment of selected hair which he has imported, enables him to make every kind of artificial hair dresses—such as *Frizettes, Tresses, Chevise, Ninons, Deshoaliers, Gabrielles*, sliding *Toupets*, which are put on and taken off with the greatest ease. His correspondent in Paris sends him every two months patterns of the newest fashions.

Mrs. Mounier executes in the neatest manner, every kind of hair work—such as bracelets, watch chains, necklaces, earrings, girdles, allegories, &c. &c. with such hair as customers chose to bring—She pledges to use the same, and work them in any manner wished for.

They have in their house a neat apartment appropriated exclusively to cutting and dressing the hair of the ladies, and a separate one for gentlemen.

I. P. MOUNIER,
OFFERS FOR SALE, AT HIS STORE,
No. 41,
, CHESNUT SRTEET,
A general assortment of most elegant
PERFUMERY.

Which he has selected himself in Paris to suit the taste of the ladies of this city.
October 28   m w f2w

A city census in 1808 counted 5,256 free blacks and thirty slaves out of a total population of 47,786. The strongest concentration of Negroes was near Cedar (South) Street just west of the Delaware River. Before the heavy European immigration began, the blacks were active in many trades and held jobs in all the variety of Philadelphia's industries. The Russian traveler-artist Pavel Svinin, to whom they were exotic, seemed to see Negroes everywhere in the city. Sawyers cut logs to heat the Bank of Pennsylvania. An oysterman offered his fare to theatergoers in front of the Chestnut Street Theatre. And the author of the Cries of Philadelphia showed them selling all kinds of wares on the streets, notably that typical local delicacy pepper-pot.

(Above) *"Pepper Pot, smoking hot,"* page from *The Cries of Philadelphia,* 1810 (HSP)
(Below) *Negroes in Front of the Bank of Pennsylvania, Philadelphia,* watercolor by Pavel Petrovich Svinin, 1814 (Rogers Fund, Metropolitan Museum of Art)
(Right) *Night Life in Philadelphia—an oyster barrow in front of the Chestnut Street Theatre,* watercolor by Pavel Petrovich Svinin, 1814 (Rogers Fund, Metropolitan Museum of Art)

PEPPER POT.

" Pepper Pot, smoking hot."

Celebrations and public gatherings were fun for all the people, and elections provided the opportunity to be part of a crowd. Voting took place at the first-floor windows of the State House, and in the street voters were cajoled; politicians discussed their chances; passers-by enjoyed the spectacle. At night the victorious party lit bonfires and paraded through the streets. Another civic function of interest was a trial, and spectators watched as cases were heard in the Mayor's Court on the first floor of the State House. The two great patriotic holidays were Washington's birthday and the Fourth of July. Winter weather and partisan Federalist politics sometimes spoiled the former, but the Fourth was always glorious for everyone. Guns, fireworks, parades, picnics, speeches, and flags made the day an exciting occasion.

(Above) *Court Scene in the State House*, pencil sketch by John Lewis Krimmel (The Joseph Downs Manuscript Collection, Henry Francis du Pont Winterthur Museum)
(Below) *Fourth of July Celebration in Centre Square*, painting by John Lewis Krimmel, 1819 (Pennsylvania Academy of the Fine Arts)

Charles Willson Peale established the city's first popular museum in rooms rented from the American Philosophical Society. When he secured several mastodon skeletons in Ulster County, New York, they proved so great an attraction that the legislature gave Peale the use of the upper floors of the State House rent free. There, particularly in the long room facing Chestnut Street, the museum exhibited stuffed birds in cases with painted backgrounds, minerals, the prehistoric skeletons, and eventually the artist's own gallery of American immortals. There was a menagerie in the State House Square. In 1816 gas was brought in to light the museum, the first such public illumination in America. One of the features for many years was a silhouette machine by which profiles were quickly and neatly cut. The apparatus was operated and the snipping done by Moses Williams, a Negro. The Philadelphia Museum Company was incorporated, and in 1829 it moved into the Arcade Building on Chestnut Street between Sixth and Seventh.

(Above) *Peale's Museum with Self Portrait*, painting by Charles Willson Peale (Pennsylvania Academy of the Fine Arts)
(Below) Silhouette by the Peale Museum (LCP)
(Right) *The Peale Museum Mastodon*, lithograph by Ed. de Montulé, from Montulé's *Voyage en Amérique*, 1821 (HSP)

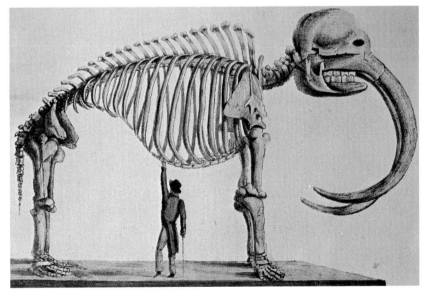

Rebecca Gratz may have been the model for the Jewess Rebecca in Sir Walter Scott's Ivanhoe, *but there is no evidence to substantiate that story first told by a nephew in 1882. She was a beautiful and cultured woman, a friend of some of the most famous authors of her day, Washington Irving, James Fenimore Cooper, James K. Paulding, and John Pendleton Kennedy. At Irving's request she introduced Thomas Sully to Philadelphians, thus launching him on his long career as the city's most prolific portrait painter. Rebecca Gratz is remembered also as a philanthropist. She was one of the founders of the Female Association for the Relief of Women and Children in Reduced Circumstances, the Female Hebrew Benevolent Society, the Hebrew Sunday School Society, and the Philadelphia Orphan Society, in all of which she played an active role.*

The Irish Catholic population of the United States grew at the end of the eighteenth century as a result of the British suppression of republicanism in Ireland. One of the results of the increasing numbers was the splitting up of the sole American diocese of Baltimore. In 1808 the See of Philadelphia was formed. St. Mary's became the cathedral of the new diocese which took in Pennsylvania, Delaware, and part of New Jersey. A Franciscan, Father Michael Egan, was appointed first bishop of Philadelphia by Pius VII. To dignify its new status the old church was so greatly altered and enlarged in 1810-12 that it became virtually a new building.

(Above) *Rebecca Gratz,* photogravure of miniature by Richard Greene Malbone (HSP)
(Below) *The Catholic Church of St. Mary,* lithograph by Kennedy & Lucas after W. L. Breton, ca. 1829 (HSP)

Rebecca Gratz.

The Reverend William Staughton was called to the pulpit of the First Baptist Church in 1805. He was fiery, eloquent, and popular. His sunrise services conducted under the willows near the Navy Yard attracted hundreds. English by birth, Staughton offended many of his congregants by his undisguised sympathy for Great Britain. In 1811 he took a number of fellow Englishmen with him to establish a new church. They built a circular brick building after the design of Robert Mills on Sansom Street between Eighth and Ninth. In the center was a pool for baptism. A historian of the Baptist Church wrote: "The largest church gatherings I have ever seen under roof were there, and regularly, too, for many years."

(Above) *A Philadelphia Anabaptist Immersion During a Storm,* watercolor by Pavel Petrovich Svinin, 1814 (Rogers Fund, Metropolitan Museum of Art)
(Below) *Sansom Street Baptist Church,* unfinished lithograph (HSP)

MORRIS IRON WORKS,

PHILADELPHIA.

Cor Schuylkill 7th & Market Sts.

Established in 1828.

I.P. Morris & Co,

Iron-Founders, Steam-Engine Makers & Machinists.

They Manufacture HIGH AND LOW PRESSURE STEAM ENGINES, STATIONARY *and for* BOATS, SUGAR MILLS, SUGAR PANS, HYDRAULIC PRESSES, PUMPS AND MACHINERY *for* MINES, BLOWING CYLINDERS *for Furnaces, and Iron and Brass Castings of every Description and Weight,*

And have provided on the DELAWARE *below the* READING RAIL ROAD DEPOT, *a commodious* SHOP *and* WHARF, *with a* CRANE, *expressly for the* Construction and Repair of STEAM-BOAT ENGINES & BOILERS.

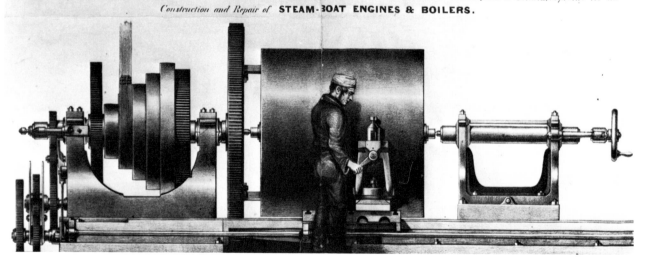

1820-1840

Coal was king. It brought prosperity to the area, which, in spite of financial ups and downs caused by banking crises, had a better economic potential as it entered the antebellum period than it had earlier. Coal made canals profitable and built railroads; it fueled factories and filled ships. Industry replaced commerce and finance as the city's underpinning, and until midcentury Philadelphia was the chief manufacturing center of the nation. However, with industry came immigrants and the upsetting of old certainties.

It was an era of rapid change. In the 1820s canals attracted progressive capital and seemed to offer sound investment. Although the opening of the Erie Canal, diverting western trade to New York, was a blow to local pride and purse, its impact was slightly lessened by the increasing tonnage of coal which came down the waterways and by rail to the city's wharves. By 1840 canals were becoming obsolete; railroads now attracted progressive capital and seemed to offer sound investment. They took over long-distance transportation, and Philadelphia quickly became a rail hub with spokes reaching out in all directions. Bridges were thrown across the Schuylkill, but the Delaware still had to be crossed by boat to connect with the Camden and Amboy Railroad for the Hudson ferry to New York.

Within the sprawling county railroads linked the center city with the old market and mill town of Germantown and the new factory settlement of Manayunk. Horse-drawn omnibuses made travel over shorter distances cheap and convenient. Networks of various other kinds brought their improvements to urban life. The new waterworks at Fairmount carried so much water to pumps and spigots throughout the city that visitors marveled at its profligate use in cleaning marble steps and brick sidewalks. In the mid-1830s another utility came into being with the establishment of the gas works at Twenty-second and Market streets after Samuel V. Merrick reported favorably to the hesitant City Councils on its use for illumination in Europe.

It was Merrick who stimulated the founding of the Franklin Institute in 1824, which soon became a major force in the promotion of American industry with its annual distribution of medals and premiums to inventors, manufacturers, and mechanics. Its influential journal spread technological information throughout the world. The presence in the city of a large number of skilled workers from colonial times on had been as responsible for the growth of industry as the

(Facing) *Morris Iron Works at 16th and Market Streets*, lithograph by T. Sinclair after M. S. Weaver, 1840 (HSP)

149

imagination and capital of the factory owners. Ample water and coal-generated steam were turned into power for all kinds of use.

The foundation of Philadelphia's varied industrial output was laid in the period. Nearly one-fourth of the country's steel and a major portion of its power machinery were produced by local industries. A confusing number of Morrises owned iron works; the Port Richmond Iron-Works of Levi, Morris & Co. and the Morris Iron Works (later Morris, Wheeler & Co.) at Sixteenth and Market streets produced heavy castings and machinery. The Pascal Iron Works of Morris, Tasker & Co. early met the demand for gas pipes. Merrick constructed superior pumpers for fire companies and his Southwark Foundry, started in 1836, made boilers. The factory of Alfred Jenks in Bridesburg, north along the river, fabricated improved machines for carding, spinning, and weaving textiles. Matthias W. Baldwin's success in building locomotives was challenged by Stephen H. Long and William Norris at their Bush Hill works and by Joseph Harrison, Jr., whose "Gowan & Marx" was the most efficient freight engine up to then built. Heavy industry was well established.

In the manufacture of textiles, too, the city was significantly engaged. British competition, seriously affecting home industries, motivated Mathew Carey to fight for high protective tariffs. With the introduction of more and more sophisticated machinery the plants were able to flourish and expand. William H. Horstmann introduced a Jacquard loom in 1825. In Germantown, long known for its stocking-weavers, John Button in 1831 established a mill which was for many years the only factory where hosiery was made by machines. Several carpet mills successfully started production in the 1830s. It was, however, the fabrication of wool and cotton into cloth, printing and dyeing it, that kept Philadelphia's mills humming along Pennypack Creek and in Manayunk and Kensington. In 1827 there were about fifty cotton manufacturing establishments in the county which turned out almost four million dollars worth of goods. The competent native and English mill-workers formed a solid Protestant economic layer which excluded blacks from all but menial jobs and found itself in turn threatened by the Irish Catholic immigration.

As a steady stream of Irish immigrants—to become a flood in the 1840s—filtered into the city, as factory work took the place of home industries, competition for jobs increased. The city's first nativist riot

(Facing) *Frank Johnson*, lithograph by A. Hoffy after a daguerreotype by R. Douglass, Jr., 1846 (HSP)

took place in 1828 when native journeymen attacked Irish weavers in a Kensington tavern. Craftsmen, members of guilds, and even the semi-skilled operators of handlooms, proud of themselves as the builders of a new country, began to shut the doors to outsiders. Blacks, although most of them, too, were natives, suffered most, for increasing prejudice kept them out of the trades which they had earlier practiced, and many went into domestic service. But they built their own churches and beneficial societies. James Forten and Robert Purvis were among those who worked with white humanitarians for abolition and took part in the 1830 National Negro Convention in Philadelphia. Some blacks achieved citywide recognition: Robert Bogle, caterer, was ubiquitous when the party season was in full swing, and Frank Johnson, composer and trumpet player, led the city's best band. He acquired such a fine reputation as a musician that he toured the United States and England, where he played before Queen Victoria— who gave him a silver bugle.

The influx of newcomers, not only from Europe but from the countryside as well, combined with natural growth nearly doubled the population of the county, from 136,635 in 1820 to 258,126 in 1840. A map from the latter year by the engineer Charles Ellet, Jr., shows the built-up area running solidly from the Delaware to Sixth Street and from the Navy Yard in Southwark to the private shipyards in Kensington. In the city proper buildings reached Broad Street with a bulge west up Market. In 1837 there was premature pressure put upon the City Councils to move the seat of the municipal government to Penn Square. Development in the Northern Liberties and Fairmount went a few squares along the city line of Vine Street, and in Southwark and Moyamensing a similar pattern occurred. Houses narrowly edged the Germantown Pike from Nicetown to Chestnut Hill, and there were small clusters in Hamiltonville in West Philadelphia, and Manayunk, Richmond, Frankford, and Bridesburg.

Growth, industrial development, and racial turmoil did not affect the city as critically as did the fight over the Second Bank of the United States. Chartered in 1816 for twenty years and ably administered by Nicholas Biddle, the Bank was the central depository of federal funds and, by virtue of its holdings of state bank notes, controlled credit. John Quincy Adams' Secretary of the Treasury, Richard Rush, declared the Bank was "an indispensable and permanent ad-

(Facing) *Procession of Victuallers on March 15, 1821, at 4th and Chestnut Streets*, aquatint by Joseph Yeager after J. L. Krimmel (HSP)

junct to our political and fiscal system." Adams' successor, Andrew Jackson, did not think so. He disliked the idea of a central bank, and, furthermore, he distrusted the aristocratic Biddle. Jackson declared a people's war on the Bank of the United States, and when Congress passed a bill in 1832 rechartering it, he vetoed the bill. A furious political fight ensued in the course of which the President ordered the withdrawal of the government's deposits as of October 1, 1833. Financial panic and business dislocation resulted. A protest meeting the following year under the auspices of the newly constituted Whig party was held on the grounds of John Hare Powel's West Philadelphia estate. Sixty thousand persons attended. Petitions and delegations sent to Washington could not change the Jackson administration's policy.

When the Bank's federal charter lapsed in 1836, the state legislature rechartered it as the State Bank of the United States. No longer was credit centrally and providently controlled. Local banks mushroomed, and inflation and speculation ran unchecked, bringing on the crisis of 1837 when all banks suspended the payment of specie. The issuance of paper money, including small notes known as "shinplasters," by the city and savings and loan companies was only an expedient. Rents declined; wages were cut; prices fell. When the Democratic legislature forced city banks to resume specie payments in 1838 and again in 1840, after another suspension, many failed, including Biddle's Bank of the United States, the Girard Bank, Pennsylvania Bank, and four others. Amid scenes of unprecedented economic distress, accompanied by loss of capital, financial power passed from Philadelphia to New York.

Nevertheless, all was not bleak. The industrial and business foundations of the city remained firm. And in a number of fields of endeavor Philadelphia continued its primacy. One of these was the field of medicine. The medical school of the University of Pennsylvania was still a magnet. Dr. William P. Dewees, professor of midwifery there, became one of the country's first bestselling professional authors. For his texts on obstetrics and pediatrics he received from the Carey publishing house higher payments than it gave such popular writers as Cooper and Irving. Dr. George McClellan, one of those attracted to the city by its medical prestige, felt that another school of medicine could perform a valuable function. In an atmosphere of

(Facing) *The Downfall of Mother Bank,* lithograph by E. W. Clay, 1833 (LCP)

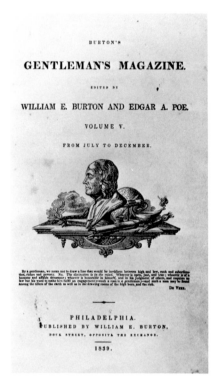

BURTON'S

GENTLEMAN'S MAGAZINE.

EDITED BY

WILLIAM E. BURTON AND EDGAR A. POE.

VOLUME V.

FROM JULY TO DECEMBER.

PHILADELPHIA.
PUBLISHED BY WILLIAM E. BURTON,
DOCK STREET, OPPOSITE THE EXCHANGE.

1839.

(Above) Title-page of *Burton's Gentleman's Magazine*, edited by Edgar Allan Poe, 1839 (LCP)

hostility he succeeded in 1826 in establishing such a school as a branch of Jefferson College in Canonsburg. A dozen years later Jefferson Medical College received a separate charter. To train men in an ancillary profession Peter K. Lehman, a druggist, took the initiative in 1821 to found the Philadelphia College of Pharmacy, the first of its kind in the country, which four years later began the publication of the *American Journal of Pharmacy*. The most important accession to the health resources of the city was the municipal hospital at the Almshouse, newly relocated in West Philadelphia. A specialized facility, the Wills Hospital for Diseases of the Eye, opened on Logan Square in 1834.

As in earlier times Philadelphia's periodicals enjoyed nationwide reputations. America's first gift annual, *The Atlantic Souvenir,* was published in 1825 by Carey, Lea and Carey and proved an immediate success. Part of the appeal of these volumes and the popular magazines lay in their illustrations, engravings, mezzotints, and lithographs done after original paintings. In Philadelphia there were plenty of good artists to meet the demand. Landscapes by Charles Doughty and seascapes by Thomas Birch were regularly shown at the exhibitions of the Pennsylvania Academy of the Fine Arts. Thomas Sully was the busiest portrait painter, but active, too, were Rembrandt Peale, Jacob Eichholtz, John Neagle, and Bass Otis. It was Otis who in 1819 made the first American lithograph; by 1830 several competent lithographic firms were established in the city. That was the process used for Edgar Allan Poe's *The Conchologist's First Book,* his first work in 1838 when he came to Philadelphia. The next year Poe became William E. Burton's assistant editor on *The Gentleman's Magazine,* but he resigned in 1840. Destined to outsell its competitors, *Godey's Lady's Book* with its monthly plates of the latest fashions began publication in 1830. It was followed in 1836 by *Miss Leslie's Magazine,* put out by Eliza Leslie whose cookbooks had brought her fame.

The city's most influential and long-lived newspapers made their debut in the decade 1829-39. The *Philadelphia Inquirer* made a modest start on June 29, 1829, as a Democratic journal. After a few months it was sold to Jesper Harding who merged it with the *Democratic Press* and turned it into an evening paper. During the altercation over the Bank of the United States, Harding tried to walk a tightrope, defending Biddle while supporting the administration. The withdrawal of the deposits was too much for him. In 1840 he came out for William Henry Harrison for President, enlarged the paper, and became a Whig stalwart. The second major newspaper to start publication was the *Public Ledger,* founded in 1836 by Swain, Abell & Simmons. It was Philadelphia's first penny paper. By printing news quickly, taking strong stands on issues, and condemning street violence, the *Ledger* soon commanded the largest circulation in the state. The *North American* first appeared in 1839, financed by some wealthy citizens who felt religious and philanthropic news received scant coverage in the other journals. Through a complicated genealogy of absorptions and mergers, the *North American* lay claim to being the oldest daily in America—a claim assumed in the twentieth century by the *Inquirer.* Within a short time it took over Zachariah Poulson's old and respected *American Daily Advertiser,* Cephas G. Childs' *Commercial Herald,* and the *Philadelphia Gazette.* The newly established papers were destined to play important civic and political roles.

In the hot summer of 1840 a Negro who had been a onetime inmate of the ward for the insane at Blockley killed a watchman in Southwark. As the latter was being buried at St. Peter's, a crowd gathered. After the service it moved as a mob to Fifth Street and Passyunk Avenue making ready to assault black neighborhoods. The would-be rioters moved up Fifth Street, swept aside the sheriff and faced Mayor John Swift and a squad of officers at Pine Street. The mayor, armed only with a cane and considerable courage, took hold of the ringleader, dragged him away and put him into the hands of the officers. The crowd dispersed, but that night the houses of some blacks were attacked. Philadelphia was entering on a stormy period.

The great century of the railroad began in Philadelphia in 1832 with the inauguration of service to Germantown. At first the stagecoach cars were drawn by horses, but soon they shared the pull with Matthias W. Baldwin's steam locomotive "Old Ironsides," which made its initial trip from Germantown to the Ninth and Green Street depot on November 23, 1832. The line was extended to Norristown in 1834, and four years later connected with the Philadelphia and Reading to reach the coal region. The west was probed, also in 1832, by the tracks of the Philadelphia and Columbia Railroad. Its double-decked cars were drawn by horses from the terminus at Third Street near Callowhill across a covered trestle bridge—the first railroad bridge in America—then pulled up the Inclined Plane of Belmont Hill by steam winch and rope, and finally were attached at Monument Road to a locomotive for the run to the Susquehanna. Pittsburgh was reached in four and a half days by way of Columbia in combination with canals and a portage railroad which amazed even the usually unimpressed Charles Dickens. The enthusiasm for railroads carried all before it. The Philadelphia, Wilmington and Baltimore Railroad, opening in 1834, serenely went north on Broad Street to connect with the Columbia line. In 1837 the freight tracks of the latter were laid down Market Street to Second, necessitating the demolition of the historic old Court House.

(Above) *Railroad Depot, 9th and Green Streets,* lithograph probably by Kennedy & Lucas after W. L. Breton, 1832 (LCP)
(Middle) *Inclined Plane up Belmont Hill,* watercolor by B. R. Evans (HSP)
(Below) *Reliance Portable Boat Company's Iron Boats for the Transportation of Goods between Philadelphia and Pittsburgh,* lithograph by P. S. Duval after Geo. Lehman, ca. 1845 (HSP)

RELIANCE PORTABLE BOAT COMPANY'S
LINE of PORTABLE IRON BOATS
FOR THE TRANSPORTATION OF GOODS BETWEEN **PHILADELPHIA** AND **PITTSBURGH.**

The city increasingly took on an appearance of pillared elegance as new churches and other public, as well as private, buildings brightened its streets. William Strickland and John Haviland, more than any other individuals, were responsible for that elegance. The 1820s saw them at the peak of their architectural activity. Typical of the classical influence was Haviland's First Presbyterian Church with its well-proportioned facade looking out on Washington Square. While St. Stephen's Episcopal Church on South Tenth Street was altered in the Gothic taste, most of Strickland's other buildings had porticos in the antique style. The Congregational Unitarian Church at Tenth and Locust streets, erected in 1828 after the arrival of William Henry Furness as minister, employed columns and marble from the recently demolished Centre Square Water Works. The United States Mint at Juniper and Chestnut streets, begun the following year, was even more impressively Greek. Another government building by Strickland, the Naval Asylum of 1827-33, also presented a bold pedimented portico. By 1840 the so-called Greek revival had passed its peak of popularity.

(Below) *St. Stephen's Episcopal Church*, engraving by Cephas Grier Childs after George Strickland, 1829 (LCP)

(Above) *First Congregational Unitarian Church*, engraving by Cephas Grier Childs after Hugh Reinagle, 1829 (LCP)

(Right) *United States Mint*, engraving by William H. Hay after William Strickland, 1829 (LCP)

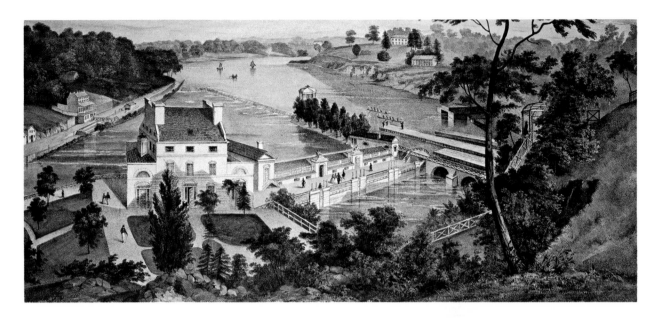

The pumps of the first waterworks kept breaking down, so a new system was built at Fairmount by Frederick Graff, then and for many years chief of the works. Water was pumped to a reservoir on top of Fairmount whence it flowed in hollow wooden pipes, later changed to iron, to Centre Square for distribution. At first the pumps were motivated by one of Evans' Columbian steam engines, but by 1822 they were converted to cheaper, more efficient water power. The City Councils saw that the lay of the land lent itself admirably for a park, so gardens were laid out, walks and gazebos were added, and Rush's nymph fountain was moved there. The public gardens and promenade, a "must" for visitors to the city, were the beginnings of Fairmount Park.

Westward lay the course of the city. The Almshouse at Tenth and Spruce streets was no longer in open fields. A new and larger facility was needed, and developers were eyeing the town land, so the combined Almshouse and Philadelphia Hospital were moved in 1833-34 across the river to still suburban Blockley Township. Out in the nearby countryside John Hare Powel in 1830 built his classicly inspired mansion, Powelton, on a family estate. Not so far west, but west of the old residential district, wealthy Charles Blight had Haviland design him a splendid house in similar style on South Thirteenth Street. Buildings simply could not be put up without columns. On the south side of Chestnut Street between Fifteenth and Sixteenth, Blight and his brother in 1828 built Colonnade Row, a handsome group with a continuous columnar

porch running the length of the development. Down a block from the old site of the Almshouse rose Portico Row. Stephen Girard was a major developer of city property in this manner, and after his death his estate continued that form of investment. The first row of Philadelphia houses with interior bathtubs and toilets was put up by the Girard Estate on the north side of Chestnut Street between Eleventh and Twelfth. Although public establishments like Swaim's Philadelphia Baths at Seventh and Sansom streets, which opened in 1828, met a need, by 1836 1,530 bathrooms were receiving water from the Fairmount Water Works.

(Above) *A view of the Fairmount Waterworks,* by J. T. Bowen, ca. 1838 **(LCP)**
(Below) *Powelton,* watercolor by David J. Kennedy **(HSP)**

As Philadelphia grew geographically, it became necessary to create a focal point for the transaction of business and for intracity transportation. The old Merchants' Coffee House was not adequate for the new generation's commerce, for Philadelphia was no longer a walking city. The Corinthian-columned Merchants' Exchange, designed by William Strickland, was built in 1834 at Dock and Walnut streets. Occupied by the Post Office and numerous businesses, it solved the need for a commercial center. Introduced at about the same time, omnibuses, which were horse-drawn carriages that traveled set routes, solved the need for convenient, inexpensive transit within the city. Gaily painted and fancifully named, the omnibuses started from the Merchants' Exchange, where they drew up beside the tracks of the Columbia Railroad. Until horsepower trolleys were introduced two decades later, omnibuses—literally "for all"—were the only city-wide public transportation.

(Above) *Merchants' Exchange,* lithograph by Deroy after Aug. Kollner, 1848 (LCP)
(Below) *An Omnibus,* lithograph by A. Kollner, ca. 1850 (HSP)

The connection of the great rivers north, south, and west of Philadelphia by canals had been a long-time dream. To bring a water supply to the city, fifteen miles of a Delaware and Schuylkill Canal had been dug in the eighteenth century, but it was abandoned. The revelation that anthracite coal would burn, a discovery attributed to many, stimulated promoters to complete plans long held in abeyance. Josiah White, proprietor of a rolling mill and wire factory at the Falls of the Schuylkill, was one of the first to bring the fuel down from the mines by water. With his partner Erskine Hazard he founded the Lehigh Coal and Navigation Company which canalized the Lehigh River from Mauch Chunk to the Delaware, landing coal at the city wharves as early

as 1820. At the same time the Schuylkill Navigation Company was finishing its complex of canals, pools, locks, dams, and a tunnel from Fairmount to Port Carbon above Reading. It was completed the full distance in 1825, a year in which canal boats brought 5,000 tons of coal to Philadelphia; three years later the tonnage rose to 47,284 and increased annually, reaching a peak of 584,692 tons in 1841— after which the Reading Railroad became the chief coal carrier. As part of its system the Schuylkill Navigation Company built a dam at Flat Rock and offered water power for sale, which led to the development of the mill town of Manayunk. A third canal, the Chesapeake and Delaware, was Philadelphia-promoted and opened trade to the south.

(Above) *Canal Locks at Manayunk*, woodcut by A. Gilbert after W. L. Breton, from *Atkinson's Casket*, 1830 (LCP)

Paints, chemicals, and drugs were Philadelphia specialities. The Wetherills' white lead was the basis of their successful paint business, and M. & S. N. Lewis turned from mercantile trade to paint manufacturing on a large property running from Fifteenth to Sixteenth Street and from Pine to Lombard. The Harrisons developed a large manufactory of sulphuric acid at their Kensington works. One of the first mills established in Manayunk to use the Schuylkill Navigation Company's water power was that of Charles V. Hagner, who there ground quantities of bark, plaster, and minerals for medical use. One of the most extraordinary figures of the period was Thomas W. Dyott, who started his career in Philadelphia selling patent medicines. In 1833 he bought a glass works just above Kensington. By acquiring adjoining land he established a kind of enclave, Dyottsville, where he housed employees, grew food for them, and erected a chapel for regular prayers, lectures, and song sessions. His Dyottsville Glass Works was soon the largest producer of glass articles in the country. Unfortunately, Dyott also operated a savings bank which overexpanded and failed in the specie crisis. In 1839 Dyott was convicted of fraudulent insolvency and sentenced to prison. The site of the glass factory became the Lehigh Coal and Navigation Company's coal depot on the Delaware.

(Above) *Wetherill & Brothers White Lead Manufactory & Chemical Works, at 12th and Cherry Streets,* lithograph probably after W. L. Breton, from Thomas Porter, *Picture of Philadelphia,* 1831 (LCP)

(Middle) *Glass Works of T. W. Dyott at Kensington,* lithograph after W. L. Breton, from Thomas Porter, *Picture of Philadelphia,* 1831 (HSP)

(Below) *View of Carpenter's Chemical Ware House,* engraving by J. Magoffin after M. S. Parker, ca. 1835 (HSP)

For visitors on business or pleasure Chestnut Street was the axis on which the city was hinged. At one of the focal points of activity, on the north side of the street opposite the Bank of the United States, stood the United States Hotel, for many years the principal hostelry in town. Converted from two large residences and subsequently enlarged, it opened its doors to guests in 1826. Among them was Charles Dickens who, as did many others before and after him, partook of its hospitality and growled over the size of his bill. Although outmoded by the much larger hotels erected after mid-century, in its day the United States Hotel was modern in comparison with the antiquated appearance of the City Hotel on North Third Street where President Jackson stayed in 1832 when he came to consult the famous surgeon Dr. Philip Syng Physick and where old John Randolph of Roanoke died the following year. Philadelphia food, much of it prepared by Negro chefs, was consistently good American fare, and famous were its oysters served in cellars throughout the city.

(Below) *City Hotel, 41 North 3rd Street*, lithograph by Kennedy & Lucas after W. L. Breton, ca. 1830 (HSP)
(Above) *Philadelphia Taste Displayed, Or, Bon-Ton Below Stairs*, lithograph by Kennedy & Lucas after James Akin, ca. 1830 (HSP)
(Right) *United States Hotel, Chestnut Street*, lithograph by P. S. Duval after D. S. Quintin, ca. 1842 (LCP)

UNITED STATES HOTEL
Chesnut Street, Philadelphia.

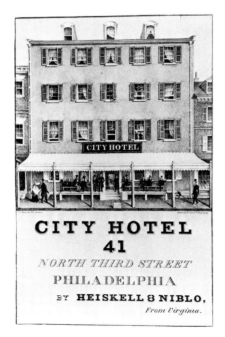

CITY HOTEL
41
NORTH THIRD STREET
PHILADELPHIA
BY **HEISKELL & NIBLO,**
From Virginia.

The city's capital flowed increasingly from mercantile adventures into transportation and manufacturing facilities. The opening of the Erie Canal further diminished the export trade, which dropped from $11,270,000 in 1826 to $3,477,000 in the depression year of 1838 but recovered to twice that amount two years later. Coal was shipped out in coastal schooners, and the import trade was fairly well maintained during the period. In the 1820s there were still Philadelphia vessels sailing to Canton and Calcutta with John McCrea and Brown Brothers & Co. among the owners. Regular transatlantic service was carried on by Thomas P. Cope's Liverpool Packet Line, started in 1821, and the New Line which soon after sailed on the twentieth of each month to Liverpool by way of Savannah. Steamboats began to make their appearance in the Delaware, notably the *Robert Morris* which carried passengers between the city and Newcastle and Burlington. On July 18, 1837, there was big excitement on the waterfront when the U.S.S. Pennsylvania, the largest and most heavily armed man-of-war in the world, was launched at the Navy Yard before a huge crowd. Designed by Samuel Humphreys, with a figurehead of Hercules carved by John Rush, she took fifteen years to build.

Philadelphia CITIZEN'S LINE of STEAMBOATS to New York.

(Above) *View of the Launch of the U. S. Ship of War* Pennsylvania, lithograph by Lehman & Duval after Geo. Lehman, 1837 (HSP)
(Middle) *Philadelphia Citizen's Line of Steam Boats at Arch Street,* lithograph after W. L. Breton, from Thomas Porter, *Picture of Philadelphia,* 1831 (LCP)
(Below) *Delaware River Water Front at Walnut Street,* lithograph, ca. 1835 (HSP)

Free education for the poor was part of the city's Quaker tradition. In 1818 the Pennsylvania Legislature established, for Philadelphia county only, a state school district. Under the leadership of Roberts Vaux, the experimental teacher Joseph Lancaster was brought in as superintendant of schools, and the Lancastrian method in which older children taught younger ones was adopted. Although there were over 3,000 children enrolled in the schools by 1820, there was some question how much education they got. The 1830s saw a reorganization of the system. New buildings were put up (there were two "colored" schools); the Lancastrian method was abandoned and a high school authorized. President Thomas Dunlap of the school board reported in 1837 that 12,000 children were being taught, in more than fifty schools, "a complete system of universal public instruction from the primary school to the proudest institute of human learning." The following year Central High School, the first of its kind in the country, opened on Juniper Street east of Penn Square. With the distinguished Dr. Alexander Dallas Bache as its organizer, the four-year school offered superior courses by competent professors. It even had an astronomical observatory with telescopes at the time better than those at Harvard and the United States Naval Observatory.

(Above) *Central High School*, wash design for diploma by Becker, ca. 1840 (HSP)

CHOLERA.
☞ Read This.

The ravages of Cholera in Montreal seem to speak out already for Temperance, and most decidedly against moderate drinkers. The deaths that have come under our personal knowledge are in many cases drunkards, (of these we have heard of one recovery) *and almost all moderate drinkers.* We some time ago said that intemperance and moderate drinking would inscribe their progress among us in letters of death. Let the moderate drinkers and scoffers at Temperance Societies now behold how fearfully our words have been verified.—[*From Montreal Courant.*

Farther and farther westward from its source and faster and faster a plague of Asiatic cholera spread around the world. The deadly pandemic had broken out near Calcutta in August, 1817, but had taken almost fifteen years to reach London and Scotland. Worried, Americans hoped the Atlantic would be a sanitary barrier, but in the beginning of June, 1832, cases were reported in Canada. By the end of the month cholera had reached New York. The Philadelphia Board of Health assisted by a committee of eminent physicians took precautionary measures. Emergency hospitals, mostly in school buildings, were set up and equipped throughout the county. On July 5th the first case occurred in Philadelphia. By August the epidemic was widespread. George Washington Dixon, a popular singer, published the Cholera Gazette to record the day-to-day progress of the disease. Before the epidemic ran its course in October 2,314 cases were reported with 935 deaths. The city was fortunate. Only one in seventy Philadelphians was stricken, only one in 173 died; in New York one in twenty-five persons died. Understandably, the most crowded sections, Southwark and Moyamensing, were the hardest hit. The heroes and heroines of the epidemic were the doctors who had volunteered their services and the Catholic Sisters of Charity who acted as nurses in the cholera hospitals.

If only the poor, the shiftless, the drunkards, the blind, and other problem people could be made to emulate their religious, hardworking, literate, clean, and temperate betters, vice, violence, and misery would disappear. Old philanthropic institutions expanded and new ones were born. The American Sunday School Union, instituted in Philadelphia in 1824, determined among other noble purposes to "circulate moral and religious publications in every part of the land." Hundreds of exemplary tales, written for children, were published in thousands of copies by this largest tract society in the country. Partly in answer to Christian missionary efforts, Rebecca Gratz, aided by the energetic rabbi Isaac Leeser, founded the Hebrew Sunday School Society in 1838. The Magdalen Society, seeking to save fallen women, and a host of temperance organizations flourished. More practical and scientific in approach were the Pennsylvania Institution for the Deaf and Dumb, founded in 1821 by David B. Seixas and housed in a handsome Greek revival building at Broad and Pine streets, and the Pennsylvania Institution for the Instruction of the Blind, established two years later and directed by Dr. Julius R. Friedlander. One major tragedy marred the progress of philanthropy when the Orphans' Asylum at Eighteenth and Cherry streets burned in January, 1822, killing twenty-three children.

(Above) *Deaf and Dumb Asylum, Broad and Pine Streets,* transfer print on Staffordshire plate (American Antiquarian Society)
(Below) Wrapper Title of *The Rainbow,* ca. 1835 (HSP)

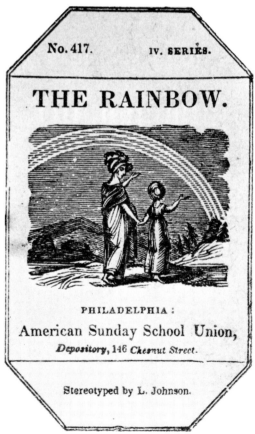

No. 417.   IV. SERIES.

THE RAINBOW.

PHILADELPHIA:
American Sunday School Union,
Depository, 146 *Chesnut Street.*

Stereotyped by L. Johnson.

It was primarily to study prisons, and particularly to observe the Pennsylvania System in Philadelphia, that the incisive commentator on American life and government Alexis de Tocqueville, and his friend Gustave de Beaumont, came to the United States. When Charles Dickens visited America, the new penitentiary and Niagara Falls were the two places he most wanted to see. The Eastern State (Cherry Hill) Penitentiary, designed by John Haviland and erected in 1823-29 with its seven rows of cells radiating out from a central tower, was built to encompass what was considered the latest in prison reform, solitary confinement at labor. Proud of its international reputation in the field of penology, Philadelphia in 1838 replaced the county's old Walnut Street jail with a new structure, Moyamensing Prison. Both of the structures had grim, turreted medieval entrances, perhaps as a warning to would-be criminals, but Thomas U. Walter, incongruously, placed an exotic Egyptian-style debtors' prison as an adjunct to the South Philadelphia building. It was never used for its designed purpose; imprisonment for debt was abolished before it was completed.

(Above) *Moyamensing Prison*, lithograph by J. T. Bowen after J. C. Wild, 1840 (LCP)
(Below) *The State Penitentiary, For the Eastern District of Pennsylvania*, lithograph by P. S. Duval & Co., on membership certificate of Pennsylvania Prison Society, 1855 (LCP)

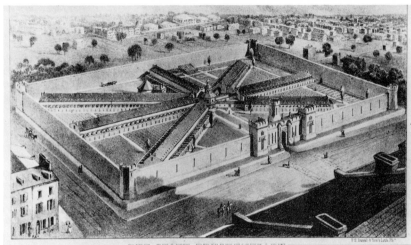

THE STATE PENITENTIARY
For the Eastern District of Pennsylvania

Late in 1819 a "very numerous and respectable meeting" was held in the State House at which the lawyer-orator Horace Binney presented resolutions opposing the extension of slavery into newly constituted states. At about the same time "the people of color," under the chairmanship of James Forten, met to protest the African colonization movement. The American Anti-Slavery Society was founded in Philadelphia in 1833, and five years later the Pennsylvania Freeman began publication with John Greenleaf Whittier as editor. But opposition to abolition on the part of many merchants with southern connections and hostility to blacks on the part of native and immigrant workers were on the increase. A racial riot, one of a continuing series, took place in a black neighborhood of Moyamensing in August, 1833. Tension became such that the abolitionists, not welcome elsewhere, built their own meeting-place, Pennsylvania Hall. When the Anti-Slavery Convention of American Women and the Pennsylvania Anti-Slavery Society met there on May 16, 1838, pent-up prejudices were loosed at the sight of blacks and whites, men and women, walking and talking together. The next night a mob stormed the hall and set it on fire. The halfhearted fire companies were prevented from playing their hoses on the conflagration. Mayor John Swift and the police were assaulted. Destruction was complete.

(Above) *Destruction by Fire of Pennsylvania Hall, on the night of the 17th of May*, lithograph by J. T. Bowen probably after J. C. Wild, 1838 (HSP)
(Facing, above) *View of the Fountain in Franklin Square*, lithograph by J. T. Bowen, 1839 (HSP)
(Facing, below) *General Lafayette's arrival at Independence Hall, Sep: 28th. 1824*, block print on linen (detail) (HSP)

As the United States approached the maturity of half a century of independence, enthusiasm grew for paying homage to the Founding Fathers. The first widespread expression of nostalgia for the past flowered during Lafayette's triumphal return in 1824. Philadelphia, which had seen him ride through its streets at Washington's side, offered him a spectacular welcome. Up Chestnut Street from the river a civic and military parade marched through an elaborately painted canvas-on-wood arch designed by William Strickland to the culminating ceremonies at the former State House, then for the first time called Independence Hall. Carrying through with the patriotic theme, in 1825 the City Councils named the compass-point squares after Washington, Franklin, Rittenhouse, and Logan, and honored the city's founder by calling the center square Penn Square.

The feeling of pride in the past stimulated by Lafayette's visit resulted in 1824 in the organization of the Historical Society of Pennsylvania, which first had its rooms in Philosophical Hall. A few years later Strickland was retained to rebuild the steeple of Independence Hall as it had been and then to bring the historic Assembly Room "to its ancient form." While all these activities were taking place, John Fanning Watson was scurrying about the city to collect bits and pieces of memories for his pioneer Annals of Philadelphia. All the manifestations of patriotism were eclipsed by the parade held in 1832 in honor of the centennial of Washington's birth. Trades each with its own float, fire companies, military troops, and state and municipal officers paraded; cannons boomed from the Arsenal and Navy Yard; ships were festooned; and at night illuminations outlined private homes and public buildings. When Chief Justice John Marshall died in 1835, the Liberty Bell cracked. Another symbol was created for the nation.

(Above) *The Gold & Silver Artificers In Civic Procession 22 Feb 1832*, lithograph by M. E. D. Brown (LCP)
(Facing, above, left) Mahogany Secretary Bookcase by Anthony G. Quervelle (Joseph Sorger, photograph by Cortlandt V. D. Hubbard)
(Facing, above, right) *Life in Philadelphia*, etching by E. W. Clay 1829 (LCP)
(Facing, middle) *Laurel Hill*, engraving by A. W. Graham, after W. Croome, for *Godey's Lady's Book* (LCP)
(Facing, below) China Pitcher by William Ellis Tucker (HSP)

It was stylish to ride in a carriage out along the Schuylkill for a stroll through rural Laurel Hill Cemetery. Inspired by Mount Auburn outside Boston, the many-faceted John Jay Smith, librarian of the Library Company, in 1836 promoted the establishment of a picturesque burial ground on the former estate of Joseph Sims. The architect John Notman designed the entrance and laid out the grounds. It quickly became one of the sights of the city. To be sure, the gentlemen strollers still wore top hats, but in the late 1830s the tails of their coats were longer than they had been a decade earlier. The sleeves of their wasp-waisted companions had diminished in size, and bonnets had replaced flowered hats. France was still the model of elegance. French craftsmen, such as Anthony G. Quervelle, vied with Joseph White and other native cabinetmakers in turning out beautifully carved furniture in a style heavier and more elaborate than that of a past generation. William Ellis Tucker successfully copied the esteemed Sèvres porcelain in his factory at Twenty-third and Market streets and was the first in America to manufacture fine china on a commercial scale. The well-to-do blacks in Philadelphia were fashion-conscious, too, as a satirist vividly pointed out.

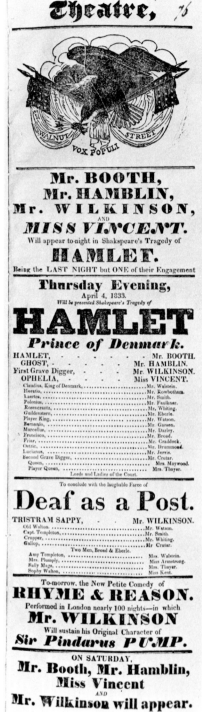

Philadelphia was theater-rich. William Warren and William B. Wood, the leading managers in the country, at first in partnership and later as rivals, brought to town the greatest actors of the day, who played in the city's three competing theaters. In 1820, after the Chestnut Street Theatre was destroyed by fire, the impresarios took over the Walnut Street where young Edwin Forrest made his stage debut, an event far overshadowed the following year by the appearance of the great Edmund Kean. The striking new Chestnut Street Theatre, designed by William Strickland and embellished with statues by William Rush, opened late in 1822. It became the most prestigious playhouse in town. A French opera company from New Orleans played there in 1829; Charles Kemble and his daughter Fanny began an engagement in 1832 when it was under new management; and three years later the dancer Fanny Ellsler performed. When the Walnut Street Theatre fell on bad days and reverted to its earlier use as a circus, Wood thought competition still could be provided to the Chestnut Street. Strickland was engaged, and the Arch Street Theatre was built and finished in 1828. It was successful in fits and starts. Instead of fading away as the Arch Street was rising, the old Walnut Street was renovated and given a new façade by John Haviland. In 1834 Francis C. Wemyss, an English actor, took over its management, renamed it the American Theatre, and tried to use principally native talent. Seasons were good and bad, but always there was something to see.

(Above, left) *Chestnut Street Theatre*, engraving by Fenner Sears & Co. after R. Goodacre, 1831 (HSP)
(Middle, left) *Walnut Street Theatre*, engraving by Fenner Sears & Co. after C. Burton, 1831 (HSP)
(Middle, right) Edwin Forrest as Spartacus in *The Gladiator* by Robert Montgomery Bird, photograph from Edwin Robin, *Twelve Great Actors* (LCP)
(Above, right) Playbill of Junius Brutus Booth in *Hamlet* at the Walnut, 1833 (LCP)

Places to go and things to do for relaxation made Philadelphia a fun city for its residents in the days before the era of self-denigration. Horse-racing, which had moved from built-up Race Street to the track at Hunting Park in open country to the north, attracted its devotees. Rowing enthusiasts formed barge clubs and competed on the Schuylkill as early as 1835. For a day's outing Fairmount beckoned with its walks and the nearby Chinese pagoda. Interest in the beguiling Orient, brought to the city by lucrative commerce, also brought visitors to Nathan Dunn's Chinese Museum. It moved from Washington Hall to the first floor of the New Museum Building at Ninth and Sansom streets, on the second floor of which the Peales in 1838 exhibited their father's popular display. For music a new auditorium on Locust Street west of Eighth, Musical Fund Hall, was remodeled by Strickland in 1824. There most of the famous vocal and instrumental musicians performed for a generation.

(Above) *The Pagoda and Labyrinth Garden,* lithograph by William B. Lucas after J. Haviland, 1828 (HSP)
(Middle) *Boat Race on the Schuylkill toward the Columbia Railroad Bridge,* lithograph by Sinclair probably after M. S. Weaver, on sheet music cover for *Schuylkill Boat Song,* ca. 1842 (LCP)
(Below) *Roper's Gymnasium, 274 Market Street,* lithograph by Childs & Inman after E. W. Clay, ca. 1831 (LCP)

1840-1860

The antebellum years were not the happiest in the city's history, but growth in many areas continued. Two economic depressions, widespread violence, and new technologies forced readjustments. Fortunes were lost in canals and banks; fortunes were made in real estate and textile and drug manufacturing. Philadelphia was able to reorder its civic administration by consolidating city and county, expand its transportation network, and, not without hardships, accommodate its work force to the machine age.

The potato famine in Ireland and the repression of democratic uprisings in Europe in 1848 sent over increasing numbers of immigrants to the land of freedom and opportunity. In 1840 Philadelphia's population was 258,037; in 1860 it had more than doubled to 565,529 —approximately a third foreign-born—making the city one of the largest urban areas in the Western world. It was the tremendous influx of unskilled Irish Catholics from a rural environment into a predominantly Protestant industrial city which created much of the tension of the times. An increase of cheap labor at a time when machines were replacing men and an economic situation which fluctuated drastically added to the problems.

Laborers were virtually at the mercy of their employers. When the Reading Railroad and the Schuylkill Navigation Company competed for coal business by lowering rates, they reduced workmen's wages. Handloom weavers were paid $4.25 a week. Although a ten-hour-day law was passed by the Pennsylvania legislature in 1848, it was largely ignored. Strikes, the crusading novelist George Lippard's Brotherhood of the Union, and over forty unions of the skilled trades were ineffectual. When the bank panic of 1857 occurred there was widespread unemployment. With the help of private philanthropy and a mild winter a major disaster was avoided.

Housing deteriorated in the older sections of Southwark, Moyamensing, the Northern Liberties, and Kensington where the blacks and most of the newcomers settled. Conditions were so appalling that, as a result of an investigation by a Sanitary Committee during a return of cholera in 1849, a massive clean-up was undertaken. A grand jury in 1853 found thousands starving and homeless in the worst of the sections from Fifth to Eighth Street and from Lombard to Fitzwater. Crime was rampant. Much of the misery was blamed by those who lived elsewhere on shiftlessness, laziness, and drunkenness.

(Facing) *The Post Office, Philadelphia*, painting by Tompkins H. Matteson, 1856 (Addison Gallery of American Art, Andover, Mass.)
(Above) *Politics in Philadelphia, Going the Split Ticket* (detail), woodcut, 1855 (LCP)

179

As more people needed homes, land increased in value. Real-estate speculators were able to make fortunes as new workmen's houses were erected around the factory complexes at Richmond, Bridesburg, Frankford, Germantown, and Manayunk, as cottages were built in the West Philadelphia settlements of Hamiltonville, Powelton, and Mantua, and as mansions rose in the rolling country from Mt. Airy to Chestnut Hill, in Fern Rock and Jenkintown. When an anonymous author estimated the wealth of the richest Philadelphians in 1845, he noted four of six millionaires, Jacob Steinmetz, James Molony, George Pepper, and John J. Ridgway, made or inherited their money from real estate. It is interesting that when the count-another-person's-money compilation was updated in 1857, among others added were two brokers, Alexander Benson and Francis M. Drexel; David Jayne, the patent medicine man; Joseph Harrison, Jr., the most successful railroad planner in the world; George W. Carpenter, drug manufacturer; and James Dundas, banker.

It was significant that most of these men of wealth were self-made, not the scions of old families who had long had money. That crusty descendant of crusty James Logan, the diarist Sidney George Fisher, commented frequently and bitterly on the prevalence of the *nouveaux riches,* the spread of Jacksonian democracy in its broadest sense, the disappearance of old values, and the rise of vulgarity. The political parties were finding it difficult to get "a gentleman" to run for office, but there were exceptions. Charles Jared Ingersoll was a Democratic congressman from 1840 to 1849, and his brother Joseph Reed Ingersoll went to Washington as a Republican in 1841. Few, however, were as colorful as Richard Vaux, a large, hearty aristocrat who, dressed in the latest fashion, delighted the Democratic voters by his enthusiastic participation in their meetings and affairs. Defeated for mayor in 1854, he won two years later. But the most outstanding Democrat was George Mifflin Dallas, vice-president of the United States from 1845 to 1849, the highest public office attained by any Philadelphian.

Politics were as confused locally as they were at the national

(Above) *View of Manayunk,* gouache drawing by unknown artist, ca. 1850 (HSP)

level. Generally speaking, the city proper, influenced by its business-men and lawyers, voted the conservative Whig ticket; the more popu-lous surrounding districts with a majority of workingmen turned in for the Democrats. When the Mexican War broke out, the Whigs opposed it because the Polk administration favored it. Nonetheless, many Philadelphians volunteered, and the militia generals Robert Patterson and George Cadwalader were hailed as heroes on their return. Seething racial, religious, and economic animosities split the major political parties and permitted the Native Americans in the 1840s and the Know Nothings in the mid-1850s to elect their own men to local and state offices and even to Congress. But violence and crime were the overriding local concerns. Police from one jurisdiction could not cross the boundaries of another in the county. After some years of political maneuvering the campaign to consolidate the city with the subdivisions of the county was crowned with success in 1854. Con-solidation brought the establishment of a strong, centralized police force, an efficient tax structure, and better control over the maverick volunteer fire companies.

Lack of a strong stand on slavery destroyed the Whig Party na-tionally. In 1856 the new Republican Party which filled the void held its first national convention in Philadelphia at the Musical Fund Hall on Locust Street and nominated John C. Fremont as its candidate for President. However, the Pennsylvanian James Buchanan, the Demo-cratic nominee, eked out a victory in the city. Philadelphians were still somewhat hesitant about supporting "black" abolitionist Repub-licans, so the local party members emphasized the tariff issue, pro-tection being unassailably popular in the industrial city. The ideo-logical foundation for the protection of manufactures was provided by Henry C. Carey, the country's foremost economist and the son of Mathew Carey, a pioneer protectionist. Without great conviction Philadelphia voted for Abraham Lincoln in November, 1860. A news-paper commented: "We never saw an election for even ward officers, that excited so little interest."

The outlook for the Negroes was bleak. They had been disen-

(Above) *Wakefield Manufacturing Company, Germantown,* lithograph by P. S. Duval after B. F. Smith, ca. 1850 (HSP)

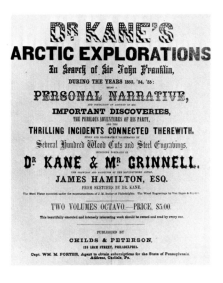

(Above) Members of the Pennsylvania Anti-Slavery Society, ca. 1860; Lucretia and James Mott at lower right (HSP)
(Below) Advertisement for Elisha Kent Kane's Bestseller, 1856 (LCP)
(Facing) *Grand, National, Democratic Banner,* lithograph by N. Currier, 1844 (HSP)
(Following spread) Photographs of McAllister's Optical Store on the South Side of Chestnut Street west of 2nd by William G. Mason, 1843 (left), and by one of the Langenheim brothers, 1856 (right) (LCP)

franchised by the state constitution of 1838, Philadelphia's schools were segregated, and blacks were denied higher education. Although some prominent Quakers such as Lucretia Mott and James Miller McKim remained uncompromising abolitionists, antislavery activity was not popular. The city's businesses had profitable and extensive connections with the South, which persuaded merchants and workmen to favor its ways. Furthermore, the head-on conflict for housing and jobs with the overwhelming number of Irish immigrants added fuel to the fire of racial hostility. Irresistably the Irish pushed the blacks into the most miserable slums and implacably they replaced them as laborers on docks and building sites.

Anti-Negro feeling was widespread. On August 1, 1842, a mob attacked a black temperance group parading in celebration of the abolition of slavery in the West Indies. Rioting, looting, and beatings raged through the black neighborhood in the vicinity of Lombard Street between Fifth and Eighth. Smith's Beneficial Hall and a church were burned. The next day Irish workers attacked blacks in a Schuylkill coal yard, and the disturbance spread east to Moyamensing where a further holocaust was prevented by a strong force of militia. Another attack on a Negro neighborhood in Moyamensing took place in October, 1849, when white ruffians stormed California House, an inn operated by a mulatto married to a white woman. The blacks fought back and for two days the battle went on. A Vigilance Committee was organized by the Negro community with William Still, Robert Purvis, and others guiding it. They kept the Underground Railroad in operation and tried to undercut the Fugitive Slave Law. Sympathy with them was minimal. A Great Union Meeting in the autumn of 1850 with such Democratic figures as John Sergeant and George Mifflin Dallas on the platform denounced the abolitionists' "imported fanaticism." *Graham's Magazine,* representing middle-class views, attacked *Uncle Tom's Cabin* in a scurrilous review. The eloquent Unitarian William Henry Furness lost many wealthy parishioners as a result of his antislavery sermons. When the body of John Brown was brought to Philadelphia in 1859 for burial, the mayor, fearing riots, forbade it; the coffin was smuggled out of town to be interred in northern New York.

Quite different had been the public sentiment at the funeral in March, 1857, of the city's greatest contemporary hero, Dr. Elisha

Kent Kane, whose daring and harrowing Arctic expeditions had won him international fame. A vast cortege of notables, naval officers, troops of militia, representatives of societies, and others followed his remains to the churchyard. There were many occasions for more festive celebration, and in the gloomy antebellum era the citizenry welcomed them. The new Concert Hall on Chestnut Street between Twelfth and Thirteenth was opened in February, 1853, with a recital by Madame Sontag, and four years later the larger and grander Academy of Music made its debut in the cultural life of Philadelphia. When the United States Agricultural Exhibition was held in the open country on Powelton Avenue in the autumn of 1856, it was estimated that about ninety thousand persons visited it, many to watch the racing of the country's fastest trotters. The first message sent over the Atlantic cable by Queen Victoria to President Buchanan was celebrated at the beginning of September, 1858, in Independence Square where the rising Republican politician Judge William B. Kelley delivered an oration. A vocal advocate of the antislavery cause and a firm believer in a high tariff, Kelley was elected to Congress in 1860, where his protectionist views for over a quarter of a century won him the cognomen of "Pig Iron" Kelley.

All the festivities and meetings previously held faded into insignificance compared with the excitement caused by the arrival in town of a Japanese embassy in June, 1860. People poured in from the countryside; the whole city, it seems, turned out to see the oriental visitors; it was reported that the incredible number of half a million persons caught the "Japanese fever." The Japanese stayed at the new Continental Hotel, where crowds gathered daily to catch a glimpse of them as they left for tours of the city. The popular favorite, especially with the ladies, was one of the delegation's interpreters, Tateish Onogero, nicknamed Japanese Tommy. It was said that the Japanese spent more than a hundred thousand dollars in stores during their week's stay; when they left they gave three thousand dollars to be divided up among the police. The visit of the Prince of Wales four months later was anticlimactic; he was quietly escorted about by Mayor Henry. The high point of his visit was a special performance at the Academy of Music at which young Adelina Patti sang.

What was becoming commonplace in the city must have seemed as strange to the Japanese as they themselves seemed to the Philadel-

(Above) *The Ambassadors from Japan Arriving at the Continental Hotel,* woodcut by E. Rogers, 1860 (HSP)
(Below) *The Gas Works at 22nd and Market Streets,* woodcut by Devereux, from *Gleason's Pictorial Drawing-Room Companion,* April 2, 1853 (LCP)

phians. Factories making all kinds of goods and machines belched forth smoke. Water channeled through sluices turned wheels which powered looms and powdered chemicals. The use of gas made from coal was general for both house and street illumination. The gas works, taken over by the city in 1841, were enlarged until 1854 when a new facility with a mammoth telescopic storage tank was opened at Point Breeze. Other works were set up for the Northern Liberties, Manayunk, and Frankford. Another improved service was the mail. Dissatisfaction with the speed of the government agency and the nuisance of going to a box in the post office led to the establishment of Blood's City Dispatch Post, a private company which promised prompt, cheap, and convenient delivery. Prompt and cheap, too, was photography, the new method of recording images. The first American daguerreotype, a view of Central High School, had been taken in 1839 by the ingenious mechanic Joseph Saxton from the United States Mint where he worked. It did not take long for the art to develop. William G. Mason, an engraver, who made a daguerreotype of a Chestnut Street scene in 1843, is credited with taking the first perfect picture by artificial light. Even better was another photograph of the same shops taken thirteen years later by one of the Langenheim brothers who were then using glass plates. By 1860 there were eighty-four Philadelphia firms engaged in photographic work, most of them supplying carte-de-visite portraits.

It was paradoxical that, emerging from an era of internal stress and about to enter one of national conflict, the city's political structure was stronger due to consolidation and most of its major industries were healthy. Philadelphia was almost, but not quite, ready to become the Republican stronghold which it remained for a century. As the southernmost of the major cities of the nation Philadelphia took a while before it uncompromisingly accepted Lincoln's program.

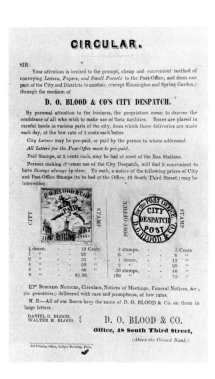

(Above) Advertisement for Blood's City Despatch, 1847 (LCP)

Chestnut Street with its stores, offices, theaters, museums, hotels, and public buildings continued to be the bustling "Broadway" of Philadelphia. Strollers, shoppers, sight-seers, carts, and omnibuses crowded the roadway and pavements. In keeping with the city's growth into a metropolis, smaller hotels such as the Franklin House gave way to grand and lavish establishments: the Girard House with its magnificent ironwork balcony and accommodations for a thousand guests, which opened in 1852, and the even larger Continental Hotel, completed in 1860, which boasted an elevator and was long the town's outstanding hostelry. Both were designed by John McArthur, Jr., and faced each other across Chestnut Street at Ninth. For patriotic visitors the main room in Independence Hall was made into a museum with the Liberty Bell elaborately enshrined. Nearby, below Fifth Street, was the city's first department store, L. J. Levy & Company's palace-like dry-goods emporium. Across on the north side of Chestnut Street G. G. Evans had his huge bookstore where he offered a gift with each book sold at retail price.

(Below) *A South West View of Sanderson's Franklin House, between 3rd and 4th Streets on Chestnut,* aquatint by John Ruben Smith, ca. 1845 (HSP)
(Above) *The Pie Man at the Corner of 5th and Chestnut Streets,* painting by William E. Winner, 1856 (HSP)
(Right) *Bookstore of G. G. Evans,* lithograph by E. Sachse, ca. 1855 (LCP)
(Facing, above) *Interior of Independence Hall,* watercolor by Max Rosenthal, 1856 (HSP)
(Facing, below) *Interior View of L. J. Levy & Co's Dry Goods Store,* lithograph by L. N. Rosenthal after Max Rosenthal, 1857 (HSP)

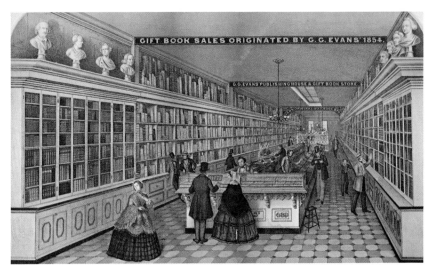

189　＜1840-1860＞

There was no doubt that Lippincott & Co. sold ready-made clothing. Philadelphia businessmen to a far greater extent than those of other American cities understood that a picture was worth a thousand words. Literally hundreds of lithographic trade cards in the form of views of stores and factories were produced by local printmakers. As advertising they must have been most effective, for they showed where and what, with the wares to be sold from stoves to wallpaper prominently and unmistakably displayed. The quality of the cards was due to the expertise of the city's lithographic printing houses, among the nation's best, including Duval, Sinclair, and Wagner & McGuigan.

(Below) Advertisement of P. S. Duval, lithograph by Alfred Newsam, ca. 1840 (HSP)
(Above) *Lippincott & Co., South West Corner of Fourth & Market St.,* lithograph by Wagner & McGuigan after R. F. Reynolds, 1853 (LCP)
(Right) *Joseph Feinour's Stove and Hardware Stores, Front Street south of Spruce,* lithograph by Wagner & McGuigan after W. H. Rease, ca. 1845 (LCP)

The basically sound foundation of the city's economy, shaken as it was by periods of depression, was expressed in the grandeur and expansiveness of the buildings erected. The architectural styles were as varied as Victorian taste. The main hall at Girard College, designed by Thomas U. Walter and under construction for many years, was finished in 1847. It was, and is, the most impressive classically inspired structure in the city. Aesthetically one of the most pleasing of the new churches was the delicate brownstone English gothic St. Mark's on Locust Street between Sixteenth and Seventeenth, consecrated in 1849. Its neighborhood near Rittenhouse Square became the most fashionable in town, and no house there was more eclectic than that at Nineteenth and Chestnut which the eccentric Dr. James Rush designed for the accommodation of his wife's salon. Mrs. Rush, the former Phoebe Ann Ridgway, corpulent, cultured, and one of the richest women in the country, was Philadelphia's most active hostess. To the east the Athenaeum's 1847 Italianate library lent distinction to Washington Square, its quiet elegance contrasting markedly with the gaudy interior of the new Masonic Hall on Chestnut Street. In the business section equally unusual buildings went up. Dr. David Jayne with the income from his patent medicines built the city's first skyscraper in 1849, also on Chestnut Street, below Third, an eight-story granite structure in Venetian gothic style. And not far away a number of stores with intricate cast-iron fronts rose to lend variety to the street scene.

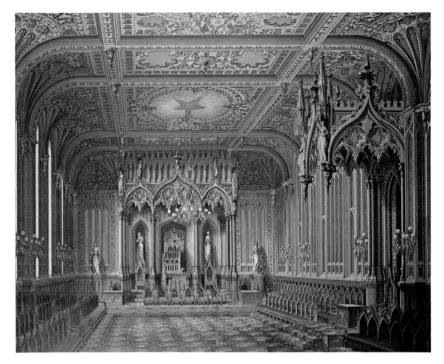

(Above) *Grand Lodge Room of the New Masonic Hall*, lithograph by Collins & Autenrieth after Max Rosenthal, 1855 (LCP)
(Middle) *Girard College*, lithograph by Deroy after Aug. Kollner, 1848 (LCP)
(Below) *Jayne Building*, engraving, 1856 (LCP)

The first great world's fair was the Crystal Palace Exhibition in London in 1851. Manufacturers from all over sent samples of their work to be compared—favorably it was hoped—with the products of their competitors. Philadelphia was well represented. Charles Oakford, the city's leading hatter, displayed his moleskin hats and Rocky Mountain beavers, and Howell & Brothers their colorful wallpaper. Cornelius & Co., whose lighting fixtures were famous throughout the United States, offered two tinted glass chandeliers for burning lard or oil, designed in an eclectic Louis XIV and Renaissance style. Two local firms, Conrad Meyer and J. R. Schomacker & Co., won prize medals for their pianos. Another medal winner was G. W. Watson; his light and speedy buggy, the "Gazelle," was constructed of polished American hickory and walnut and hung on "endless elliptical springs." H. P. & W. C. Taylor, soap-makers and perfumers, entered as their exhibit a stained glass window made of transparent soap for which they, too, got a prize. In an era when the only treatment for compound fractures was amputation, Franklin B. Palmer's ingenious, articulated artificial legs impressed the judges and won their inventor not only a medal but a London outlet for his ware. Obviously, light industry was flourishing in Philadelphia.

(Below) Chandeliers, lithograph, from Cornelius & Sons' trade catalogue, ca. 1860 (HSP)
(Above) Watson's Gazelle Carriage, woodcut, from *Official Descriptive and Illustrated Catalogue* (of the Crystal Palace Exhibition), 1851 (LCP)
(Right) Advertisement for Palmer's Patent Leg (New-York Historical Society)

PALMER'S PATENT LEG,

As Exhibited at the WORLD'S EXHIBITION, LONDON, 1851, and NEW YORK, 1853, with the Gold and Silver Medals awarded.

The Cut represents Mr. J. M. SANFORD, of West Medford, (near Boston, Mass.,) as he appeared in the CRYSTAL PALACE, walking *without the aid of a cane*, even, upon TWO OF PALMER'S PATENT LEGS, one applying ABOVE THE KNEE.
Mr. S. appears so perfect, both in form and motion, as to *entirely conceal the nature of his misfortune.*

"Palmer's Patent," differs radically from all other artificial limbs, both in its mechanism and external appearance. The articulations of knee, ankle, and toes, are united upon a new principle, and in such improved manner as to present the most natural and symmetrical shapes and proportions.
The exterior is covered with a strong material, indissolably fastened, which prevents the possibility of splitting. This covering is fitted without perceptible seam, and then coated with a cement impervious to water, which gives an enameled surface, and color so natural that the most delicately wrought hose and slipper are sufficient to conceal the work of art.
It is adapted to every form of amputation, and successfully applied to the shortest and tenderest stumps. The peculiar characteristics of this limb, are *life-like elasticity and flexibility, excessive lightness, durability, adaptability, and perfection of exterior appearance.*
"I have examined carefully the artificial Leg invented by Mr. B. Frank. Palmer, of this country. Its construction is simple, and its execution is beautiful; and what is most important, those who have the misfortune to require a substitute for the natural limb, and the good fortune to possess it, all concur in bearing practical testimony to its superiority in comfort and utility."
NEW YORK, JANUARY 29, 1851.   VALENT NE MOTT.
                                                                                                Professor of Surgery in the New York University.
"I have seen several of the Artificial Legs manufactured by Mr. B. F. Palmer in use, and consider them superior to any with which I am acquainted."   WILLARD PARKER, M D
New York, January, 29, 1854.   *Professor of Surgery in the College of Physicians and Surgeons, New York.*
                                                                                                PHILADELPH-A, MARCH 28, 1851.
"I have examined, with great care, the Artificial Leg invented by Mr. B. F. Palmer and do not hesitate to recommend it in the *strongest terms,*   THOS. D. MUTTER, M. D.
                                                                                Professor of Surgery in the Jefferson College, Philadelphia.

Thirty GOLD and SILVER MEDALS, (or First Premiums) have been awarded the Inventor; among which are the great PRIZE MEDALS of the WORLD'S EXHIBITIONS in LONDON and NEW YORK.

376 Chestnut St., Philadelphia, } Manufactories, { Burt's Block, Springfield Mass.
378 Broadway, New York,   }   { 24 Savile Row, London.
    All applications from the Middle, Southern and Western States should be directed to Philadelphia.

PALMER & CO.

The lacy ironwork balconies which graced Jackson Square in New Orleans were shipped down by boat from Philadelphia. The largest manufactory of ornamental railings in the United States was Robert Wood's on Ridge Avenue east of Twelfth Street. Cuba too was within the city's business orbit; more raw sugar was shipped to Delaware River wharves than to any other American port. Great refineries were established, that of Harrison & Newhall among the largest, making Philadelphia the sugar center of the nation. From the South had come exotic plants and shrubs since the days of the Bartrams. In that tradition John MacAran built a sophisticated conservatory at Seventeenth and Arch streets where evening entertainments were offered in his long and spacious hothouses. David Landreth on Federal Street near the Arsenal, Robert Buist at 140 South Twelfth Street, and Henry A. Dreer on Market Street maintained thriving nurseries and carried on an extensive trade in seeds. With the flourishing Pennsylvania Horticultural Society which had held annual shows since 1839 these establishments made Philadelphia a major gardening center.

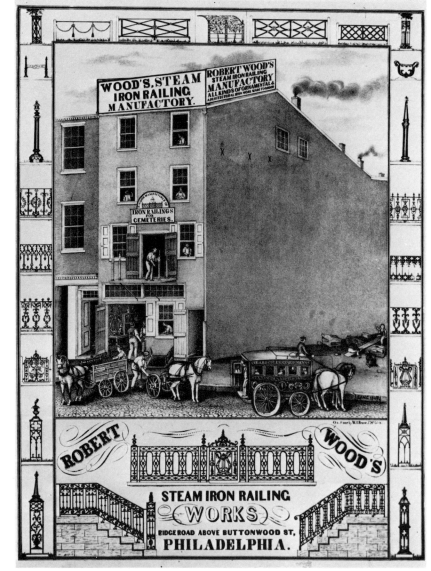

(Below) *Harrison & Newhall, Corner of Race and Crown Streets,* lithograph by Wagner & McGuigan after W. H. Rease, 1856 (HSP)
(Above) *Robert Wood's Steam Iron Railing Works, Ridge Road above Buttonwood St.,* lithograph by W. H. Rease, 1847 (LCP)
(Right) *View of Robert Buist's City Nursery & Greenhouses, No. 140 South Twelfth Str.,* lithograph by Wagner & McGuigan after Alfred Hoffy, 1846 (LCP)

Wood-burning locomotives were dirty, noisy, and fire hazards. All tracks were at grade level. A coalition of Kensington workingmen and property owners by tearing up tracks and by political pressure in the early 1840s prevented a southern extension of the Philadelphia and Trenton Railroad down Front Street from its Tacony depot. But there was no opposition when the Reading Railroad delivered the first coal to its Richmond wharves, and there was general approval when the Pennsylvania Railroad was chartered in 1846 to replace the rail, canal, and portage system with a regular rail line to Pittsburgh, thereby competing with the Erie Canal for the freight business of the west. While the steam engines puffed through the outlying sections, an ordinance banned them from the city proper, down whose streets the coaches and freight vans were drawn from the depots by horses or mules. It was but a small step to lay down more tracks and substitute horse cars for omnibuses to provide short-haul passenger service. Against considerable opposition street cars drawn by horse on rails began operating in 1858 from Frankford to Southwark south on Sixth Street and north on Fifth. Within two years the city's streets were crisscrossed by eighteen separate systems whose stock was subscribed to in a frenzy of speculative eagerness.

(Above) *Philadelphia & Reading Rail Road Depot, Southeast Corner of Broad and Cherry Streets,* watercolor by David J. Kennedy (HSP) (Below) *Eli Hess' Penn Steam Marble Mantel Manufactory, with Horse Car of Exchange & Fairmount Line,* lithograph by W. H. Rease, ca. 1859 (HSP)

One of Philadelphia's early large-scale real-estate speculators, Isaac S. Lloyd, knew good property when he saw it. He bought two estates, Lemon Hill and Sedgley, comprising eighty acres along the east bank of the Schuylkill. Alas, Lloyd was wiped out in the panic of 1837. In order to protect the purity of the water flowing down to the waterworks, the city in 1844 bought Lemon Hill. The house, built by Henry Pratt to replace one formerly owned by Robert Morris, was for a while operated as a beer garden, a favorite spot for picnics and entertainments. In 1855 Lemon Hill became the first section of what was then officially dubbed Fairmount Park. Two years later, partly by private subscription and partly with public funds, the Sedgley estate to the north was purchased from Ferdinand J. Dreer and added to the park which then extended from the Spring Garden Water Works south to Landing Avenue near Fairmount. The river was one of the city's major attractions. The wildness of its tributary Wissahickon Creek, the monumental sculptures and tree-shaded walks of Laurel Hill Cemetery, the gardens at Fairmount, boating in the summer and skating in the winter, all brought people in coaches, on horseback, or on foot to spend the day or a few hours. There were plenty of inns and taverns nearby to cater to the visitors.

(Above) *A Pic-Nic on the Wissahickon*, engraving by Rawdon, Wright & Hatch after W. Croome, from *Graham's Magazine*, 1844 (LCP)
(Middle) *Spring Garden Water Works*, gouache drawing by unknown artist, ca. 1840 (HSP)
(Below) *Lemon Hill*, wash drawing by B. R. Evans, 1852 (HSP)

If the Schuylkill between the Falls and Fairmount was largely picturesque, its serenity invaded only by occasional canal boats taking coal to the wharves down-river, the Delaware was commercial and bustling—except during cold spells when ice delighted the populace but hindered navigation. The winter of 1856 saw the river frozen solid from bank to bank. This was, of course, one of the disadvantages under which the port of Philadelphia suffered in its ceaseless competition with New York and Baltimore. But Philadelphia had its shipyards and the coastal coal trade which continued to grow. One of the busiest yards was that of William Cramp in Kensington. By 1857 when he took his sons into partnership, Cramp's was launching the heaviest tonnage on the river. Abreast of the change in marine architecture, the firm in the immediate antebellum era switched from building wooden vessels and became expert in the construction of iron ships. Sailing vessels found all manner of equipment and supplies available in the stores along Delaware Avenue and elsewhere near the river. Steamboats found fuel close at hand, for most of the coal was carried to the city by the Reading Railroad direct to its wharves at Port Richmond. In spite of the activity shad fishing was still a profitable business, and Delaware River shad and roe were among the city's epicurean delicacies.

(Above) *Scene on the Delaware River*, lithograph by P. S. Duval & Co. after James Queen, 1856 (HSP)
(Middle) *The W. Cramp & Sons Ship & Engine Building Co.*, engraving by John A. Lowell & Co., ca. 1860 (HSP)
(Below) *Francis Bacon & Co's Coal Yard, Spruce Street Wharf, Schuylkill*, lithograph by T. Sinclair after W. H. Rease, ca. 1853 (HSP)

In the summer of 1849 the Killers, a gang of toughs allied with the Irish Catholic and Democratic Moyamensing Hose Company, set four fires and then ambushed the Native American Shiffler Hose Company on its way to put them out. Not only fires but guns blazed. The divisiveness which was setting one political party, one ethnic group, violently against another was nowhere more marked than in the fire companies. What had been sporting rivalry to be first at the scene degenerated all too frequently into a vicious riot. The engine or hose house was a workingman's club where companionship, political partisanship, and also prejudice thrived. In 1858 there were forty-five engine, forty-two hose, and five ladder companies in the city. A rash of serious fires made the need clear for better equipment, including horse-drawn steam pumpers, and more rational organization. Shortly after a fire in a cotton mill in 1851, when women workers had to jump out of third-story windows, the first hook-and-ladder company was formed. Another conflagration on July 5, 1854, destroyed the whole south side of Chestnut Street, including the popular Chinese Museum and the National Theatre. Worse disasters took place in 1856. In March the steamer New Jersey caught on fire just offshore and sank with the loss of fifty lives. In July sixty persons were killed and a hundred injured when a train of Catholic excursionists collided with another on the North Pennsylvania line at Camp Hill and burned. By then the nation was also in a tinderbox condition.

(Above) *The Dreadful Accident on the North Pennsylvania Rail-Road*, lithograph by John L. Magee, 1856 (LCP)
(Middle) *View of the United States Hose House & Apparatus, York Avenue and Tammany Street*, lithograph, ca. 1855 (LCP)
(Below) *Fighting a Fire with Steam Pumper and Ladders*, lithograph by P. S. Duval & Son after J. Queen, detail from membership certificate in Columbia Hose Co., ca. 1860 (LCP)

Thunderstorms of violence had long been brewing, and gangs provided irresponsible manpower for any riot. When Bishop Kenrick in 1842 asked the school board to allow Catholic children to use their own Bible, the not-so-latent anti-Catholic feeling took on the dimensions of a Protestant crusade with the clergy, the demagogic press, and xenophobic politicians joining in. On May 6, 1844, a meeting of the nativist American Republican Association in Kensington became the scene of a melee when shots were fired from the Hibernia Hose Company house nearby. Eighteen-year-old George Shiffler was killed, the story went, as he was defending an American flag from the Irish mob; he became the American Party's hero-martyr. As a sequel to the day's events, a crowd assembled on May 8th in the State House yard was aroused by oratory and swarmed north to attack and set fire to the Hibernia Hose house. The First Brigade under General Cadwalader finally was able to quell the riot the next day, but not before St. Michael's Catholic Church, at Second and Jefferson streets, and St. Augustine's, on Fourth Street below Vine, were burned. On July 5, 1844, another riot broke out in Southwark, this time centering on the church of St. Philip de Neri on Queen Street between Second and Third. For several days its Irish Catholic defenders, a hostile mob, and intervening militiamen surged back and forth through the area; eventually the military prevailed. It was a sign of the times that a grand jury found the Irish guilty of the earlier May tragedy.

(Above) *Death of George Shi[f]fler in Kensington,* lithograph by J. L. Magee, 1844 (HSP)
(Below) *Riot in Philadelphia, July 7th 1844,* lithograph by J. Baillie and J. Sowle after H. Buchholtzer (HSP)

On February 2, 1854, the state legislature passed the Consolidation Act uniting Philadelphia city and the nine incorporated districts, six boroughs, and thirteen townships into which the county was splintered. The occasion was celebrated with a large ball at the Chinese Museum. The new municipality was divided into twenty-four wards, each of which was to elect three members (four in the two large wards in the northeast) to the Common Council and one to the Select Council. The city debt, to which nearly four and a half million dollars had been added in a last-minute pre-consolidation splurge, stood at $17,000,000; five million dollars of that was in Pennsylvania Railroad stock. The first mayor elected under the new law was Robert T. Conrad, who squeaked into office with the help of the Know Nothing vote. It was his successor and former Democratic opponent Richard Vaux who increased the police force to a thousand and effectively suppressed gangs such as the Killers. Vaux's policemen wore only a badge on their civilian suits, but under Mayor Alexander Henry in 1860 they were put into full uniform. The handsome commissioners' halls in the Northern Liberties and Spring Garden, completed as recently as 1848, lost their functions.

(Above) *Commissioners Hall, Spring Garden,* lithograph by P. S. Duval after C. C. Kuchel, 1851 (LCP)
(Right) Map of the Consolidated City by R. L. Barnes, 1854 (LCP)
(Below) *Two of the Killers,* lithograph by J. Childs, 1848 (LCP)

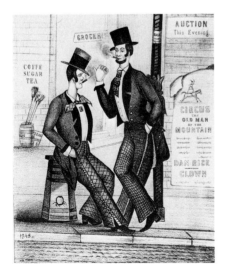

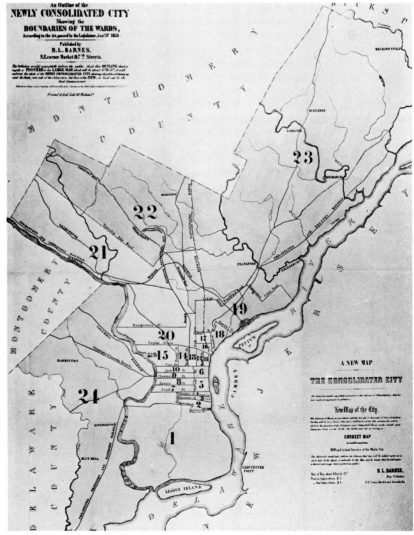

By midcentury Jefferson Medical College was graduating more physicians than its older rival at the University of Pennsylvania. To match its growing stature, in 1845 Jefferson enlarged its building on Walnut Street and added an impressive six-column façade. The new curative system of the German physician Samuel Hahnemann was established in the city when Constantine Hering founded the Homeopathic Hospital in 1852. The venerable Pennsylvania Hospital, needing larger quarters for its department for the insane, erected a handsome building on a large tract of land in West Philadelphia. It was opened in 1841 under the direction of Thomas S. Kirkbride, a leader in the treatment of the mentally ill, by whose name the institution became known. Religious groups, too, began to put up their own hospitals, the Catholics founding St. Joseph's in 1849, and the Episcopalians theirs three years later. It was recognition of Philadelphia's medical preeminence which persuaded the founders of the American Medical Association to hold its organizing meeting there in 1847. Yet, better known than all the medical men were the purveyors of patent medicines. William Swaim's "Panacea," good for every ailment including cancer, Benjamin Brandreth's pills, and David Jayne's "Vermifuge," "Expectorant" for lung conditions, and "Carminative," a cure for cholera and other diseases, made fortunes for their proprietors.

(Below) Jefferson Medical College, Walnut Street, ca. 1855 (LCP)
(Above) *Pennsylvania Hospital for the Insane*, engraving by W. E. Tucker after W. Mason, ca. 1845 (HSP)
(Right) Advertisement for Swaim's Panacea, 1848 (LCP)

NANCY LINTON.
After she was cured by Swaim's Panacea.

SWAIM'S PANACEA.   11

THE FOLLOWING
REMARKABLE CURE
IS WORTHY OF PUBLIC ATTENTION.

The annals of medicine cannot furnish a parallel; it should be extensively known, for it is feared that thousands are labouring under diseases which may produce consequences equally disastrous unless arrested by the agency of SWAIM'S PANACEA.

CASE OF NANCY LINTON.

NANCY LINTON, at the age of twelve years, was attacked with scrofulous swellings of the glands of the neck, a small ulcer appeared on the palate, which gradually extended itself to all the surrounding internal parts, destroying in its rapid and relentless course, integuments, muscles and bones; from the throat and face it next extended itself to the left shoulder, and from thence down to the lower extremities, during a period of fourteen years, in which time all that medical skill could possibly devise proved unavailing.

At this period (in the spring of 1824) the ulceration in the throat had extended in such a manner as to open a medium of communication between the nose and mouth, by the destruction of the velum palati and portions of the palatine and upper maxillary bones, in consequence of which fluids introduced into the mouth passed out from the nostrils, the whole of the nose, the nasal bones, and the nasal processes of the upper maxillary bones being destroyed, and presenting a deep open cavity, from which you could *see down to the basis of the skull*; the gums participated in the disease, and several of the teeth came out from their sockets. The whole of this extensive surface was in a state of ulceration, from which there was a constant discharge of highly offensive matter.

From the face, the left shoulder was next affected with corroding ulceration, which destroyed a considerable portion of the deltoid muscle; but the points on which the whole force of the disease seemed to expend itself were the lower extremities.

Both the knee joints were in the first place attacked with inflammation, which soon terminated in ulceration; on the left side the ulceration extended higher up than the hip, and as low down as midway between the knees and feet. The whole of the muscles in this situation were laid completely bare; several of them were separated from each other, and an opening was thus formed, through which several fingers could be passed between the flexors of both legs and the bone. A con-

When Jenny Lind came to town in 1850, her impressario P. T. Barnum auctioned off the tickets for the two performances at the Chestnut Street Theatre. There, too, in 1845 William H. Fry's *Leonora*, the first opera by an American, had been played. But there was no hall in the city large enough to seat all those who would have come to hear the Swedish Nightingale and no hall quite satisfactory for the performance of grand opera. To fill the need subscriptions were raised to construct the Academy of Music at Broad and Locust streets. Napoleon Le Brun was selected as architect and, basing his interior on La Scala in Milan, he built an almost acoustically perfect shell. The Academy opened with a ball on January 26, 1857; the first opera, *Il Trovatore*, was performed by Maretzek's company a month later. The Chestnut Street Theatre had closed down, but the Arch Street, where Edwin Booth made his first local appearance, and Walnut Street, where in 1842 Charlotte Cushman was named manager, held full seasons. Less serious amusement was offered by Sanford's Minstrels, Barnum's Museum, and the City Museum. Signor Antonio Blitz was renowned for his ventriloquism, sleight-of-hand, and performing birds. Theatergoers and others patronized Parkinson's ice cream salon on Chestnut Street above Tenth, the most popular in the city.

(Below) *Garden View of Parkinson's Cafe*, woodcut, 1853 (Free Library of Philadelphia)
(Above) *Barnum's Museum, northwest Corner of 9th and Chestnut Streets*, watercolor by B. R. Evans, 1851 (LCP)
(Middle left) *Interior of the Academy of Music*, woodcut (HSP)
(Middle right) Playbill of Rachel in *Les Horaces* at the Walnut, 1855 (HSP)

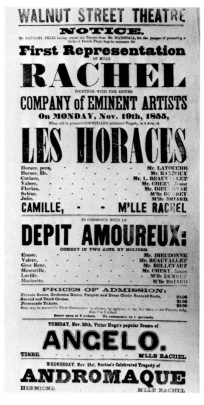

Women were beginning to make their mark in the male-dominated world. In the theater they had long shone. The notorious divorce suit of the talented and determined actress Fanny Kemble against her husband Pierce Butler underlined a woman's independence, while the printed accounts of the suit and of the sale of the bankrupt Butler's slaves titillated the public. The activity of women sparked the antislavery and the temperance movements, and the latter flourished in combat with 902 taverns recorded in the county in 1841. It received added impetus in 1854 from Ten Nights in a Bar-Room by the local author Timothy Shay Arthur. It was women editors and authors such as Sarah Josepha Hale who proved to be the molders of morals and taste. Mrs. Hale, the editor of the uplifting and sentimental Godey's Lady's Book since 1837, moved to Philadelphia in 1841, and by 1860 Godey's had 150,000 subscribers. Among Mrs. Hale's interests was the Female (Woman's) Medical College, founded in 1850, the first institution in the United States to open the door of medical education to women. The same year the School of Design (now Moore College of Art) began to train girls in the useful arts. Almost in an apologetic manner there was even a two-year normal school for girls established in 1848; it was some years before it was transformed into Girls' High School.

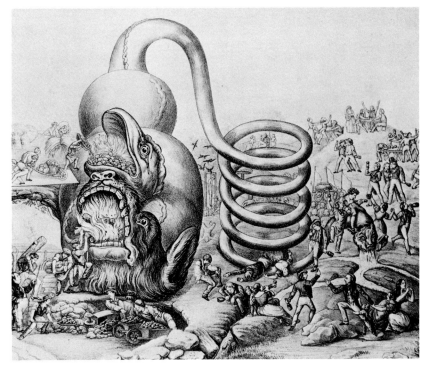

Baseball really started in Philadelphia in 1833 when two teams of Townball Players or Rounders founded the Olympic Club at Twenty-fifth and Jefferson streets. The game according to modern rules came later with the formation of the Minerva Baseball Club in 1857, the Keystones in 1859, the well-known Athletics in 1860, and the Mercantiles about the same time. An older sport, cricket, flourished in the United States uniquely in Philadelphia. English immigrant hosiery workers at the Wakefield Mills in Germantown organized a club early in the 1840s, which was followed in 1842 by the Union Cricket Club. Among the stars of the latter team were James Turner, a sawmaker from Sheffield, and Tom Barett, owner of a well-patronized gymnasium. There was, however, but mild general interest in the game until the founding of the Philadelphia Cricket Club and the Germantown Cricket Club in 1854. The next year the Young America Cricket Club was organized by Walter S. Newhall, one of the country's finest cricketers.

(Facing, below) *Sarah Josepha Hale*, engraving (HSP)
(Facing, above) *A Bloomer Girl on Chestnut Street*, lithograph by P. S. Duval after J. Queen, on sheet music cover for *The New Costume Polka*, 1851 (HSP)
(Facing, below right) Temperance Cartoon, lithograph, ca. 1845 (HSP)
(Above) *The Mercantile Base Ball Club at 18th and Master Streets*, lithograph by T. Sinclair, on sheet music cover for *Home Run Quick Step*, ca. 1860 (HSP)

HOME RUN QUICK STEP.

RESPECTFULLY DEDICATED
to the
MEMBERS OF THE
MERCANTILE BASE BALL CLUB
OF
PHILAD^a
by
JOHN ZEBLEY, JR.

Philadelphia E & WALKER 722 Chestnut St

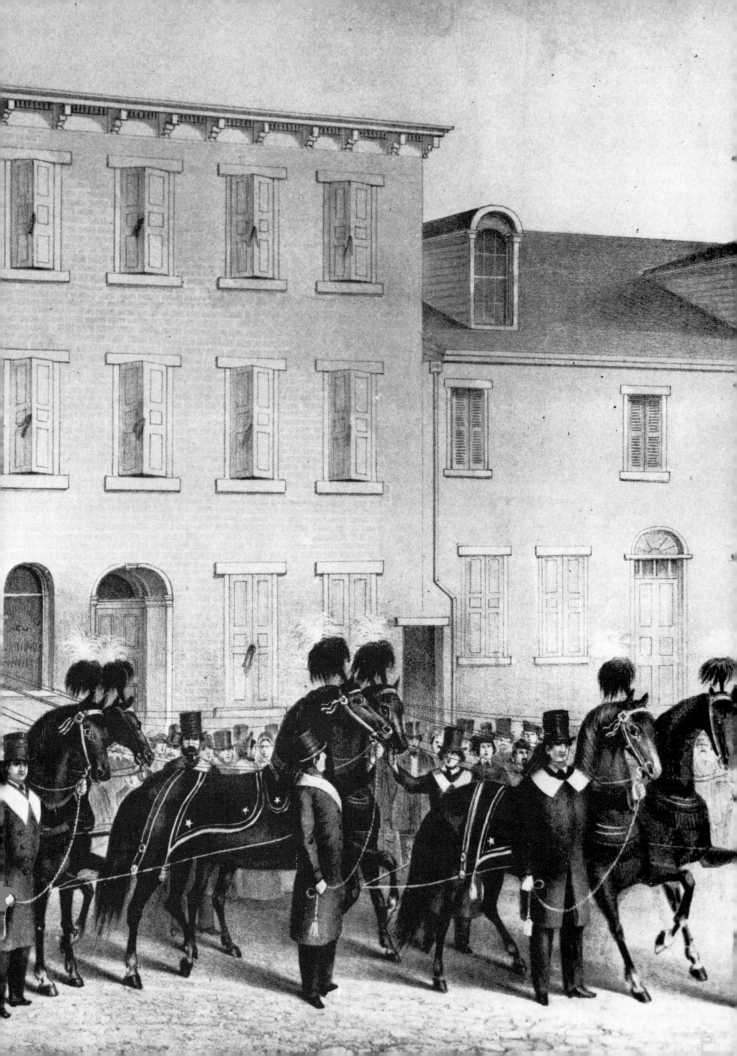

1860-1876

On Washington's Birthday in 1861 President-elect Abraham Lincoln stopped off on his way from Springfield to the capital to raise a thirty-four star flag at Independence Hall in honor of the new state of Kansas. There he re-enunciated the egalitarian principles of the Declaration of Independence and stood firm on the integrity of the Union. When he spoke from the balcony of the Continental Hotel to a huge crowd he declared that "there is no need of bloodshed and war"; the crowd applauded its approval. Lincoln left town surreptitiously to avoid assassins said to have been lying in wait in Baltimore.

He left a large, growing, and politically schizophrenic community. Philadelphia, according to the census of 1860, could boast of 565,529 inhabitants, making it the second city of the United States and possibly the fourth most populous in the Western world. It was just above the Mason-Dixon line and had the largest black population, 22,000, of any Northern city, only four percent of the total, but concentrated and highly visible in the wards of the old city. There were five times as many foreign-born, most of them Irish. By the Centennial year 1876 the population was estimated at 817,000, a remarkable growth in half a generation. While the Civil War cut off immigration, the city's role as a major supplier of goods and as a nexus of transportation—in brief, war prosperity—had proved a magnet.

The politics of the city was a tangled web of shifting sentiment, expedient alliances, and the pressures of the progress of the war until the Republican Party established a dominance that seemed to many eternal. In 1858 an uneasy coalition of a toned-down nativist American Party and Republicans elected Alexander Henry mayor. He was an able and confident leader who in the immediate antebellum period and during the war won election after election until he retired at the end of 1865. Henry preserved his balance between radical abolitionists and anti-Negro sympathizers with the South. He used his police powers tactically and tactfully to preserve law and order. Although explosive situations were just below the surface, there was no violence in Philadelphia comparable to the draft riots in New York.

When Fort Sumter was fired on and hostilities broke out, an initial upsurge of enthusiasm for the preservation of the Union quite submerged Philadelphia's traditional attachment to the South. The mob which but a few years earlier had attacked blacks and abolitionists turned on southern sympathizers. An excited crowd gathered

(Facing) *Major Genl. Meade*, lithograph by Gibson & Co. (LCP)

207

before the building near Fourth and Chestnut streets where *The Palmetto Flag*, a secessionist paper, was published and was only prevented from violence by the intervention of Mayor Henry. President Lincoln's call for troops was quickly met. The Washington Brigade, without uniforms or arms, was one of the first to leave and, following the 6th Massachusetts into Baltimore, was attacked by a hostile mob. German-born George Leisenring, who died of stab wounds, was Philadelphia's first war casualty. Within a comparatively short time the city supplied eight regular infantry regiments, the 17th to the 24th Pennsylvania, and other independent companies.

The service of troops was complicated by the different terms of enlistment. The first soldiers joined up for three months, others later for three years, and a few for the duration. Even before the three-month men came home, Philadelphians volunteered for a three-year tour of duty. The 28th, 29th, 31st, 32nd, 33rd, 36th, and 41st Pennsylvania Regiments were filled largely from the city by mid-summer of 1861. Thereafter, forty-seven other three-year infantry and cavalry regiments, some nine-month regiments, artillery units, and, after the Emancipation Proclamation, eleven black regiments went to war with substantial numbers of local soldiers on their rolls to a total of almost 90,000 Philadelphians.

After the first outpouring of support for the Union, the city resumed its ambivalence. It elected an anti-Negro Democrat, Charles J. Biddle, to Congress in the fall of 1861 and turned him out in the next election. Conservatives who did not completely approve of Lincoln's radical measures were eventually won over by the overriding feeling that the rebellion must be put down. Yet the Emancipation Proclamation was provocative enough to give the peace Democrats another chance. When Lee invaded Pennsylvania in June, 1863, they took heart; there was no immediate surge of concern in the city.

(Above) *The Arrival of Mr. Lincoln at the Continental Hotel*, pencil drawing heightened with white by Thomas Nast, 1861 (M. & M. Karolik Collection, Boston Museum of Fine Arts)

It did become necessary to organize for defense as the fighting swirled nearer, and the city did so slowly. Undermanned and unenthusiastic militia were of little consequence. The War Department sent in a New Englander, Major-General Napoleon Jackson Tecumseh Dana, to put muscle into Philadelphia's preparations. When he asked Mayor Henry for 2,000 men to dig entrenchments, a hundred laborers and two hundred clergymen turned out. Governor Curtin came to town to stir up the citizenry, and emergency troops were finally brought together. Recruiting was intensified and recruits were forthcoming.

The victory at Gettysburg gave Philadelphia its greatest war hero, Major-General George Gordon Meade. It was maliciously and inaccurately said that he was picked by Lincoln to command the Army of the Potomac after Joseph Hooker's resignation because he had been born in Spain and hence could not by law become a candidate for the presidency. No matter; Meade was a good organizer, quickly appraised the situation, and, when the battle was joined, had his troops concentrated where they were most needed. Although General Grant became the recognized military savior of the Union, no one, least of all his fellow-citizens, took away from Meade the glory of having won the bloodiest and most crucial contest of the Civil War.

As the war dragged on to an end, the Republican Party, with the effective help of the newly formed Union League, became dominant in local politics. Lincoln carried the city in 1864. Men who had made their reputations as liberal supporters of the Lincoln administration, considered vulgar by the acerbic diarist Sidney George Fisher, adopted more materialistic principles. In Philadelphia commerce and industry dominated. The post-bellum period, with capital freed for investment in more than wasteful war products, was one in which the

(Above) *U. S. Iron Clad Steamer, New Ironsides,* lithograph by W. H. Rease, ca. 1864 (LCP)

makings of things for a growing consumers' market encouraged manufactures. Protectionism and industrialism solidified the Republican control which lasted for three-quarters of a century.

Philadelphia's Baldwin locomotives, which had taken troops and supplies to the army, puffed their way across Europe and South America. During the war Merrick & Son supplied the steam engine for the ironclad frigate *New Ironsides* constructed by Cramp & Sons, who in peacetime remained the most active shipbuilders in the country. Their four ships for the American Steamship Company gave Philadelphia the advantage of regular transatlantic service to Liverpool. Few machines were more efficient than those manufactured by William Sellers & Co., and the saws of Henry Disston & Sons became proverbially the best in the nation. On an established base, the Franklin Sugar Refinery of Harrison, Havemeyer & Co. grew to be the largest in the world; together with its other refineries, Philadelphia in 1870 produced almost $26,000,000 worth of sugar. In the field of textiles, long a major local industry, Thomas Dolan established a knit-goods factory, and John Bromley made carpets. Small towns grew up around the factory, creating enclaves of a sort where the mill-owner, the foremen, and the workers lived in vastly different homes but near each other. On a more intellectual, but no less profitable, level the house of J. B. Lippincott & Co., with a widely circulated magazine and a perennial list of old and new bestsellers, was near the top of the nation's publishing houses in output and literary influence. During the postwar years the Board of Trade, with John Welsh, Philadelphia's man for every occasion, as its president, performed the promotional functions of a Chamber of Commerce. Looking toward the celebration of the Centennial, a committee of Congress visited the city on June 16, 1870.

Not realizing that they were creating a monster which would control them, the City Councils wrote into the ordinance establishing a municipal gas works a provision that a trusteeship should survive until all the company's loans were paid off. A "Gas Trust" came into being which saw to it that there were always loans outstanding. The trust's guiding genius was "King" James McManes, a north-of-Ireland Republican ward leader, who became a trustee in 1865. He recognized that control of many hundreds of jobs gave him great political leverage. McManes was almost everything a Boy Scout was supposed to be: loyal, friendly, helpful—to his friends—but not trustworthy. He established the Gas Ring which dominated the city's politics for a quarter of a century and lined the pockets of its members by providing kickbacks from the coal sold to the gas works.

In 1871 the city was filled with violence. The independent fire companies were making trouble as they had a generation earlier. Elections were won by the use of "repeaters," paid to vote again and again, and by the importation of voters from as far away as Baltimore and Washington. Thus, Daniel M. Fox, a Democrat, had been elected mayor in 1867. But William B. Stokley seemed to be a candidate of a different stripe. As a councilman he had attacked the fire companies and opposed the "Gas Trust." In the election of 1871, during which riots against Negroes resulted in the death of Octavius V. Catto, principal of the Philadelphia Institute for Colored Youth, Stokley was elected over his opponent James S. Biddle. The new mayor effectively reestablished law and order. The police were strengthened and a paid city fire department supplanted the unruly volunteers. But Stokley was a machine politician; he gave contracts to his friends; and he was not above stuffing ballot boxes. The "better" people, including newspaperman George W. Childs, book publisher Joseph B. Lippincott, railroader Joseph Harrison, banker Anthony J. Drexel and others, formed a Citizens' Municipal Reform Association to extirpate corruption. As with similar groups thereafter, they made but an evanescent impact. William B. Mann, a McManes henchman, was defeated in 1874 by a Democratic opponent, but Stokley proved perennial. The prevailing Republican tone had been underlined in 1872 when the National Republican Convention was held at the Academy of Music, where General Grant was unanimously renominated.

Newspapers played a major role in politics. Robert T. Conrad and Morton McMichael, editors of the Whig-turned-Republican *North American,* had both previously been elected mayor. Although the volatile Colonel John W. Forney had been a backer of Buchanan after his election, the Democratic attitude in the Bleeding Kansas affair turned Forney and his paper, *The Press,* into strong supporters of Lincoln and the Union. He was an imaginative editor whose paper reflected his own political views; it was Forney's *Press,* as in New York it was Greeley's *Tribune.* The *Public Ledger* was, however, becoming the most successful and conservative daily in town. George W. Childs,

who had been briefly in partnership with the book and magazine publisher Peterson and even more briefly with J. B. Lippincott, bought the *Ledger* late in 1864. Under Childs' direction circulation and influence increased to such an extent that the paper moved in the summer of 1867 to a new building at Sixth and Chestnut streets, described as "the most complete, perfect, and beautiful building in the United States for newspaper purposes." The *Philadelphia Evening Bulletin,* without an editor of fame, survived a fire to occupy a newly built home in 1866 between Third and Fourth on Chestnut Street. As the voice of the extensive German-American community, the *Philadelphia Demokrat* under Dr. Edward Morwitz grew rapidly.

There was excitement for reporters to record. On January 7, 1866, the thermometer at the Merchants' Exchange registered eighteen degrees below zero. An outbreak of cholera occurred in July of that year. When word spread that Moyamensing Hall was going to be used as a cholera hospital, the people of the area burned it down. A year later fire broke out in the New American Theatre on Walnut Street above Eighth during a performance of the "Demon Dance"; the building was destroyed, but there were no casualties. During the summer of 1868 the city was thrown into a panic by a strike of the employees of the gas works. Fear of a second night of darkness forced compliance with the strikers' demands. In October, 1872, an epizootic affected most of the horses in the city, crippling the passenger and freight railways; men and boys substituted for horsepower on some streets. The most sensational news story of the period was the kidnapping on July 1, 1874, of four-year-old Charles Brewster Ross. The search for him was the widest and best publicized up to then ever held in America. The two kidnappers ultimately were killed in a robbery attempt, but Charley Ross was never found—although pseudo-Charleys kept turning up year after year.

(Above) *Dock of Pennsylvania Sugar Refining Company,* ca. 1870 (HSP)

World and national events made their impact on the local scene. Irish Catholics supported the Fenian nationalists; Germans rallied for their countrymen during the Franco-Prussian War. When the Fifteenth Amendment was adopted, blacks marched jubilantly through the streets. Philadelphia turned in Republican majorities both times that Grant ran for the presidency. Yet, in spite of the depression sparked by the failure of Jay Cooke & Co., the city was alert and constructive as the Centennial year drew near. The lawyer Henry Armitt Brown orated at Carpenters' Hall on September 5, 1874, to celebrate the anniversary of the First Continental Congress. The Franklin Institute, as an aperitif to 1876, held a large exhibition of the products of local industry in the old Pennsylvania Railroad freight depot at Juniper and Market streets; almost 300,000 tickets were sold. The First City Troop on its hundredth anniversary in November, 1874, dedicated its Twenty-First Street armory. On July 4, 1874, the Girard Avenue Bridge was opened; the cornerstone was laid for "the public buildings," as City Hall was still called; ground was broken for the exhibition buildings at Lansdowne in Fairmount Park; and 10,000 members of the Catholic Total Abstinence Beneficial Societies paraded. By the Fourth of July the following year a concert could be held in Machinery Hall and ground was broken for Agricultural Hall. Shortly thereafter work was begun to spruce up Independence Square. Within two years the Jewish (now Einstein North), University, and German (later Lankenau) hospitals were put into operation. In November, 1875, the South Street Bridge was opened, and in December the temporary bridge at Market Street, replacing one just burned down, was finished, with tracks laid down, in less than twenty-one days. Philadelphia was getting things done.

(Above) George W. Childs, photograph by F. Gutekunst Co. (HSP)

PHILADELPHIA ZOUAVE CORPS.
PENNSYLVANIA VOLUNTEERS.

Before the fighting started soldiering was romantic. As long as militiamen did nothing but parade, as they had in the United States for almost half a century, appearance was all. The most fashionable costume for would-be-heroes was that of a Zouave, a tribute to the world-renown of the French Algerian troops. Philadelphia, like other cities, had its Zouave Corps, but the grim realities of warfare quickly put an end to colorful dress. Union blue became standard, and it was the soft-goods industry of Philadelphia which made it. The production of officers' uniforms and their accessories of braid, epaulets, sword belts, and dress hats was almost exclusively in the hands of the local firms of Horstmann, Stokes, and Oakford, while seamstresses at home sewed the uniforms of enlisted men on contract for the Schuylkill Arsenal. Less prestigious necessities such as underwear, shirts, socks, and camp supplies made quick profits for a host of lesser manufacturers. There was no dearth of ladies to roll bandages and knit mittens on a volunteer basis.

(Above) *Philadelphia Zouave Corps, Pennsylvania Volunteers,* lithograph by P. S. Duval & Son after James Queen and August Feusier, ca. 1861 (HSP)
(Below) Advertisement of E. W. Carryl & Co., Army and Navy Goods, ca. 1863 (LCP)

More troops passed through Philadelphia during the Civil War than through any other city in the Union. It was the gateway to the South, and that is where the war was fought, Gettysburg excepted. From New England, New York, and New Jersey regiments were landed at the foot of Washington Avenue where the cars of the Philadelphia, Wilmington and Baltimore Rail Road took them on their way. A local grocer, Barzilai S. Brown, had the happy thought that men on the move to the front would be heartened by food, washing facilities though primitive, and drink though non-alcoholic. Thus came into being the Union Volunteer Refreshment Saloon down near the docks. By the end of the war 900,000 men had been heartened at the unbelievably low cost of $100,000. The Union Saloon and the Cooper Shop Volunteer Refreshment Saloon nearby were financed by private contributions and manned by willing, unpaid workers.

(Above) *Union Volunteer Refreshment Saloon*, lithograph by T. Sinclair after James Queen, 1861 (LCP)
(Middle) *Interior of the Cooper Shop Volunteer Refreshment Saloon*, watercolor by an unknown artist, 1862 (HSP)
(Below) *Cooper Shop Volunteer Refreshment Saloon*, lithograph by M. H. Traubel, 1862 (LCP)

A small Union Club was founded in November, 1862, by Judge J. I. Clarke Hare, George H. Boker, Morton Mc-Michael, Horace Binney, Jr., and others to counteract the social prestige of the peace Democrats such as Charles Ingersoll, George W. Biddle, and John C. Bullitt. A little over a month later they decided to increase the political effectiveness of the group by organizing the Union League. By the end of the war its several thousand members had raised and equipped nine regiments, two battalions, and a troop of cavalry and issued millions of copies of pamphlets supporting President Lincoln and the war effort. The League's membership came to be dominated by the newly rich businessmen and industrialists who after the war devoted their energies to the maintenance of the protective tariff and the Republican Party. The sumptuous red brick and brownstone club house in the French Renaissance style, with its somberly impressive rooms, at Broad and Sansom streets was opened on May 11, 1865. A month later, on the day the Philadelphia troops returned to the city, the military hero General U. S. Grant was tendered a reception at the Union League, the first of many festive occasions celebrated there.

In spite of Philadelphia's Quaker background and the abolitionists and voters' support of the Republican Party, strong anti-Negro feeling was widespread. Before the threatening Southern offensive in the spring of 1863, black recruits had to be sent away at night to New England regiments. Lee's advance changed that. On June 19th, under the auspices of the Union League a committee of leading citizens was appointed to raise black regiments. Across the city line in Cheltenham Township where Lucretia Mott and her husband had their farm, Camp William Penn was set up to receive volunteers. As the movement gathered momentum, black soldiers could be seen marching through the city to entrain for the front. Eleven black regiments were trained at Camp William Penn, of which the 6th and 8th saw the bloodiest and most active service on the James River, at Fort Fisher in North Carolina, and during the unhappy Florida campaign. The 22nd, which had fought before Richmond, was detailed as part of the Lincoln funeral escort. When the black veterans came marching home they found that they were not permitted to ride on street cars. White workers in the Navy Yard and government clothing factories strongly supported the discrimination. In spite of kind words from substantial citizens, nothing was done to end the exclusion until the state legislature, not particularly sympathetic to blacks, but less sympathetic to Philadelphia, passed a law ordering street-car lines to permit Negro passengers.

(Facing, above) *Celebration of the Abolition of Slavery in Maryland before the Buildings of the Supervisory Committee for Recruiting Negro Troops and the Union League on Chestnut Street between 11th and 12th*, woodcut, from *Frank Leslie's Illustrated Newspaper*, November 19, 1864 (LCP)
(Facing, below) The Union League at Broad and Sansom Streets (HSP)
(Above) *United States Soldiers at Camp "William Penn,"* lithograph by P. S. Duval & Son, 1864 (LCP)
(Below) Top Portion of Petition for the Colored People of Philadelphia to Ride in the Cars, with Original Signatures, 1866, and Slip for Poll of Street Car Riders, January 30, 1865 (HSP)

PETITION FOR THE COLORED PEOPLE OF PHILADELPHIA TO RIDE IN THE CARS.

To the Board of Managers of the various City Passenger Cars.

The Colored Citizens of Philadelphia suffer very serious inconvenience and hardship, daily, by being excluded from riding in the City Passenger Cars. In New York City, and in all the principal Northern Cities, except Philadelphia, they ride; even in New Orleans, (although subject to some proscription,) they ride in the cars; why then should they be excluded in Philadelphia, in a city standing so pre-eminently high for its Benevolence, Liberality, Love of Freedom, and Christianity as the City of Brotherly Love!

Colored people pay more taxes here than is paid by the same class in any other Northern City. The Members of the *"Social and Statistical Association,"* although numbering less than fifty members, pay annually about *Five Thousand Dollars* into the Tax Collector's Office.

Therefore, the undersigned respectfully petition that the various Boards of the City Passenger Cars rescind the rules indiscriminately excluding colored persons from the inside of the Cars.

The transportation system which took troops through Philadelphia to the front brought the wounded back. With its resources of physicians and medical institutions, the city soon became the hospital center of the Civil War. The Union Refreshment Saloon set up the first tiny military hospital; additional facilities were created in existing buildings. When casualties poured into town after McClellan's Virginia campaign in 1862, the Citizens' Volunteer Hospital with 400 beds was established on Broad Street opposite the Philadelphia, Wilmington and Baltimore Rail Road station. The advances in firepower were making the war the most lethal ever waged. The unprecedented number of wounded moved the government to build two huge facilities: the 3,100-bed Satterlee General Hospital near Forty-third Street and Baltimore Avenue in West Philadelphia and the 4,000-bed Mower General Hospital at Wyndmoor Station in Chestnut Hill, then the largest complex of medical buildings in the world.

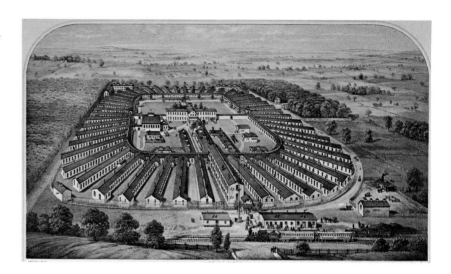

(Above) *Mower U. S. A. General Hospital, Chestnut Hill,* lithograph by P. S. Duval & Son after James Queen, ca. 1863 (HSP)
(Below) *Ambulance of the United States Fire Engine Company for Transporting Wounded Soldiers,* woodcut after F. Schell, from *Frank Leslie's Illustrated Newspaper,* May 27, 1865 (LCP)

"*Enlarged views, refined taste, and unflagging energies have originated, planned, and matured this grand undertaking,*" Mayor Henry stated on June 7, 1864, as he opened the Great Central Fair. The receipts were to go to the Sanitary Commission for the benefit of sick and wounded soldiers and sailors. The erection of the huge temporary buildings which covered the whole of Logan Square had been made possible by benefits and contributions from individuals and businesses, many of the latter donating one day's receipts. A vaulted gallery, Union Avenue, ran through the center of the fair from Eighteenth to Logan (now Nineteenth) Street. Commercial exhibits of all kinds—glassblowers, a horseshoe machine, wax fruit, and "Gents' Furnishing Goods," among dozens of others—were shown under roof with a floral display, an art gallery running the full block along Vine Street, and historical relics. When the very recently renominated President Lincoln visited the fair on June 16th, the press of crowds was so great that he could barely make his way through the buildings. "A Magnificent $2500 Sword" was presented to General Meade, the hero of Gettysburg, who was voted the visitors' favorite general. Over a million dollars was turned over to the Sanitary Commission when the fair closed on June 28th.

(Below) Art Gallery of the Great Central Fair, photograph by John Moran, 1864 (LCP)
(Above) *Buildings of the Great Central Fair, In aid of the U. S. Sanitary Commission, Logan Square*, lithograph by P. S. Duval & Son after James Queen, 1864 (LCP)
(Right) *The Opening of the Great Central Fair in the Vaulted Gallery*, woodcut from *Frank Leslie's Illustrated Newspaper*, June 25, 1864 (LCP)

The watershed years of the 1870s were the last time visitors could have seen the old brick city which Philadelphia essentially had been. The press of speed, change, profit, and Philistinism tore down or commercialized most of the charming street faces and byways which the redevelopers of the twentieth century have striven so hard to restore. After a hundred years or more of independence, the city close to the Delaware River still retained the flavor of its past. Front, Water, and Dock streets, notably, could easily have been—commercial signs removed —streets where the Founding Fathers walked.

(Above) Nos. 44-46 North Water Street, 1868 (LCP)
(Below) Wise & Co., Ship Chandlers, Dock and Spruce Streets, photograph by Bonsell, 1860 (HSP)
(Facing, above) The Lincoln Funeral Car at 5th and Chestnut Streets, 1865 (HSP)
(Facing, below) *Funeral Car, Used at the Obsequies of President Lincoln, in Philadelphia, April 22nd, 1865*, lithograph by J. Haehnlen (LCP)

"Richmond is ours" came over the wires on the morning of April 3, 1865. Crowds had gathered in front of newspaper offices as rumors of a major victory spread through the city. When the mayor received confirmation from Secretary of War Stanton, the State House bell was rung and triumphant peals echoed from churches everywhere. When, six days later on a Sunday, news was received of Lee's surrender, the city went wild: steam whistles, bells, fireworks, and bonfires, firemen with their colorful equipment and, amid much else, a salute of two hundred guns "by order of the Union League." The exuberance at the end of the bloody, dragged-out, fraternal war was suddenly checked when President Lincoln was shot in Ford's Theater. The city was draped in black. On Saturday, April 22nd, the remains of the President arrived in town on their way to Springfield. A funeral procession several miles in length wound its way through somber, crowded streets to Independence Hall where the body lay in state. By midnight, when the doors of the hall were finally closed, 85,000 persons had passed before the bier and thousands were still in line waiting to pay homage to the martyred president.

The surge of the city was westward away from the center of its eighteenth-century activities. In an abortive effort in 1837 progressives had tried to persuade the municipal government to lead the movement by resettling in Penn Square. After the Civil War irresistible pressure grew to follow residences, hotels, and businesses toward and across Broad Street, but there was no unanimity. Old roots were hard to pull up. In the fall of 1870 a Solomonic decision was reached to offer the voters a choice: build a new City Hall in Penn Square or in Washington Square. The vote was 51,623 to 32,825 in favor of the former. At first four municipal buildings were planned for the square, but by the time the cornerstone was laid on July 4, 1874, the huge mansarded structure designed by John MacArthur, Jr., and Thomas U. Walter had been approved. Like much city work on and around Penn Square, the towered building took many years to complete.

(Above) *West Penn Square from Filbert and Merrick Streets toward the Southeast,* watercolor by David Kennedy, 1859 (S. Robert Teitelman) (Middle and below) City Hall under Construction, 1873-75 (HSP)

Nobody who was anybody lived north of Market Street, according to an old dictum, but a great many of the men who controlled the red-blood flow of Philadelphia's industrial and political arteries moved there. A promenade, worthy of New York's Fifth Avenue, stretched north on Broad Street from the Odd Fellows' Hall at Spring Garden Street and the new Saracenic synagogue of Rodeph Shalom nearby, past the luxurious homes of men like the actor Edwin Forrest above Master Street and the toolmaker Henry Disston near Jefferson. In recognition of its status the brick sidewalks along Broad Street were replaced in 1873 with flagging. Just off the wide avenue, on Spring Garden, Fairmount, and Girard Avenue, other mansions, some on large lots, lent an aristocratic tone to the "unfashionable" part of town. Farther away from the center of town, the long north-south axis of Philadelphia became a country road, dead-ending at a strategically placed inn where the Germantown Pike crossed it.

(Above) *Odd Fellows' Broadway Hall, Broad and Spring Garden Streets,* lithograph by Rease & Schell, ca. 1855 (HSP)
(Middle) *Sleighing on Broad Street near Jefferson,* woodcut by Schell & Hogg, from Edward Strahan, *A Century After: Picturesque Glimpses of Philadelphia and Pennsylvania,* 1875 (LCP)
(Below) *Markley's Tavern, Broad Street at Germantown Avenue,* watercolor by B. R. Evans (**LCP**)

It was all so elegant. Rittenhouse Square was surrounded by handsome mansions in every style which imaginative Victorian architects could conjure up on their drawing boards. On Eighteenth Street stood the great Italianate house of Joseph Harrison, Jr., who had made a fortune building railroads for the Czar of Russia. Brownstone fronts, such as lined the Walnut and Locust streets approaches to the square, set off the typical red bricks and white trim of the nineteenth-century colonial-revival houses. The Church of the Holy Trinity with its Romanesque façade, designed by John Notman and finished in 1859, became the most fashionable church in town. Nursemaids watched Philadelphia's future lawyers, doctors, bankers, and industrialists feed the pigeons whose descendants, unlike those of the children, still strut in the park. Here Philadelphia society lived and entertained for half a century after the Civil War.

(Below) The House of Joseph Harrison, Jr., on 18th Street, 1866 (Free Library of Philadelphia)
(Above) *Rittenhouse Square,* woodcut by C. H. Reed after F. E. Lummis, 1884 (HSP)
(Right) Walnut Street looking East past the Church of the Holy Trinity (HSP)

The streets of the city continued to show the contrasts of a metropolis. There was the fascination of variety in the solid blocks of the commercial sections. Comings and goings centered on the Continental Hotel where distinguished visitors to Philadelphia customarily stayed, but many of them walked west along Chestnut Street to Broad where the General Telegraph Office housed Thomas Cook's travel agency and railroad ticket offices. Not far away was the School of Design for Women on West Penn Square, where the Pennsylvania Railroad's station would rise. To the south the curious mix of the elegant and the ordinary which had been characteristic of eighteenth-century Philadelphia still prevailed. At Thirteenth and Locust streets General Robert Patterson's charming Italianate villa with its hothouse occupied a large area while only a few blocks away old houses framed a wooden tavern on the corner. In the poorer sections along South and Lombard streets and in contiguous Moyamensing clapboard houses in rundown condition created the city's worst slums.

(Below) *Business Exchange and Lobby of the Continental Hotel*, woodcut, ca. 1860 (HSP)
(Above) *General Telegraph and Ticket Office on the Northeast Corner of Broad and Chestnut Streets*, watercolor by B. R. Evans, 1879 (LCP)
(Middle) *Fifth Street near South*, watercolor by B. R. Evans, 1883 (LCP)
(Below, right) North Side of Arch Street East of 7th, 1858 (HSP)

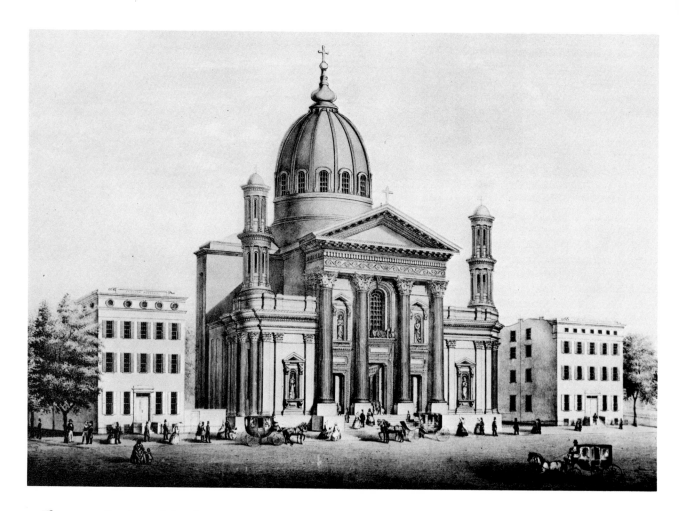

These were the times of church building and religious enthusiasm. The Cathedral of SS. Peter and Paul facing Logan Square, begun by Bishop Kenrick in 1846, was finally finished under Bishop Wood in 1864. It is, as a historian of architecture has stated, "one of the grandest nineteenth-century statements in the vocabulary of the Italian Renaissance." So great was the demand for priests in the Catholic diocese that work was begun in 1864 on the grandiose Theological Seminary of St. Charles Borromeo at Lancaster Pike and City Avenue. It was ready for students in 1871. In North Philadelphia within a six months' period in 1869 cornerstones were laid for Zion German Lutheran Church at Franklin Street above Race, First Reformed Church at Seventh and Oxford streets, Synagogue Rodeph Shalom at Broad and Mt. Vernon streets, and Messiah

Evangelical Lutheran Church at Sixteenth and Jefferson streets. More churches may have been built in a half generation following the Civil War than at any other period in the city's history. By far the biggest and most ostentatious manifestation of religiosity was the Moody and Sankey revival meetings in the old Pennsylvania Railroad freight depot at Thirteenth and Market streets held nightly from November 21, 1875, to January 28, 1876. Over a million people attended and, it was said, John Wanamaker, who owned the building, never missed a session.

(Above) *Cathedral of St. Peter and St. Paul,* Logan Square, lithograph by W. Boell, 1864 (HSP)
(Facing, below) Advertisement of Jay Cooke & Co., 1862 (LCP)
(Facing, above) *Jay Cooke's Mansion, "Ogontz,"* woodcut by R. F. Goist (HSP)
(Facing, right) Farmers' and Mechanics' Bank, Chestnut Street above 4th, photograph by McClees, ca. 1865 (LCP)

The name of Jay Cooke was synonymous with money during the war and the Reconstruction era. His splendid house, Ogontz, in the northern suburbs was a nationally cited example of financier's grandeur; it was said to have cost the immense sum of $1,000,000. After the battle of Bull Run in July, 1861, the Federal Government's credit was at a low ebb. Cash to prosecute the war could not be raised. At that juncture Cooke got the needed money from banks in Philadelphia and New York. Through extensive advertising thereafter Jay Cooke & Co., as the fiscal agent of the United States, sold hundreds of millions of dollars of bonds. What was good for Cooke and the government was good for Philadelphia's financial institutions, which grew in size and number. By 1875 there were in the city over forty banks, including four savings banks, almost as many insurance companies, and several dozen private banking houses. Impressive rows of solid structures along Chestnut Street gave evidence of their soundness. Suddenly, in September, 1873, having overextended itself in underwriting securities of the Northern Pacific Railroad, Jay Cooke & Co. failed. In the ensuing financial panic E. W. Clark & Company and the Union Banking Company also went under, but the rest of the city's banks weathered the succeeding years of depression in a remarkably stable fashion.

With the Union saved, it was time to save the picturesque quality of the Schuylkill River to say nothing of the quality of its waters. The small Fairmount Park of the prewar days was vastly enlarged in size and importance when the Lansdowne property on the west bank, bought protectively from the Baring banking interests of London by private individuals, was turned over to the city at cost. The land at George's Hill was soon added. In 1867 the ecological and esthetic role of the whole river area was made official by the establishment of the Fairmount Park Commission with powers of condemnation. The park thereafter expanded rapidly and dramatically by gift and purchase until, less than a decade from the establishment of the commission, it included both sides of the Schuylkill to the Falls and the main stream of the tributary Wissahickon Creek as well. On the west bank the Philadelphia Zoo, the first of its kind in the nation, opened in 1874 after access was given to it by the elegant iron Girard Avenue Bridge. Drives were leveled to enable riders and coaches to trot along the river banks. "Thousands of carriages file by," the tourist-writer Lafacadio Hearn later wrote, "each with a pair of lovers in it. Everybody in the park seems to be making love to somebody. Love is so much the atmosphere of the place." In 1871 the Fairmount Park Association, a private organization, was formed to beautify the landscape in more permanent shape with statuary, an artistic service it still renders.

The era of expansion of the University of Pennsylvania began, while Charles J. Stillé was provost, with its move to West Philadelphia. A trustee, Nathaniel B. Brown, in 1868 suggested that the Ninth and Chestnut Street property be sold (which it was in 1872 to the government for a Federal building), that the city turn over part of the Almshouse farm at a nominal price, and that the University with the college and flourishing medical and law schools reestablish itself on a greater acreage and on a grander scale. And so it came to pass. The professor of architecture Thomas W. Richards designed the destined-to-be ivy-covered buildings which were erected on ten and a half acres of the old Hamilton estate bought from the city. In June, 1871, the cornerstone of College Hall was laid. The following year the Towne Scientific School was added to the university by bequest. As the academic development took place, the city granted additional ground for a medical-school-operated hospital which by 1874 was completed on Spruce Street.

(Facing, above) *Girard Avenue Bridge, Fairmount Park*, lithograph by Currier & Ives, 1874 (HSP)
(Facing, below left) *Fairmount Park from the Pennsylvania Railroad Bridge*, woodcut, from *Philadelphia and Its Environs*, 1875 (LCP)
(Facing, below right) *Interior of the Monkey House at the Zoo*, woodcut, from *Illustrated Guide and Handbook of the Zoological Garden*, 1875 (HSP)
(Above) College Hall and the Medical School of the University of Pennsylvania, ca. 1874 (University of Pennsylvania Archives)

In the postwar years the gradual settling of the suburbs along the Pennsylvania Railroad's line to the west took place. Few persons of substance lived out there all the year round, but the area became an increasingly popular summer resort. At first only six trains daily served the stations which pushed their way beyond Mantua, Hestonville (at Fifty-second Street), and Overbrook (there was a bridge over a brook) into the old Welsh Tract where a few houses and some mansions were built in Wynnewood, Merion, and Haverford. By the time of the Centennial there were hotels and boarding houses there. It was fashionable to stay at the Wildgoss (that was the name of the proprietoress) Boarding House which had a waiting list every year, in spite of no baths and outside toilets. Soon, however, development crept in. In order to eliminate a detour around an established hotel, the Pennsylvania Railroad bought up a large tract. The suburb of Bryn Mawr came into existence when it sold off lots and built the Bryn Mawr Hotel where Alexander J. Cassatt, later president of the railroad, led a host of friends and sycophants to estivate.

(Above) *Bryn Mawr Hotel*, woodcut, from *The Railroad Scenery of Pennsylvania*, 1875 (LCP)
(Below) Merion Station on the Pennsylvania Railroad, 1865 (HSP)

Although Edwin L. Drake drilled his successful oil well in Titusville, Pennsylvania, in 1859 and speculation in oil quickly followed, the petroleum industry did not become regularized until after the war. Refined into kerosene and used almost exclusively for illumination, petroleum replaced whale oil in the lamps of the world. From the northwestern part of the state the Pennsylvania Railroad brought crude oil down to the Atlantic Petroleum Storage Company's facilities at Point Breeze on the lower Schuylkill and those of other companies there and nearby on the Delaware. William L. Elkins built the foundation of a fortune with his Belmont Oil Works. In 1875 the city exported 61,000,000 gallons of petroleum to foreign countries. Easy access by rail and water created a commercially attractive site for the growing oil industry.

(Above) *Atlantic Petroleum Storage Company for Refined Oil*, lithograph, 1866 (LCP)
(Below) *Oil on the Brain*, song sheet, 1864 (HSP)

1876-1900

The eyes of the Western world may have been on Philadelphia in 1776, but the eyes of a much more extended world, including Japan, Australia, India, Algeria, Brazil, and Turkey among others, were on Philadelphia in 1876. The Centennial Exhibition was the greatest, grandest, most extensive, inclusive, and splendiferous, to say nothing of the most hospitable, ever held. At the Paris and Vienna fairs visitors were charged for ice water; in Philadelphia it was free. The Quaker City shed its proverbial gray modesty and flowed into the mainstream of American territorial and industrial expansion.

It took a man, John Welsh, and a community attuned to the voluntarism that became a habit during the Civil War to create the mammoth show the Centennial turned out to be. The practice exercise for Welsh and his fellow-citizens had been the Great Central Fair of 1864. A dozen years later the success was repeated. Welsh had the help of such unusual individuals as Frederick Fraley, who had headed many of the city's cultural institutions and opposed the introduction of gas, electricity, and trolley cars; the German-born architect-engineer Hermann Schwarzmann, who designed the major buildings; and Elizabeth Duane Gillespie, an energetic proto-feminist descendant of Franklin, whose civic spirit was unquenchable. One of the methods used to finance the extravaganza was the sale of stock at ten dollars a share; over 20,000 Americans bought shares for a total investment of $2,800,000.

As early as July, 1874, the Centennial Board of Finance accepted the low bid for the construction of Memorial Hall and the Main (Industrial) Building, the latter covering eighteen acres. From then on progress continued. Foreign nations were solicited to send their best of everything—machines, produce, art, whatever they chose as outstanding or representative. Foreign nations, curious about the United States, were delighted to accept the invitation. Only the Federal Government dragged its feet. It was not until February 11, 1876, that an appropriation of $1,500,000 was passed. And then, after the exhibition was over, the government sued to recover that amount, which the Supreme Court finally awarded it at the expense of the private shareholders.

From May 10th when the exposition opened until November 10th, the day it closed, 9,910,966 persons (just over eight million paid) entered the fair grounds. A heat wave for a month beginning the mid-

(Facing) *The Corliss Engine*, lithograph by Cosack & Co., from Charles B. Norton, *Treasures of Art, Industry and Manufacture represented in the American Centennial Exhibition,* 1877 (LCP) (Above) *The Crush on Opening Day of the Centennial at the Intersection of Elm and Belmont Avenues,* woodcut after Schell and Hogan, from *Harper's Weekly,* June 3, 1876

dle of June, with the temperature hitting ninety degrees almost every day, kept down the size of the crowds in the first months, but as the summer drew on attendance increased. Three times as many people visited the Centennial in November as had come in May. Not only were the varied exhibits the most exciting and novel which had ever been shown, but the arrangements for lodging, transportation, public comfort, health and police protection were unprecedented. With planning, leadership, and sound execution Philadelphia achieved a success which still echoes after a hundred years.

The high level of international fame was not matched on the level of local politics. Perhaps the *éclat* of the Centennial inspired the city's plunderbund to greater depredations. William S. Stokley, the reformer-turned-rascal, managed to be re-elected in spite of the opposition of, among others, Colonel A. K. McClure, the aggressive independent editor of the *Philadelphia Times,* which, because of his hard-hitting journalism, began to challenge the popularity of Childs' more conservative *Public Ledger.* These were the times when the police, with Marine and regular army troops in reserve, in July, 1877, summarily put down incipient labor riots which threatened to be a sequel to the earlier bloody set-to of railroad workers in Pittsburgh. It was generally believed that the police—and most other city employees—were under the control of James McManes' "Gas Ring," which had consolidated its hold since that worthy had taken over control of the city's politics as a trustee of the Gas Works after the Civil War. Certainly many of the municipal officers owed their position to McManes and paid him fealty.

As happened so frequently in Philadelphia's history, excessive corruption once again generated a reform movement. Late in 1880 the Committee of One Hundred was formed, which included almost every important nonpolitical member of the business and industrial community from young Rudolph Blankenburg, who came into his own in the twentieth century, and the banker Anthony J. Drexel, the movement's treasurer, to Justus C. Strawbridge, a rising Quaker department-store owner. The reformers did manage to elect Samuel G. King mayor in 1881, but, as in similar liberal uprisings before and

(Above) *Horticultural Hall,* watercolor by David J. Kennedy, 1876 (HSP)

after, when the heat died down, the reformers failed to sustain their momentum. The "Gas Ring" elected its candidate in the next balloting.

What came out of the churning up of opinion was a new city charter. John Christian Bullitt, a prominent lawyer, played the leading role in framing it and, with the aid of the rising politician Boies Penrose, pushed it through the legislature in 1885. It went into effect two years later. The new municipal instrument centralized power and responsibility; the mayor's hand was strengthened and his term extended to four years. The twenty-five city bureaus were consolidated into nine departments, the most important of which were public safety, public works, and public health, whose heads were appointed by the mayor. The trustees of the Gas Works were ousted. The Committee of One Hundred was so satisfied that it had succeeded in legislating civic decency that it dissolved.

In 1887 Edwin R. Fitler, a wealthy cordage manufacturer, became the first mayor under the new charter. He appointed the hoary politician Stokley his director of public safety, since he did pretty much whatever the City Hall gang asked him to do. Contrary to the reformers' expectations a succession of grafters continued to occupy the city offices. As gas and electricity played an increasing role in the day-to-day welfare of the people by providing illumination and power for telephones, trolley cars, and machinery, the utility barons who controlled franchises became richer and more powerful. Peter A. B. Widener, Thomas Dolan, William L. Elkins, William G. Warden, and others who invested in, combined, and arranged financing for gas and electric companies were equally involved in the consolidation of street railways and then their electrification and extension. Allied with bankers, chiefly Drexel and Company, and city officials who gratefully received the leavings of the giants, the large stockholders in gas, electric, and traction companies were not only suppliers of power, but powers themselves. It was not difficult for Dolan on behalf of the United Gas Improvement Company to get a new lease on the city works from the City Council in 1897 no matter how many consumers met to protest it.

The state political boss, Matthew B. Quay, who had supported

(Above) *Northwest Corner of Eleventh and Pine Street,* watercolor by B. R. Evans, 1885 (**LCP**)

It is TIME to drink **Hires'** Rootbeer.

the Bullitt bill to dislodge his increasingly insubordinate local hench-man McManes, installed David Martin as his new Philadelphia lieu-tenant. In the political structure he replaced McManes men with his own followers. According to Lincoln Steffens, whose *The Shame of the Cities* contained a study of Philadelphia's corruption and be-came a classic, Martin "took away from the rank and file of the party and from the ward leaders and office holders the privilege of theft, and he formed companies and groups to handle the legitimate business of the city. It was all graft, but it was all to be lawful and, in the main, it was public franchises, public works and public contracts."

Sooner or later other bosses and other contractors would want to "Shake the Plum Tree," as Boss Quay charmingly expressed it. In an internecine Republican fight in 1895 Martin put up former city soli-citor Charles F. Warwick as mayor; Quay wanted Boies Penrose. Martin swung the city committee to his candidate, but won the enmity of a Quay-Penrose alliance which shortly thereafter dethroned him and put in his stead as the city boss Israel W. Durham, leader of the Seventh Ward, a successful vote-getter and shrewd political manipu-lator. The consolidation of the new regime took place when, in two successive encounters, it beat down John Wanamaker's attempt to get the Republican nomination for senator. Philadelphia was showing the rest of the nation how an efficient political machine worked.

Surges of constructive activity did, nonetheless, take place. In 1887 there were 5,773 licensed retail liquor dealers in Philadelphia County. The term "corner saloon" was aptly descriptive since so many corners were graced—or disgraced—by wooden shacks where beer, whisky, and gin were freely dispensed. At its spring session in 1887 the state legislature passed the Brooks' Law putting a price of $500 on city liquor licenses, requiring the licensees to be of good character, and regulating the sale of intoxicants in various ways. Only 1,343 applicants for retail licenses passed judicial review the following year.

The closing of the saloons did not inhibit the members of the Clover Club, organized in 1881, whose motto was "While We Live We Live in Clover; When We're Dead We're Dead All Over." It was composed chiefly of leaders and supporters of the Republican Party, the movers and shakers of the 1880s and 1890s, who relaxed con-vivially at its banquets where "the note of seriousness is very seldom tolerated from even the most sedate statesmen." The club still exists,

(Above) Trade Card of Hires' Rootbeer (HSP) (Facing) *Between Rounds*, painting by Thomas Eakins, 1899 (Philadelphia Museum of Art, Gift of Mrs. Thomas Eakins and Miss Mary A. Williams; photographed by Alfred J. Wyatt)

(Above) Susan Tyson Rorer in her Model
Kitchen, photogravure, from *Ladies' Home
Journal*, February, 1897 (Emma Seifrit Weigley)

the bibulosity of its members undiminished. One of the city's prominent statesmen was Samuel Jackson Randall. He had been elected
to the House of Representatives as a Democrat during the Civil War
and served term after term until his death in 1890. In a Republican
city it was Randall's unfailing support of protectionism which made
him immune to the winds of party. He was chosen Speaker of the
House in 1875 and remained in that post until 1883, presiding during
the controversy over the disputed Hayes-Tilden election in 1876.

Not only Philadelphia politicians but, more favorably regarded,
Philadelphia products became household words in the last quarter
of the century. John B. Stetson, who started making hats himself in
1865, succeeded so well that twenty-one years later he built a huge
plant at Fourth Street and Montgomery Avenue to turn out broad-
brimmed Stetsons and more conservative headgear in quantities.
Robert H. Foerderer discovered a process for glazing goatskins which
resulted in "Vici" kid, the glossiest and most supple made in a day
when kid gloves were long and frequently worn. Foerderer was one
of the few owners of a large manufacturing firm to be elected to Congress, a position of political influence which enabled him to share in
the spoils of the franchise-hungry traction magnates.

Much of the selling of goods was being done by advertising
which, as an American way of life, was being nurtured by N. W. Ayer
& Son. That agency was a pioneer in popularizing trade names; its
1899 campaign on behalf of the local National Biscuit Company, the
most intensive up to then conducted, made "Uneeda Biscuit" a nationally known product. Other Philadelphia firms which grew into major
national industries with the help of advertising offered Burpee Seeds,
Hires Root Beer, Fels-Naptha Soap, and Whitman's Chocolate. As
an emporium of second-hand books Leary's had no peer.

One prominent citizen, the autocratic physician S. Weir Mitchell,
needed no agency to make him known. A pioneer in the then un-
designated field of psychosomatic medicine and an author of great
local esteem, Dr. Mitchell by force of personality dominated the
cultural and scientific life of the city. At the Retail Grocers', Manufacturers and Pure Food Exposition held at Horticultural Hall on
Broad Street from 1889 to 1901, Sarah Tyson Rorer, a forerunner of
Julia Child, demonstrated improved methods of cooking to thousands
who flocked to see her dramatic culinary performances.

There was exuberance in the air. George W. Childs, owner of the *Public Ledger* was an indefatigable host. Every Fourth of July he gave a dinner for hundreds of newsboys, usually at a restaurant in the park such as Proskauer's Belmont. When ex-President Grant returned from his round-the-world trip in 1879, after 300,000 spectators watched 40,000 marchers strut through the streets, Childs feted the notables at his home at Twenty-second and Walnut streets. And in January, 1893, when Columbus' descendant the Duke of Veragua stopped on his way to the Columbian Exposition in Chicago, once again it was Childs who entertained him. Hardly an occasion was permitted to pass without a celebration. The bicentenary of the founding of Philadelphia in 1882 brought forth crowds who watched from the waterfront as a procession of tugs and steamboats accompanied a replica of Penn's *Welcome*. The day was further enlivened by a bicycle meet, archery contest, and regatta on the Schuylkill. The centennial of the Constitution in 1887 was national in its significance, and President Cleveland honored the city during three days filled with food and speeches. On one of them, after ceremonies in Independence Square, the President had dinner with the Hibernian Society in midafternoon and attended a banquet given by the learned societies at the Academy of Music that night. While her husband was thus engaged, Mrs. Cleveland was entertained by Mrs. Childs.

One of the great happenings of the period was the blizzard of March, 1888, which paralyzed the city. Other events were more pleasant. President McKinley came to town in 1897 to unveil the spectacular Washington Monument created by the German Rudolf Siemering, the gift of the Society of the Cincinnati of Pennsylvania, now in front of the Art Museum. The brief Spanish-American War made but a small impact on Philadelphia, although its yards continued to build ships for the Navy, upon which most of the wartime attention focused. When the Peace Jubilee was held at the end of October, 1898, the President returned. A Naval Day saw a pageant on the Delaware River with a squadron of warships as guests of honor. Then a heavy rain intervened and the festivities were postponed. They resumed with a military parade, featuring the famed Rough Riders, which was reviewed by the President as 25,000 soldiers and sailors passed under a large arch on Broad Street at Sansom. Philadelphia was looking forward to the new century.

(Above) Rough Riders on Market Street in the Peace Jubilee Parade, photograph by William H. Rau, 1898 (HSP)

Herman Melville called it "a sort of tremendous Vanity Fair," as John Maass has recorded, and Ralph Waldo Emerson was "dazzled and astounded." At the Centennial Exhibition there was so much to see and do (227 buildings), such distances to cover (284½ acres), and so many people. The Main Building, with the pavilions of the nations arranged within, covered twenty acres. The slightly smaller Machinery Hall, a spider-web of iron pillars and trusses, was over a quarter of a mile long. Its feature and one of the marvels of the whole exhibition was the Corliss Engine, a steam monster of seven hundred tons weight, which was started up on opening day in the presence of President Grant and Emperor Pedro of Brazil. It provided the power to run the hundreds of machines ranged through the hall. The engine was a pragmatic symbol of the American technological accomplishments which the Centennial made known to the industrial nations of Europe. They were impressed. The exposure to new ideas was not all one way. Americans from Maine to California came, picked up a complimentary copy of the facsimile of the first issue of the Public Ledger, bought a Japanese vase or bowl, ate exotic foods they had never dreamt of before, and thronged in to see the sculpture and painting exhibits in Memorial Hall—particularly the Italian gallery—after which they were able to express Puritanical disapproval of the displayed nudities they so eagerly sought out. The variety was almost infinite, from the Cataract with its cool jets of water, very popular during the steaming summer, to the telephone which received its now fabled introduction to the world, and innumerable products, gimmicks, and novelties from South Africa to Norway.

(Above) *Our Artist's Dream of the Centennial Restaurant,* woodcut after Walter F. Brown, from *Harper's Weekly,* July 1, 1876 (LCP) (Facing) Centennial Trade Cards and Labels (HSP)

City Hall, begun in 1872, was to have been completed in ten years at a cost of $10,000,000; it took longer and cost much, much more. The tower was finished in 1887, the statue of Penn raised in 1894, and the clock installed five years later. On a site about 475 feet square with a courtyard in the center, the massive structure when built was larger than any other single building in America. Alexander Milne Calder, grandfather of the modern sculptor of mobile fame, spent half a generation making plaster models of the sculpture with which City Hall is luxuriantly embellished; a troop of skilled workmen chipped the granite after his designs. The statue of William Penn, 37 feet high, which stands atop the 547-foot-high tower, was Calder's final contribution; in its creation he was aided by John Casani, an immigrant from Venice. Visible for miles on a clear day, it has become both a landmark and a symbol. By municipal ordinance no new building may top Penn's hat. The structure, an ebullient nineteenth-century interpretation of French Renaissance grandeur, has been maligned, praised, almost torn-down, and even cleaned. With a kind of supercilious attitude, City Hall looks out over much of the city's new building and asks, "Après moi, quoi?"

(Above) City Hall, phototype by F. Gutekunst, 1887 (HSP)
(Below) Statue of William Penn in City Hall Courtyard, 1894 (HSP)

In the burst of building which marked the Centennial era the busiest architect in Philadelphia was Frank Furness. His style has challenged the adjectival powers of architectural historians to describe. Robert Venturi spoke of "an array of violent pressures within a rigid frame." To nonprofessionals Furness appears to have been exuberant on the grand scale and finicky in details. The list of major buildings he, with his partners, designed is almost like a litany of Philadelphia saints: some of its solid banks, the Pennsylvania Academy of the Fine Arts finished in 1876, Library Company of Philadelphia at Juniper and Locust streets opened in 1879, the Undine Barge Club on the Schuylkill of 1882-83, the squat First Unitarian Church at Twenty-second and Chestnut streets, the castellated library of the University of Pennsylvania, alterations to the monumental Broad Street Station completed in 1893, and a series of structures for the Jewish Hospital at Tabor and Old York roads which occupied him from 1871 to 1907. Brick was Furness' favorite medium, but it was in the design of shapes and embellishments that his touch was made evident.

(Above) *Guarantee Trust and Safe Deposit Co., 316-320 Chestnut Street,* lithograph by Bunk and McFetridge, 1886 (HSP)
(Below) Library of the University of Pennsylvania, ca. 1890 (HSP)

As the cloud-scraping tower of City Hall slowly rose, across the street the Pennsylvania Railroad built its central city depot, designed by John M. Wilson. When it opened in 1881, it was a convenience; the luxurious trains of the nation's foremost railroad entered into the very heart of the city. The tracks were laid by the master contractor of railroad engineering, Patricious McManus. However, the masonry barrier at street level which enclosed the tracks, the "Chinese Wall," as it became known, was also a barrier to the development of Market Street to the west. Crowds poured into the terminal; a bridge at Fifteenth Street took pedestrians from the station, over the traffic, and south to where high office buildings were making a city skyline. To the east the Philadelphia and Reading Railroad at Twelfth and Market streets put up a neo-Venetian station to which the largest and finest market in the city was a kind of rear adjunct. The Reading Terminal, shorn of some of its pristine glory, still stands. Once-upon-a-time its restaurant on the second floor was one of the most satisfactory in the city.

(Below) *Interior of the Farmers' Market,* woodcut after J. M. Weiker, from Edward Strahan, *A Century After: Picturesque Glimpses of Philadelphia and Pennsylvania,* 1875 (LCP)
(Above) Broad Street Station, photograph by R. Newell & Son, 1889 (Kean Archives)
(Right) Pullman Buffet Car Interior, 1890 (HSP)

It is incredible that the Quaker City should have nurtured Thomas Eakins, the greatest artistic realist of his time. He saw Philadelphians with a clear eye, and with a sturdy brush painted them in their many faceted forms: scullers on the Schuylkill, great surgeons at work, a succession of Catholic dignitaries, boxers in the arena, a four-in-hand bowling along the park drive, and portrait after portrait of friends and patrons delineated without the usual painter's nod to flattery. Eakins, trained in Paris, came home to teach at the Pennsylvania Academy of the Fine Arts where his devotion to the drawing of male and female anatomy—a subject he had studied at Jefferson Medical College —brought him into conflict with contemporary mores. But he was a great teacher who led a generation of students, among them Thomas Anschutz, Alice Barber, and Alexander Milne Calder, to an understanding of the beauty of life forms. Today he is recognized as the most important artist the city has ever produced.

(Above) *The Gross Clinic*, painting by Thomas Eakins, 1875 (Jefferson Medical College of Thomas Jefferson University; photograph by Alfred J. Wyatt)

In 1867 on behalf of a coalition of cultural institutions—the Academy of the Fine Arts, Academy of Natural Sciences, Library Company, Philosophical Society, and Franklin Institute —the City Councils had petitioned the state legislature to permit the societies to build on Penn Square. The bill failed in the House of Representatives. Following the trend, most of the institutions relocated to the west anyway. The venerable Library Company doubled its facilities when, almost simultaneously, in 1879 it moved into a new building at Juniper and Locust streets to serve its members and reluctantly occupied Addison Hutton's Parthenonic Ridgway Library at Broad and Christian streets in order to benefit from the estate of Dr. James Rush. The Academy of Natural Sciences, raising the unheard-of sum of $239,160, built a huge structure in collegiate Gothic style at Nineteenth and Race streets, finished in 1876, to care for its internationally famous collections. That same year the Pennsylvania Academy of the Fine Arts, entering one of its most productive and exciting periods as a teaching institution, completed its splendid Furness home at Broad and Cherry streets. The fast-growing Historical Society of Pennsylvania, which had moved from the Athenaeum to the "Picture House" of the Pennsylvania Hospital in 1872, moved again ten years later to the mansion of General Robert Patterson at the corner of Thirteenth and Locust streets onto which an assembly hall was built.

(Above) Reading Room of the Ridgway Library, ca. 1890 (LCP)
(Below) Assembly Hall of the Historical Society of Pennsylvania, Locust Street, ca. 1890 (HSP)

On February 23, 1882, the S.S. Illinois *landed 225 Jewish refugees from Russia at a Philadelphia pier. Since accounts of the Czar's cruelty had preceded them, the immigrants were given a municipal reception, and $20,000 was raised to help them settle. Ship after ship brought more and more Jews fleeing persecutions and pogroms, while less dramatically came thousands of Italians leaving the hopelessness of poverty and the burnt-out land of southern Italy and Sicily. The Eastern European Jews found jobs in the needlework trades and the cigar industry; they peddled from pushcarts and opened small shops. The Italians made their livelihood as laborers, and the more skilled as masons, on the booming road-building and construction projects. Poor, unable to speak English, the new Americans could find lodgings only in the old, run-down section of the city, south of Pine Street and east of Ninth, where they dislodged blacks who moved west and north. With Poles joining the foreign-born population, a large, exotic element was added to the Quaker City. Sectarian charities sprang up to aid the newcomers, but tensions existed between the newcomers and the earlier Irish, German, and English arrivals. Social, economic and religious prejudice intensified throughout the city.*

(Below) Store of Frank Cuneo, 801-805 Christian Street, photogravure from George W. Englehardt, *Philadelphia, Pa. The Book of the Bourse and Co-operating Public Bodies*, 1898-99 (LCP)
(Above) *Scene in St. Mary Street, South Philadelphia*, woodcut by F. Juengling after W. L. Sheppard, from Edward Strahan, *A Century After: Picturesque Glimpses of Philadelphia and Pennsylvania*, 1875 (LCP)
(Right) Advertisement of Immigrant Service of Pennsylvania Railroad and American Line, ca. 1900 (Philadelphia Maritime Museum)

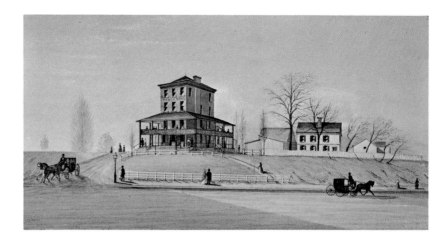

The villages within the city ceased to be separate factory-based settlements as the open spaces between them were built up. In 1891 an account of the spread of houses stated: "The marble pile at Broad Street is hardly in the centre of the south-western part of the city; old Fairmount is chiefly notable because of the number of good building lots it covers in the heart of the town; for miles down and up Broad Street there are row after row of massive or ornate buildings; over the Schuylkill it is difficult to find a good vacant place to build. The Punch Bowl [an inn on Broad Street north of Diamond] is swallowed up; Suffolk [a race track near Penrose Ferry Road] is obliterated under blocks of well-built houses; Kensington is in the city as much as Southwark; you can go to German-town, Frankford or Chestnut Hill over well-paved streets solidly built up, and then hardly have more than a faint idea of Philadelphia's advance in real estate improvement." There were two- and three-story brick houses for solid workingmen and shopkeepers. On the wider avenues rows of more pretentious homes rose, each with its front porch which the builders of the era made a Philadelphia tradition. Philadelphia was, indeed, a city of homes, most of them owner occupied.

(Above) *Punch Bowl on North Broad Street,* watercolor by David J. Kennedy, 1889 (HSP)
(Middle) *Twenty-ninth Street North from Goldbeck Street,* ca. 1900 (HSP)
(Below) *Northeast Corner of Fifteenth Street and Erie Avenue,* photogravure from George W. Englehardt, *Philadelphia, Pa. The Book of the Bourse and Co-operating Public Bodies,* 1898-99 (LCP)

Now forgotten, William M. Singerley was typical of the booming last decades of the century. He began his career with the Germantown Passenger Railway, his father's business, and managed it so well that in 1878 he was able to sell his inherited shares for $1,500,000. A year earlier he had bought control of the Philadelphia Record, turned it into a penny daily, livened it up, espoused, in Republican protectionist Philadelphia, Democratic free trade and increased the circulation from 5,200 to 100,000 copies. In 1881-82 for his paper he erected a granite building of exotic appearance next to the new Post Office on Chestnut Street which echoed, more conventionally, one of the pavilions of the Louvre. Singerley at the time had begun to invest heavily in building operations, in the words of a contemporary, "probably the most extensive ever inaugurated in Philadelphia by one person at any one time." His development included about a thousand houses west of Seventeenth Street between Diamond and York which overran the racetrack adjoining the Lamb Tavern in that area. Singerley raised Holstein cattle on a six hundred acre farm in Gwynedd, had a mansion on North Broad Street, raced horses in Kentucky and ran ineffectually as the Democratic nominee for governor in 1894. The Chestnut Street National Bank of which he was president failed in 1898; he died suddenly a few months later leaving such tangled affairs that receivers were appointed to straighten them out.

(Above) *Philadelphia Record Building, Chestnut Street above Ninth,* woodcut by J. Brown after P. F. Goist, from J. Thomas Scharf and Thompson Westcott, *History of Philadelphia,* 1884 (LCP)

Never in the history of the city had the life of the rich been so perfect and so cloudless. With the floodgates of immigration open, servants for home and garden were available at the lowest rates. Even householders of moderate means had cooks, maids, coachmen and gardeners. Neatly clipped hedges and manicured lawns were delightful to see on estates in Germantown and Chestnut Hill and in the suburbs along the Whitemarsh Valley, the Main Line, and Old York Road. What had been summer houses were turned into or replaced by all-year-round residences, some baronial in size and design, as commuter train services were vastly improved. Henry H. Houston, the largest landowner within the city limits in Roxborough and Chestnut Hill, was largely responsible for the full development of the latter area, building the Wissahickon Inn to attract visitors and giving a large tract of land across the street to the Philadelphia Cricket Club. Even in the city, particularly in West Philadelphia near the expanding University of Pennsylvania and north on Broad Street where the millionaires Peter A. B. Widener and William L. Elkins built mansions, large houses boasted at least gardens and hothouses.

(Above) *House of William M. Singerley at Broad and Jefferson Streets on Sunday Afternoon,* woodcut by VanIngen & Snyder after F. Schell, from *Philadelphia and Its Environs,* 1875 (LCP)
(Middle) "Lindenwold," the Residence of Dr. R. V. Mattison, Ambler, Exterior and Sitting Room, photogravure from George W. Englehardt, *Philadelphia, Pa. The Book of the Bourse and Co-operating Public Bodies,* 1898-99 (LCP)
(Below) House of Peter A. B. Widener at the Corner of Broad Street and Girard Avenue, ca. 1890 (Free Library of Philadelphia)

John Wanamaker expected his hired help to go to Sunday School every week, and he did not trust an employee who smoked Cuban cigars. In spite of or because of his high moral standards Wanamaker successfully set a pattern for sales of varied goods in a vast store. He had begun his career in Philadelphia as a Jack-of-all-trades in Bennett's Tower Hall clothing store while he moonlighted as secretary of the YMCA. In 1861 with Nathan Brown he opened Oak Hall, a men's and boy's store at Sixth and Market streets, pioneering with special sales after Christmas and offering one-price merchandise with returnability of goods. Success followed. To match it, Wanamaker bought the old railroad station on the south side of Market Street facing Penn Square, and on May 6, 1876, on the eve of the Centennial, he opened the largest store in the city. Wanamaker's Grand Depot was the granddaddy of all Philadelphia department stores. The imaginative owner himself became a philanthropist with an ultra-conservative bias; he was appointed postmaster general by President Harrison; and, not so effectively as he sold merchandise, he supported a succession of reform movements in the city.

(Above) Interior of Wanamaker's Grand Depot, Lithograph, ca. 1880 (Free Library of Philadelphia)
(Below) Advertisement for Wanamaker's, from Evening Star, July 9, 1876 (LCP)

WHETHER YOU GO
OUT OF TOWN
OR
STAY AT HOME
THESE
HOT JULY
DAYS,

It must be a comfortable reflection, if you think of it at all, that you can so readily accommodate yourself in the matter of

CLOTHING

in a house like WANAMAKER'S, where every possible requirement in cool raiment for summer wear for Men and Youths and Boys and Children, can be so amply met, and at such extremely low prices, lower in fact than was ever known before for equally desirable articles.

WHAT KIND.

Cool Coats and Suits, all sizes.
All-wool Light Cassimeres,
All linen White Duck Pants.
Men's White Vests, Ducks, Marseilles, &c.
Men's Drap d'Ete Coats.
Lustrous Alpacas,
Mohair and Seersucker Goods.
Serges and Light Weight Cloths.
All Summer Fabrics called for.

WHAT FOR.

Suits for Traveling and Pleasure.
Suits for Business and Street.
Suits for Vacation and School.
Suits for Dress and Party.
Suits for Seashore and Mountain.
Suits for Country and City.
Suits for Workshop and Store.
Suits for Bathing and Fishing.
Suits for All Purposes and Occasions.

ESPECIALLY
UNDERWEAR,
FURNISHING GOODS,
AND
TOILET NOTIONS.

50 cents will buy - - Six pairs good Half Hose.
50 cents will buy - - Four fine Linen Collars.
50 cents will buy - - Two good Linen Handkerchiefs.
50 cents will buy - - One Summer Undershirt.
50 cents will buy - - A Pair of Summer Drawers.

And so on, at equally attractive prices, through the long list of everything for Men and Boys' Wear.

WANAMAKER,
THE NEW ESTABLISHMENT,
THIRTEENTH AND MARKET STREETS.

Clubs became a way of life—for food, fellowship, and fun. At the Philadelphia Club men of old families dined, wined, and played sniff; businessmen gathered at the Manufacturers' Club; upward mobile German-Jews played pinochle and gave balls at their splendid Mercantile Club; leaders in literature, science, and art formed the Penn Club; and socially prominent women in 1894 organized the Acorn Club. The Grand Army of the Republic, Redmen, Odd Fellows, Knights of the Golden Eagle, Masons of all degrees, members of Bnai Brith, and Knights of Columbus held conventions, parades, and picnics. These were the days when German clubs were in their prime and tens of thousands celebrated folk festivals at Schuetzen Park. In 1880 all but ten of the sixty-three city singing societies and most of the bands were German. Every cluster of immigrants established a nostalgic old-country beneficial and social association. Where the grass was green, cricket clubs blossomed as Philadelphia cricketers, foremost of whom were the Newhalls, played international matches and sometimes won. Lawn tennis was added to society's popular sports, and courts soon became more common than cricket pitches. By the end of the century golf courses were laid out at several country clubs. Along the river the Schuylkill Navy held sway, with boat races a regular feature of the spring season; there and also on the Delaware yacht clubs sprang up.

(Above) *Grounds and Club-house of the Belmont Cricket Club, 58th Street and Darby Road,* lithograph by H. I. Kurtz, 1885 (HSP)
(Below) *Flags of the Schuylkill Navy,* lithograph by Duval Steam Lith. Co., ca. 1880 (HSP)

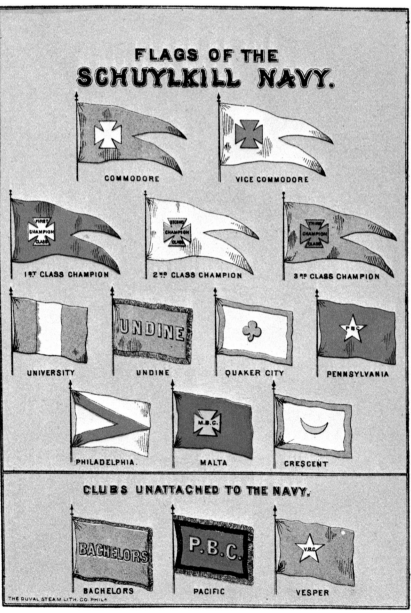

The last two decades of the nineteenth century saw a boom in education in the United States unmatched until after World War II. Philadelphia contributed to the boom by establishing new colleges and expanding its major university. Under Quaker auspices, Haverford College had been founded much earlier in the rustic suburbs, Swarthmore shortly after the Civil War, and Bryn Mawr, academically the bellwether of all women's colleges, in 1884. In town, for the children of less well-endowed parents, Russell H. Conwell, the dynamic Baptist minister whose Acres of Diamonds was an inspirational bestseller for years, developed his informal educational meetings into Temple College, chartered in 1888. Thinking in terms of industrial development, the banker Anthony J. Drexel gave a large sum in 1893 to found the Drexel Institute of Art, Sciences, and Industry (later shortened to Technology). But it was the prestigious University of Pennsylvania under the leadership of the provosts Dr. William Pepper and Charles Custis Harrison which brought high honors academic and athletic to the city. In 1880 the university graduated 86 students; twenty years later the graduating class had grown to 950. The last years of the century saw Penn's greatest football team with the All-American T. Truxtun Hare as its star. In the bloom of success the dental school was opened in 1878, the Wharton School of Business and Finance in 1881, and the veterinary school three years later. It was then socially respectable to go to Penn.

(Above) Main Hall of Temple College, photogravure, ca. 1898 (HSP)
(Right) Football Team of the University of Pennsylvania, 1897 (University of Pennsylvania Archives)

It was the age of clutter. Late
Victorian taste was partial to a pro-
fusion and variety of shapes. For
example, the standard method of
display, as followed by the University
Museum, founded in 1889, was to
show as much of everything as possible
in the available space. The Free Library of Philadelphia was indeed
cramped in its early quarters on the
north side of Chestnut Street between
Twelfth and Thirteenth in the ornate
old Concert Hall, but the obviously
posed readers reflected the times' satis-
faction with chockablock rooms. One
wonders if the Welsbach gas mantles
gave enough light to read by on dark
and dreary days. Perhaps the finest
surviving Philadelphia period room
is the library of the great historian
of the Inquisition, Henry Charles
Lea. It was built in 1881 as an
appendage to his house at the corner
of Twentieth and Walnut streets and
is now incorporated into the Rare
Book Department of the University
of Pennsylvania. Ladies' dresses
matched the exuberance of architectural decoration and house furnishings.

(Below) Interior of the University Museum,
photograph by William H. Rau, 1898 (Uni-
versity of Pennsylvania Archives)
(Above) *Les Modes Parisiennes—An October
Afternoon*, lithograph by Illman Brothers, from
Peterson's Magazine, October, 1888 (LCP)
(Middle) Library of Henry Charles Lea, 2000
Walnut Street, ca. 1900 (HSP)
(Below right) Circulation Room of Free Library
of Philadelphia, 1221-27 Chestnut Street, photo-
gravure, ca. 1900 (HSP)

Electricity was coming of age when the Franklin Institute held its International Electrical Exhibition in September, 1884. There Thomas A. Edison proved to the world that his incandescent lamp was the best lighting there was. In Philadelphia a forest of cluttered poles had carried the wires of the police and fire alarm system, of the telegraph company and, after 1878 when the first telephone directory was published with forty-seven subscribers, of the Bell Telephone Company. Soon electric light poles were added. Brush carbon arc lamps were tried successfully in John Wanamaker's, the Continental Hotel, and Thomas Dolan's Keystone Knitting Mills. Forming a company, Dolan offered to light Chestnut Street from river to river free for a year as a demonstration, a feat accomplished late in 1881. From then on the Councils granted franchises to one after another local company for street lighting. In 1889 the Edison Electric Light Company, guided by Professor William D. Marks, went into operation with a generator at Sansom Street near Ninth, miles of underground conduits, and an instant demand for household lighting by incandescent lamps. Electricity furnished the power not only for the operation of lights and machines, but for the formation of new companies, political and financial maneuvering, mergers, and the ultimate creation of a monopoly, the Philadelphia Electric Company.

(Above) View South on Broad Street from Chestnut, ca. 1880 (Mrs. Robert H. Nones, Jr.)
(Below left) Bell Telephone Company of Philadelphia Directory, November 12, 1878 (Atwater Kent Museum)
(Below right) The Illuminated Fountain at the International Electrical Exhibition, woodcut after W. P. Snyder, from *Harper's Weekly*, September 13, 1884 (LCP)

Technology made its impact. The increased amount of power which the electric companies generated made the horseless trolley car feasible, so the owners of traction franchises sought the right to introduce electric cars. In 1892 Mayor Edwin S. Stuart vetoed the ordinance permitting them; the Councils overrode the veto. Philadelphians loved their new trolleys and they rode on gaily lit-up ones at night for sheer fun. The transit system spread rapidly. Shortly afterwards a new gadget, the automobile, made its appearance. The Swiss-born baker, Jules Junker, was said to have owned the first motorcar in Philadelphia, although his fresh-baked rolls continued to be delivered in horsedrawn wagons for years. Quite divorced from such everyday life then was the experimental work of Eadward Muybridge under the auspices of the University of Pennsylvania. In a well-screened area, with an ingenious setup of trip wires attached to cameras, he took the first photographs, thousands of them, showing men, women, and animals in motion, a tentative step toward the creation of the cinema, and an immediate aid to artists and anatomists.

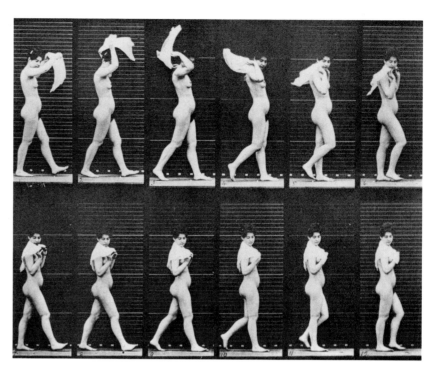

The official seal of the city adopted
in 1874 had as one of the charges
on the coat-of-arms a ship in full sail.
The Delaware River continued to be
a major economic asset; old fashioned
schooners, coal-burning freighters,
and coastal tugs with chains of flat-
boats brought in a vast variety of
raw materials and carried away refined and manufactured goods. In
1880 almost forty-five million bushels
of grain came into the port and as
much again came from the interior for
use in the local bakeries and for trans-
shipment. At this period the major
manufactured products of Philadelphia industries were boots and shoes,
carpets, men's and boy's clothing, the
coinage of the Mint, hosiery, knit
and worsted goods, and sugar. The
wagons along Delaware Avenue were
evidence of the activity which was
increased during the summer months
by passenger traffic onto the ferries
for Camden where trains took vaca-
tioners to Atlantic City and Cape May.
In August, 1881, a fast train of the
Camden and Atlantic Rail Road made
the run to the shore in seventy-six
minutes. Less light-hearted was the
crash program to build up the United
States Navy. The final decade of the
century saw Cramp's Shipyard launch
such vessels as the armored cruiser
New York, *said to be "the fastest and
most powerful seagoing ship in the
world," and the battleship* Indiana
*which President Harrison watched
slide down the ways.*

(Facing, below) "The Trolley as a Popular Fad
in Philadelphia," photogravure after F. Cresson
Schell, *Frank Leslie's Illustrated Newspaper*,
July 25, 1895 (LCP)
(Facing, above) Woman Walking, photogravure,
from Eadward Muybridge, *Animal Locomotion*,
1887 (LCP)
(Facing, right) Trolley Loop at the Foot of
Market Street, photograph by W. N. Jennings,
ca. 1901 (HSP)
(Above) Delaware Avenue at Market Street, ca.
1890 (HSP)
(Below) *U. S. S. New York*, painting by Hart,
1893 (Philadelphia Maritime Museum)

1900-1930

The twentieth century began in Philadelphia in a blaze of glory. At the stroke of twelve on New Year's Eve, City Hall, outlined by 12,000 electric lights strung from the rim of Billy Penn's hat down to the four arches of the courtyard, became a gigantic Roman candle.

Samuel H. Ashbridge, known variously as "Stars and Stripes" Sam or "Sunday School" Sam because of the assiduity with which he spoke at patriotic gatherings and prayer meetings, was mayor. Ashbridge, Lincoln Steffens wrote, "broke through all the principles of moderate grafting." In 1901 when the state legislature pushed through a bill to set up fourteen new transit companies, Ashbridge threw away John Wanamaker's letter offering $2,500,000 for the franchises without reading it and signed the charters for the politically faithful. It was Steffens in 1904 who called Philadelphia "the most corrupt and contented" city in the nation. The city's elite and its political henchmen, the bankers and lawyers "on the inside," did indeed benefit from traction franchises, the issue of electric company stocks and street railway bonds, and contracts for bridges, subways, streets, and schools. Graft in the Edwardian era was an American way of life, interrupted occasionally by the activities of grim-jawed reformers, of a grinning ex-police commissioner and Rough Rider, Theodore Roosevelt, or of a studious ex-college president, Woodrow Wilson.

But in Philadelphia in the first decades of the twentieth century there was built—no doubt, at greater expense than was necessary—an urban transportation network second to none in the nation. Resources for electric power and an efficient gas works were created to meet the demands of ballooning use. Horn and Hardart opened its first automat. Department stores, offering a wide variety of merchandise at moderate prices, blossomed on Market Street. Oil reached Marcus Hook through a new pipeline. The modern mint on Spring Garden Street began to turn out coins. A reincarnated battleship *Maine* was launched from Cramp's Shipyard. Old businesses and industries were expanded and new ones established.

In 1900 the city's population was nearly 1,300,000, an increase of almost twenty-five percent in a single decade; by 1930 there were 1,950,000 inhabitants in the city, and the overflow into the surrounding suburban counties had already become substantial. The sprawl of privately owned houses covered wide areas. As successive waves of would-be Philadelphians arrived, they settled first in the old warrens

(Facing) Trolley Cars on Chestnut Street looking East from Wanamaker's Store, ca. 1905 (HSP)

of courts and alleys of the Northern Liberties, Southwark, and Moyamensing. The newest immigrants were like pebbles in a pond, landing where the housing was the poorest and sending out concentric circles of the upwardly mobile. By the end of the 1920s it was the blacks newly come from the South who found the only housing they could afford in the South Street area and in parts of West and North Philadelphia.

Persons from the same European background tended to live near and work with each other and, when the opportunity presented itself, to occupy newly built-up blocks together, although sometimes the homogenous neighborhoods formed small checkerboard squares across the city. As the Germans left the section between Girard and Columbia avenues east of Broad Street for Olney, they took with them their singing clubs and assorted varieties of wursts. Well-to-do German Jews settled around their social center, the Mercantile Club, on Broad Street near Jefferson. Eastern European Jews began to move out from the southern slums, the more successful of them to Wynnefield and Strawberry Mansion, others to the houses of Marshall Street once occupied by the German Jews. Their synagogues followed them. South Philadelphia, from Catherine Street down in a wide band, was "Little Italy," where the customs, churches, sounds, and smells of Naples and Sicily filled the area. The mills of Manayunk attracted the Poles, and soon their own distinctive Catholic churches rose on the hills overlooking the Schuylkill. Philadelphia, as it had been since the villages first began to cluster around mills and factories, was an amalgam of neighborhoods: Fishtown, Port Richmond, Torresdale, Nicetown, Tioga, Francisville, Manayunk, Logan, Mount Airy, Mantua, and Moyamensing.

In the ferment of expansion, the political life remained consistent. At the beginning of the century the Philadelphia triumvirate of the organization boss Israel W. Durham, James P. McNichol, *de facto* but not *de jure* official contractor for the city, and the promoter and financier of franchises John W. Mack ran the Republican machine. The Vares were then only beginning to consolidate their power. Reform movements and reform candidates gently ebbed and flowed; no tidal flood cleansed the city for long. Mayor John Weaver, put into office by the gang, surprised his sponsors by turning on them and refusing to extend the lease of the gas works to the United Gas Improvement

(Above) Anti-Republican Machine Cartoon, *Public Ledger*, February 17, 1907 (HSP)
(Facing, above) Broad and Arch Streets looking toward City Hall, ca. 1900 (HSP)
(Facing, below) Horn & Hardart's Automat, photogravure, ca. 1910 (Horn & Hardart Company)

FIRST HOLIDAY TODAY; STORES ASKED NOT TO OPEN, EVEN HEATLESS

Closing Order for Today

Officially Defined By the Federal Fuel Administration

It is the desire of the United States fuel administration that department stores and other retail establishments close on Mondays, food stores and drug stores excepted, only. The United States fuel administration has not issued any special order dealing with department stores.

As a result of information furnished by the United States food administration to the effect that confusion exists in the minds of the public as to the closing of food-distributing stores on Monday afternoons, the order of the United States fuel administration, dated ...

Only Food and Drug Stores Exempt From Use of Fuel

REPORTS SHOW GAINS IN APPROVAL OF ORDER

Operation of Elevators to Be Restricted on Coming Mondays

COLD CAUSING DELAYS

Movement of Coal to Tidewater and Return of Cars Increasing

Public Ledger Bureau ⎰
Washington, Jan. 20 ⎱

THE SECOND COAL-LESS DAY

Coal for homes and ships moving more rapidly as factories close.

Empty cars at seaboard being sent westward.

Compliance with order general, reports to Washington indicate. Complaints now few.

Potter makes more concessions to factories in Philadelphia.

Coal receipts for city at new low level.

Speeding cars back to mines for tomorrow's shipments.

Theatres' closing day shifted from Monday to Tuesday.

CITY SALOONS TO BE CLOSED TIGHT MONDAY

Garfield Shutdown Brings Action by Liquor Dealers' Federation

FUEL SHIPMENTS FALL TO NEW LOW LEVELS

Modification in Rules Suspending Factory Operation Made by Potter

COAL SHIPMENT SPEEDS UP AS FACTORIES STOP

Movement of Fuel for Ships and Homes Shows Improvement

INDUSTRIAL EMBARGO COSTS U S. $50,000,000

Smith Reports Empty Cars Are Being Sent Westward From Seaboard

(Above) The Coal Shortage, *Public Ledger*, January 20-21, 1918 (Free Library of Philadelphia)

Company. Weaver's boldness and the election of Teddy Roosevelt in 1904 encouraged the sober elements in town to believe that they could beat the politicians. The Committee of Seventy brought into existence a reformist City Party with Franklin Spencer Edmonds at its helm. Its nominees won the off-year election for minor offices in November, 1905, but the new era ended almost as soon as it had begun. Weaver fell back into line; the City Party lost the next election.

The reformers' next chance came in 1911 when William S. Vare wanted to be mayor. The all-powerful state boss Senator Boies Penrose offered as his candidate George H. Earle, Jr., lawyer and real estate speculator. Earle won the Republican nomination in a bitter primary fight. The split enabled the new reformist Keystone Party, with the aid of the few Democrats, to elect Rudolph Blankenburg mayor. Even his enemies admitted that he was a man of integrity, although some said the real brains were supplied by the formidable, feminist Mrs. Blankenburg. The new mayor promised a businessman's administration and delivered it. Hundreds of thousands of dollars were saved for the city by the negotiation of graft-free contracts. Four years later, in 1915, the Penrose–Vare–McNichol combine was happily reunited to share power and profit; out went the reformers.

The 1920s brought no improvement. J. Hampton Moore, personally so honest that he leaned over backward, might have set the city on the path of rectitude had not the City Council consisted of hew-to-the-line organization men. Philadelphians liked Moore, who somewhat resembled Caspar Milquetoast in appearance, but they never gave him the power to accomplish much. The city charter of 1919 had given primacy to the Common Council at the expense of the mayor; the voters continued to elect the same politicians to Council, thus effectively negating change. W. Freeland Kendrick, rarely pictured without his Shriner's fez, succeeded Moore in 1924. He presented no problem to the bosses. He is remembered, if at all, and that with a certain amount of justification, for the failure of the Sesqui-Centennial. What may have seemed in the eyes of the participants cataclysmic campaigns for local offices over the decades were the substitution—and frequently prostitution—of one Republican nominee for another. The few Democrats were completely dependent upon the Republican machine for their widow's mite of patronage.

The politicians did, however, change the face of the city. Huge areas within the city limits were converted from farm lands to streets of row houses. Roosevelt Boulevard, cutting northeast from the old Hunting Park race track, and the Frankford Elevated, following the curve of the Delaware River, opened up a huge underdeveloped section. The Market Street Elevated, forging its way west, brought another area close to downtown. North through Logan, Old York Road made its way, and a paved Broad Street crept slowly north and south as a subway was tunneled under it. And with the slicing through of the Parkway, a tree-lined boulevard brought the green of Fairmount Park to City Hall.

World War I was a powerful uniting factor. Most Philadelphians, from those who claimed descent from the barons of the Magna Charta to those whose more immediate ancestors spoke Italian, Yiddish, Polish, Greek, or Russian, were on the side of the Allies from the beginning. After the invasion of Belgium, the wide circulation of cartoons showing the atrocities of the Huns made the large German–American population uncomfortable, but no major confrontation or violence took place. Grover Bergdoll, of German extraction and heir to a brewery fortune, achieved notoriety by becoming the city's most widely publicized draft-dodger. In the main, however, a powerful surge of patriotism brought volunteers into the army, money into government bonds, workers into factories, and a fighting spirit into every national and civic enterprise. Philadelphia, with her industrial and commercial might, became "the Arsenal of Democracy."

Wartime shortages were made more acute in January, 1918, when twenty-eight inches of snow fell on the city. An already existing coal shortage forced many who were connected to gas lines to use it for heat as well as for cooking and illumination. Ice in the river threatened the water supply. For lack of coal, plants and businesses were shut down completely for five days and Mondays became forced holidays for a period of nine weeks as the state fuel administrator ordered dealers to supply dwellings before stores. Trolleys skip-stopped to conserve electricity; people were urged to turn out unessential lights; and daylight saving time was introduced on March 31, 1918. The price of coal doubled. Mobs raided coal cars. Bread was rationed in hotels and rose in price to such an extent that there were scattered bread riots. Victory gardens greened in city backyards. Inflation brought on some strikes, but most of the citizens considered their problems neces-

(Above) The Train Shed at Broad Street Station on Fire, *Public Ledger*, June 17, 1923 (Free Library of Philadelphia)

sary sacrifices for victory and kept a stiff upper lip.

In the postwar Red scare that shook the nation, Philadelphia had its own alarms. At the end of December, 1918, the homes of three influential citizens, Justice Robert von Moschizker, the president of the Chamber of Commerce Ernest T. Trigg, and Judge James E. Gorman, were bombed as part of a widespread terrorist plot. Amateurishly printed circulars were found around the ruined buildings. On May Day, 1919, to protest the imprisonment of Eugene V. Debs and his fellow radicals, some waiters and cooks struck and paraded. Early in June a bomb exploded at a Catholic church in West Philadelphia. Raids on clandestine hideouts in various parts of the city turned up copies of the *Soviet Bulletin* and "suspicious appearing liquids." It was not until November that a nationwide roundup of radical elements including the I.W.W., anarchists, and Russian agitators ended Philadelphia's latent concern. Locally, a number of Russians including Paul Yakimov, Michael Lestschuk, and Paul Yurkwicz were arrested at a meeting where Matthew Furshtmann was lecturing on "The Principles of Anarchy."

Philadelphia's greatest bonfire of the 1920s could not be attributed to anarchism. This conflagration, which gutted the train shed at the Pennsylvania Railroad's Broad Street Station in the night of June 10, 1923, was one of the city's spectaculars. In a surprisingly short time the damage was repaired. The Pennsy in those days could make anything good whatever the price. It was a political power to which governors and mayors were beholden, a steady employer of thousands and a safe investment for widows. In the first quarter of the twentieth century, politically, financially, and socially, the Pennsylvania Railroad was the biggest thing in town.

Philadelphia's police were polite, punctilious, and well-groomed as they directed traffic along the important business streets where leading citizens saw them every weekday. The Fairmount Park guards, too, in grey rather than blue looked equally spruce as they saluted the well-known cars of magnates being driven through the Park on their way to town from Chestnut Hill and the Main Line. At Christmas time five-dollar gold pieces were pressed into receptive hands to assure the chauffeurs of the great the courtesy of the road. With all the city's political ups and downs, the police department was modernized and motorized and did its best within the limits set by influential pres-

(Above) Philadelphia Policeman at Eighth and Chestnut Streets, photograph by David W. Garrigues, ca. 1910 (HSP)
(Facing) Poster for a Meeting of the Cloak and Shirt Makers Union, 1917 (Amalgamated Clothing Workers Union Records, Urban Archives, Temple University)

WORKERS!

Do the wages you receive enable you and your family to live as human beings should live?

Do you know that to work more than eight hours is harmful to your health and detrimental to the welfare of the working class?

Do you realize that unless you are organized and establish the principle of collective bargaining, there is neither Liberty nor Freedom in the shop.

A SHOP MEETING

of all the people working for J. M. Susskind will be held

Monday, August 20th, 6 P. M. sharp

at Cigar Makers Hall, 232 N. 9th St.

Come all. Let us unite.   The workers united are invincible.

THE JOINT COMMITTEE
of the Cloak and Skirt Makers Union
and D. C. No. 2, Amalgamated Clothing Workers of America

אַרבייטער! קענט איהר, מים אייערע פֿאַמיליען, מאַכען אַין
אנשטענדיג לעבּען פון דיא נעהאַלטען וועלכע איהר
בעקומם? וייסט איהר אז אַרבּייטען מעהר פון 8
שמונדע אַ מאָן איז שעדליך פיר אייער נעזונד און פאר דער וואָלשעטינקיים פון דעם אַרבּייטער
קלאַס? בּעגרייפט איהר, אז אַזיי לאַנג איהר זיים נים אַרנאַנזירם קענם איהר נים ערוואַרמען
אז דער פרינציפּ פון קאָלעקטיווע מעטינגקיים זאָל בּריינגען פרייהיים און פערבּעסערונג אין אייער שאַפ.

✷ ⊛ אַ שאַפּ מיטינג ⊛ ✷

פון אלע אַרבּייטער פון דוש. מ. סוסקינד, וועט שטאַטפינדערען

מאַנטאַג, דעם 20טען אויגוסט, 6 אוהר אבֿענדס
אין סינאר מייקערס האָל, 232 נ. 9טע סטריט.

פערפעהלם נים צו קומען. לאָמיר זיך פעראיינינען וייל—איהר וויסם דאָך—אין אייינקיים ליענט מאַכט
דיא דזשאַינט קאָמיטע פון קלאָוק און סקוירט מייקערס יוניאן
אונד ד. ק. נו. 2, אַמאַלגעמייטעד קלאָדינג וואָרקערס אָף אַמעריקא

LAVORATORI!

Sono le paghe che ricevete sufficienti per vivere decentemente voi e la vostra famiglia?

Sapete che il lavorare piu di otto ore e' dannoso alla vostra salute e di ostacolo all' elevazione della classe lavoratrice? Avete mai pensato che se non siete organizzati voi non potete essere ne' liberi ne' indipendenti dentro la fabbrica?

UNA RIUNIONE

di tutti gli operai di J. M. Susskind sara tenuta

Lunedi 20 Agosto, alle 6 P. M. precise

al Cigar Makers Hall, 232 N. 9th St.

Venite tutti. Uniamoci. I lavoratori uniti sono invincibili.

IL COMITATO RIUNITO
della Cloak and Skirt Makers Union
e del D. C. No. 2, Amalgamated Clothing Workers of America

(Above) Club Madrid (formerly the Residence of Charlemagne Tower) at 1313 Locust Street, 1924 (HSP)

sures to keep order. Then came Prohibition. It was mocked and the law was broken widely. Social clubs, the quickly organized equivalents of London's gin mills in working class neighborhoods, and the ubiquitous speakeasies served good, bad, or almost lethal alcoholic beverages strictly in accordance with the patron's ability to pay. Everybody who was anybody and many nobodies besides had their own bootleggers. In an inconvenient fit of revulsion against lawlessness, Mayor Moore in 1924 brought in a Marine Corps general, Smedley D. Butler, as head of the police department to clean up the city. Butler was tough. After raids on socially and politically sensitive outlets for bootleg liquor, he was abruptly relieved of his office.

The war had been like a shot of adrenalin for Philadelphia. The city found that once again it could get things done. In spite of the brief postwar depression, the 1920s saw old projects brought to completion and new ones begun. The buildings on the Parkway, notably the Free Library and the Art Museum, as they rose gave the city an air of distinction. The Sesqui-Centennial Exposition in 1926 was to have underlined the urban revitalization. Unfortunately, civic leaders, businessmen, and politicians stumbled over each other's feet with unfortunate results. Nobody had much good to say about the resultant fair and celebration.

Philadelphia could shake off the disappointment. Of the large American cities it was still the most pleasant in which to live. Its industries were diversified and the boom of the later 1920s kept the factories humming. Oil refineries, coal transportation companies, the manufacturers of heavy machinery, textiles, pharmaceuticals, and, across the river in Camden, of victrolas and canned goods provided steady work for native-born and hyphenated Americans, most of whom discovered the American way and were absorbed into the culture of the majority. The teeming activity was a fertile ground for the burgeoning labor unions and a vital force in the process of Americanization. The melting-pot theory was in the ascendant; only the older generation sorrowed at the loss of old-world ways.

John G. Johnson, who had won the critical Northern Securities antitrust case in 1904, was the nation's most esteemed lawyer. He had also formed one of the most distinguished collections of Old Master paintings of his day. Somewhat later the irascible, eccentric Albert C. Barnes, having made a fortune from his sore-throat medicine argyrol, quietly gathered a sensational collection of works by the then-undiscovered artists of the School of Paris. A. S. W. Rosenbach was the unchallenged monarch of the rare-book world. In their own peculiar Philadelphia way, Christopher Morley, Agnes Repplier, and A. Edward Newton wrote of books and of the city and enjoyed a somewhat more than local fame for their essays. Strictly local was the *succès de scandale* of novels by young, socially prominent Francis Biddle and William C. Bullitt whose tales featured Philadelphia gentlemen and their lower-class loves. Far better known is Owen Wister's *The Virginian,* published in 1902, the first "Western" novel and an instant success. Dominating the literary scene was the Curtis Publishing Company founded by Cyrus H. K. Curtis. The first quarter of the twentieth century was the era of the *Saturday Evening Post* with its warmly sentimental Norman Rockwell covers and remarkable mix of short stories and articles so carefully chosen by the editor, George Horace Lorimer. The Curtis School of Music was founded by Curtis' daughter Mary Louise Curtis Bok, wife of Edward Bok, reform-minded editor of another Curtis magazine, the *Ladies' Home Journal.* Philadelphia was ready to face the world, confident that although it was not the richest, the largest, the noisiest, the busiest, the most exciting city in the world, it had something for everybody.

(Above) Sales Division of the Curtis Publishing Company, ca. 1920 (Curtis Publishing Company)

Boies Penrose, a descendant of early Philadelphia shipbuilders and merchants, with the help of the political boss Matthew S. Quay was elected United States senator from Pennsylvania over John Wanamaker in 1897. When Quay died in 1904, Penrose took over his organization and became the unquestioned, all-powerful leader of the Republican party in the state. Huge in size and equally disdainful of his social peers and hoi polloi, Penrose's appetite for power was equalled only by his appetite for wine, women, and steak and potatoes. Independently wealthy, he sought no graft for himself, but he was the friend and champion of the industrial tycoons of his era whom he served faithfully and well. He was elected and reelected to the Senate until his death in 1922. The Republican hegemony in Philadelphia during the first quarter of the twentieth century was in a large measure the product of his control of patronage and his forceful, arrogant, but usually effective leadership.

(Above) Boies Penrose, 1919 (HSP)

Boies Penrose Sr.

The Vare brothers, George A. (who died in 1908) and Edwin H., who were state senators, and Congressman William S., dominated Philadelphia politics for a generation. Brought up on a farm in "The Neck" where the family raised pigs, the Vares quickly learned how to have their cake and eat it too. The city paid them to collect garbage; their pigs grew fat. The paving of a street, turkeys grandiosely distributed at Christmas, the quashing of petty indictments, and the judicious distribution of franchises, contracts, and bond underwriting made devoted followers and influential friends. It was, however, the instinctive political sense that grass-roots support well organized was the base of power which made them perennially effective. The Vares expanded their own interests to street cleaning and ultimately contracting. "Hail, hail, the gang's all here" was sung in their honor as torchlight parades celebrated repeated election victories—aided by the dead who cast their votes in the Vare-controlled wards.

(Above) Edwin H. Vare, 1914 (HSP)

The watchwords of business and industry were merge, unify, monopolize, and control. In 1902 the Philadelphia Electric Company and the Philadelphia Rapid Transit Company successfully completed the financial, legal, and political measures which enabled them to operate citywide, integrated systems. Electricity, at first generated for its own lines by the transit company but later supplied by Philadelphia Electric, sparked the expansion of the trolley system. It was possible to get in a car at Sixteenth and Chestnut streets and ride, without changing, to Willow Grove, a suburban amusement park with sensational roller coasters and John Philip Sousa's band. Subways made travel quicker. In spite of some strikes, one in 1909 as violent as any the city had seen, it was a remarkably efficient network of tracks, tunnels, wires, and cars with fares, in 1926, at two tokens for 25 cents.

(Above) Generator Room of the Christian Street Station of the Philadelphia Electric Company, from *Electrical World*, LIII, 1909 (Philadelphia Electric Company)
(Below) Map of the Philadelphia Rapid Transit System, 1919 (HSP)

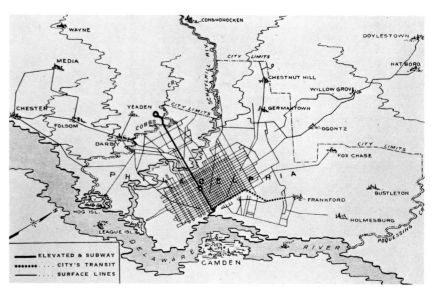

During the first decades of the twentieth century Philadelphia's streets were torn up as underground tunnels were constructed and overhead steel networks spun. A subway under Market Street was built to send surface cars across the Schuylkill for local stops and elevated trains in the middle of the street to the western limits of the city at Sixty-ninth Street. In the shadows of the elevated, neighborhoods deteriorated, for aesthetics were not a consideration, although political connections for contracts were. "Sunny Jim" McNichol of the City Hall gang got the contract. At the other end of Market Street another spider web of elevated tracks brought Frankford and the Northeast closer to hand. After World War I Broad Street became a ripple of planks as the subway was dug from City Hall to Olney Avenue in the north. The Keystone State Construction Company, of which Jerome H. Louchheim, a major contributor to the Republican Party, was head, won the contract for that, the longest underground trackage built in the city.

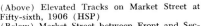

(Above) Elevated Tracks on Market Street at Fifty-sixth, 1906 (HSP)
(Below) Market Street between Front and Second during the Building of the Subway, 1907 (HSP)

By today's standards there were comparatively few vehicles on the streets paved with Belgian blocks, and it was only where the skyscrapers were rising that one saw a rushhour crowd of pedestrians. The generally calm flow of trolleys, putt-putting automobiles, and horse-drawn wagons was regulated by policemen who manually turned stop-and-go signs. Streets did get better. The tracks of the Reading Railroad which cut through residential areas at street level were raised to eliminate grade-crossings and to give vehicular access to the homes. The tollhouse on Bethlehem Pike in Chestnut Hill was done away with in 1904, but that on Old York Road at City Line (now Cheltenham Avenue) was still collecting tolls much later.

(Below) Traffic Policeman with Semaphore at Eleventh and Market Streets, 1924 (HSP)
(Above) Toll Station on York Road at City Line (now Cheltenham Avenue), ca. 1915 (HSP)
(Right) Tracks of the Reading Railroad between Brown and Parrish Streets, 1909 (HSP)

During the war thousands made enough money to consider buying houses, financed, to be sure, through the mushrooming savings and loan associations, with down payments and mortgages. People moved from shabby sections of the old city to areas where new homes, new industry, and easy transportation beckoned. One of the first such developments was in West Philadelphia along the elevated line to Sixty-ninth Street. Farm land was transformed into rows of houses, all, in the manner of the day, with front porches. John McClatchy, the first of the builder-developers to operate on a comprehensive scale, not only put up homes, but also created a commercial center at the Sixty-ninth Street terminal for the convenience of their owners. When Roosevelt Boulevard was pushed through and a Sears, Roebuck store built, a new community was created in that section. And later as the Broad Street subway crept north, Logan and Olney became shopping and residential neighborhoods.

(Above) Row Houses on Sixtieth Street North of Market, 1907 (HSP)
(Below) Advertisement for Houses in West Philadelphia, 1909 (HSP)

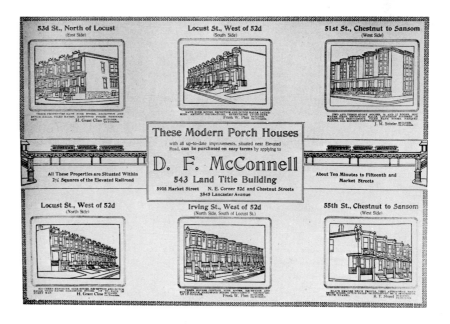

(Above) Joseph E. Widener's Lynnewood Hall in Elkins Park, ca. 1910 (HSP)

The old Philadelphians had estates in Chestnut Hill and the Main Line; the new money moved north to the Old York Road area just beyond the city limits. There the intertwined families of Widener, Elkins, Tyler, Sinkler, and Dixon settled luxuriously on vast holdings on both sides of Washington Lane. It may have been pique at his social rejection that moved Joseph E. Widener to have Horace Trumbauer build Lynnewood Hall, a mansion on the scale of Versailles. Space was provided for a gallery for one of the finest private collections of paintings in the country and a library which included a Gutenberg Bible. Across the road were stables and a full-size exercise track. Not far away Cyrus H. K. Curtis had his house, complete with concert hall and surrounded by a private golf course. John B. Stetson, the manufacturer of hats, had an estate close by on York Road, and farther north department-store Wanamakers and ice-cream Breyers had handsome establishments. It remained for the most influential financier of the era, Edward B. Stotesbury—urged by his wife, it was said, to provide a refuge for the Pope should the Germans take Rome—to erect during World War I another Trumbauer extravaganza, Whitemarsh Hall.

Although many of the leaders of society moved away from the city in the 1920s, backwaters of gentility remained. Walnut, Locust, and Spruce streets west of Sixteenth managed to retain their residential hauteur until the Depression of the 1930s. Rittenhouse Square, surrounded by elegant homes, was a green oasis which stabilized the neighborhood. Small streets seemed to flourish on their own. Clinton Street backed up to the Pennsylvania Hospital, Camac Street with its artistic and cultural clubs, and Delancey Place within the orbit of Rittenhouse Square were well-maintained, quiet, brick-faced byways. By 1924 Panama Street had been metamorphosed from run-down workmen's houses to stylish homes for the well-to-do, an early example of the reclaiming of the center city. Visitors to Philadelphia, notably Britishers, came, saw, and were impressed by the nostalgically English atmosphere of the tree-lined streets where the artistic and the properly descended lived in urban harmony.

(Below) *The Little Street of Clubs, Camac Street above Spruce*, lithograph by Joseph Pennell (HSP)
(Above and right) Panama Street, before 1920, and Panama Street, after 1924 (HSP)

All was not elegance and new homes.
The new Philadelphians, immigrants
from Italy, Poland, and Russia and
blacks from the South, lodged in old
houses lacking inside toilets, running
water, and all but the most primitive
heating equipment. Private sectarian
charities, relatives who had come
earlier and moved up and on, the
municipal Department of Welfare, and
a number of private housing agencies
tried to better their condition. The
Federation of Jewish Charities was
organized in 1901, and the citywide
Welfare Federation in 1920. If there
were too many people and too few
cheap but adequate dwellings, at least
in Philadelphia the tenements did not
rise up for many stories to block out
light and air. Ethnic neighborhoods,
moreover, provided the familiarity of
language and customs. Here, as in other
seaboard cities, a pushcart was the
easiest way to get a start in business.
The drive was to earn enough to
move out.

(Below) 322 Fitzwater Street (Housing Asso-
ciation Records, Urban Archives, Temple Uni-
versity)
(Above) Father and Son in Cellar Room on
Rodman Street between Reese and Randolph
in House owned by Lady Aberdare (Housing
Association Records, Urban Archives, Temple
University)
(Middle) Fourth Street South of Fitzwater, 1932
(copyright, National Geographic Society)
(Below, right) 724 Bainbridge Street (Housing
Association Records, Urban Archives, Temple
University)

With visions of the Champs Elysées in his head, civic leader Eli Kirk Price II worked through, around, and above municipal authorities to create a Parkway which would be lined with monumental buildings and would bring the green of Fairmount Park into the heart of the city. This idea had been projected as early as 1902, but languished until political palms were duly crossed with the silver of advantageous purchases, so that the slashing boulevard could go through. Finally, in 1917, the imaginative concept of Jacques Auguste Henri Gréber came into being. The Free Library's main branch on the north side of the Parkway at Nineteenth Street, a replica of the Chateau Crillon in Paris and designed by Horace Trumbauer, was finished in 1927. It replaced a building at Thirteenth and Locust streets, once the home of the College of Physicians, that had grown too small to serve as the headquarters of a library complex which by the end of the first quarter of the century was circulating over 4,000,000 books. Twenty-three branch libraries had been added to the system through Andrew Carnegie's $1,500,000 gift. The imposing temple of the Art Museum rose on the site of the old reservoir at the top of Fairmount to close the vista at the Park end of the new Parkway. A "Greek garage" some artistic snobs called it, and for quite a while there was an amplitude of echoing space in the galleries. The Vares, paid for excavating the site, in true political fashion sold the city the stone they had removed.

(Above) The Parkway looking West, 1924 (HSP)
(Middle) Art Museum at Fairmount under Construction, ca. 1922 (Aero Service Division, Western Geophysical Company of America)
(Below) Free Library of Philadelphia on Logan Circle, 1931 (Free Library of Philadelphia)

In 1912 wavy-haired Leopold Stokowski, with an acquired but unquestionably romantic accent, was appointed conductor of the twelve-year-old Philadelphia Orchestra. He was a superb musician and a great showman. Guided by the motions of his expressive fingers the orchestra was cajoled and disciplined until it became one of the finest in the world. "Stoky's" aggressiveness produced the first American performance of Mahler's gargantuan Eighth Symphony, his boldness played Edgar Varese's modern compositions, and his charm delighted a generation of children with their own concerts. The orchestra played what he wanted it to play, and he persuaded the city's musical patrons that what he wanted was good for both the performers and the audience. Until he resigned in 1934, Stokowski kept the local musical world in a titillating balance between shock and delight.

(Above) Leopold Stokowski, photograph by Adrian Siegel, 1937 (Adrian Siegel)
(Below) The Performance of Mahler's Eighth Symphony by the Philadelphia Orchestra, March 2, 1916, photogravure (Free Library of Philadelphia)

Philadelphia Chippendale chairs, Syng silver, and portraits by Peale and Sully were not the stock-in-trade of the Old Curiosity Shop, a pioneer antique store on Pine Street in the first decade of the century. The primitive wares displayed then have become the treasures of American folk art. One wonders what was the price of the cigar-store Indian, for example, or the cast-iron settee or the weather vanes. Rows of antique shops now line Pine Street where one can buy an eighteenth-century chest of drawers or vintage souvenirs of the Sesqui-Centennial.

(Above) The Old Curiosity Shop, 1237 Pine Street, ca. 1910 (HSP)

The center of the city moved west
with City Hall. Banks and trust
companies, hotels, lawyers and businessmen, all it would seem but insurance companies, joined forces to
form a new business district with its
hub at Broad and Chestnut streets. The
Land Title Building, the North American Building, and the Real Estate
Trust Building framed the new Rialto
with skyscrapers. The elegant Dundas-
Lippincott house at the northeast
corner of Broad and Walnut streets
was torn down, and in 1905 the entrepreneur Felix Isman erected there a
number of temporary rentables, years
later to be replaced by the Fidelity
Bank's building. Although high-rise
buildings were generally favored for
permanent development, the conservative Girard Trust put up a distinctive
Pantheon-like temple of banking by
way of contrast. Two small hotels at
Broad and Walnut streets by merger
became the prestigious Bellevue-
Stratford. Its chief competitor, the
Ritz-Carlton, settled down across the
street. Theaters and restaurants replaced private homes. The high
buildings brought more bustle and
more workers to the area, but drovers
were able to walk their meat-on-the-
hoof down Broad Street to the South
Philadelphia abattoirs for some time
to come without seriously impeding
traffic.

(Below) *Girard Trust Company*, lithograph by
Joseph Pennell (HSP)
(Above) Broad Street with the Ritz-Carlton
Hotel at Walnut Street, ca. 1920 (HSP)
(Right) Broad Street looking North from Locust,
1905 (HSP)

Much of the commercial activity of the city took place on or near lower Market Street. Here, on the fringes of the high-rising buildings to the west, the streets retained their modest scale. Private homes had been remodeled or replaced with new structures of similar proportions. No lighted signs blazed forth, but advertisements painted on walls and a multitude of hanging signs blatantly proclaimed the shopkeepers' business. The three gold balls of pawn shops were common sights. A modest A. & P. grocery store even then offered S. & H. stamps, while Riggs' optical house boasted its life-size figure of a mariner with his sextant. In those prewar days "slightly used" automobiles could be bought for $150 where the 1782 president of Congress, Elias Boudinot, once lived and suits next door for $11.80. Nothing could have been more dramatic than a clothing company's exterior display or more varied than the firms doing business cheek by jowl with one another. The finest ice cream made anywhere, Bassett's, was sold near Fifth and Market streets. It was fun to walk the streets. Street lights were few in the Lower Market Street area, as in the other parts of the city, and at first they were arc lamps which incandescent bulbs gradually replaced after 1923.

(Below) Market Street between Third and Fourth, 1905 (HSP)
(Above) Southeast Corner of Ninth and Arch Streets, 1913 (HSP)
(Right) Southwest Corner of Fifth and Market Streets, ca. 1905 (HSP)

The change in the appearance of the city during the first quarter of the twentieth century would not be matched until after World War II. Although John Wanamaker rebuilt his department store across from City Hall to make it one of the largest and finest in the nation, lower Market Street was almost unchanged. The strong amalgam of cast-iron and ornamental masonry fronts of the other major department stores, Lit's, Strawbridge and Clothier's, and Gimbel's, was altered at the street level as new show windows were inserted but remained above— to the delight of sky-gazers. If Broad and Chestnut streets was the center of the banking community after 1900, Eighth and Market streets played a parallel role in merchandising. The magnetic appeal to shoppers was reinforced in the 1920s when both Strawbridge and Clothier's and Gimbel's built large additions to their stores.

(Above) Market Street looking East from Juniper Street with Wanamaker's New Store, 1907 (HSP)
(Below, and facing) Lit Brothers' Store on Market Street at Eighth, 1905 (HSP)
(Facing, above) Strawbridge & Clothier's Store on Market Street at Eighth, ca. 1910 (HSP)

Every era had its public spectacles.
The Mummers who had marched for
years along secondary streets inaugurated their annual Broad Street
spectacular in 1901. The capes, the
comics, the female impersonators, and
the string bands grew more elaborate
and more numerous each year as
"Oh, dem Golden Slippers" became the
Philadelphia song. The city also
erected fancy pillars and arches for
special occasions and conventions.
Independence Hall was graced with
columns to welcome home the Keystone (28th) Division from the Argonne
and Chateau Thierry at the end of the
war. When the Moose came to town in
1927 the city fathers, anticipating the
modernists of the Art Museum, painted
a welcome mat leading to Jack Lynch's
Walton Roof Garden where girls
shimmied and bootleg liquor flowed.

(Above) The Mummers' New Year's Day Parade,
Public Ledger, January 14, 1912 (HSP)
(Below) Decorations for a Moose Convention at
Broad and Locust Streets, 1927 (HSP)

The city was sport rich and sport
happy in the early decades of the century. Before World War I Connie Mack
managed the Athletics to World Series
victories in 1910, 1911, and 1913.
Pitchers Rube Waddell and Chief Ben-
der, "Home Run" Baker, and the greatest second baseman of all time, Eddie
Collins, were among his outstanding
players. To handle the enthusiastic
fans a new field, Shibe Park, was built
at Twenty-second Street and Lehigh
Avenue. The National League Phillies,
with the great pitcher Grover Alexander and slugger Sherry Magee, won
a league pennant in 1915. "Philadelphia Jack" O'Brien dominated the light-
heavyweight division of boxing for
seven years and in the late 1920s handsome, gentlemanly Tommy Loughran,
a local favorite, took over the title.
Benny Leonard, technically the finest
of the city's boxers and one of the great
tacticians of the ring, was the light-
weight champion of the world. The all-
Philadelphia bout in 1923 between
Leonard and challenger Lew Tendler
was a classic encounter. It could not,
however, match the excitement when
the underdog Gene Tunney beat Jack
Dempsey in the then-new Municipal
(now Kennedy) Stadium on September 23, 1926, in a steady rain before
120,000 fans. William T. "Big Bill"
Tilden held the national singles tennis championship from 1920 to 1925
and regained it in 1929. With Vincent
Richards, another local player and
survivor of the Titanic, R. Norris Williams, 2nd, won the doubles in 1925
and 1926. It remained for a woman to
put Philadelphia in the limelight on
the golf course. Glenna Collett (later
Mrs. Edwin H. Vare) won the national
woman's championship in 1922 and
four more times thereafter.

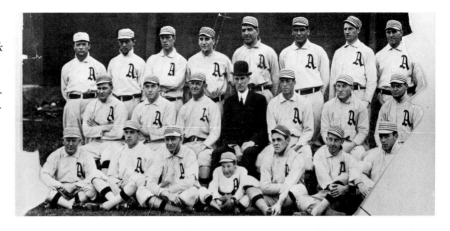

(Above) Athletics 1911 World Champions
(Philadelphia Inquirer)
(Middle) Tilden Playing in the Davis Cup,
September 3, 1921, photograph by Bains News
Service (HSP)
(Below, left) Dempsey–Tunney Fight, *Public
Ledger*, September 24, 1926 (Free Library of
Philadelphia)
(Below, right) Glenna Collett (later Vare),
1927 (HSP)

The first crude motion picture on flexible film was shown at Keith's Bijou on North Eighth Street as early as 1895, but the real pioneer of the cinema in Philadelphia was Sigmund Lubin. Lubin first set up a primitive studio at 916 Arch Street, but soon established enlarged indoor facilities at Twentieth and Indiana Avenue. By 1915 Lubin's film company, also with outdoor studios at a former beer baron's estate at Betzwood, near Valley Forge, was one of the largest in the country. Jules Mastbaum in 1905 opened a nickelodeon at the corner of Eighth and Market streets to show motion pictures. Later, in partnership with his brother Stanley, he created the largest local chain of movie theaters, the Stanley Company of America, eventually taken over by the Hollywood giant, Warner Brothers.

(Above) Lubin's Studio at Twentieth and Indiana Avenue, photogravure from J. Berg Esenwein and Arthur Leeds, *Writing the Photoplay,* 1913 (Wallace E. Davies)
(Below, left) The Lubin Motion Picture Theatre, 923 Market Street, 1908 (HSP)
(Below, right) Advertisement of the Stanley Company, *Public Ledger,* October 15, 1922 (Free Library of Philadelphia)

The theater flourished in the first quarter of the twentieth century. On the eve of the Sesqui-Centennial there were over fifty theaters and 164 movie houses in Philadelphia. The Arch Street Theatre, long managed by Mrs. John Drew, had become the home of a colorful Yiddish stage. But memories of the town's great theatrical family were revived when her son John came to play at the Broad Street Theater, and later with appearances of her Philadelphia-born grandchildren, Ethel, Lionel, and John Barrymore. With the Adelphi and Lyric on North Broad Street and the Forrest and Schubert on South Broad Street, the Schuberts were the chief theatrical impresarios. Vaudeville with its varied fare of acrobats, slapstick comedians, trained animals, and jugglers was still popular, particularly at neighborhood theaters. When the master magicians Houdini or Thurston came to town, performances were sold out; and popular singer Harry Lauder's "It's a wee doch an' doris" brought down the house. Philadelphians never forgot that performers as unlike one another as W. C. Fields, Jeanette Macdonald, and Nelson Eddy had roots here.

(Above) Broad Street Theatre on South Broad Street, at Time of Benefit for the Kishinev Sufferers, 1903 (HSP)
(Below, left) Advertisement for John Drew at the Broad Street Theatre, January, 1907 (HSP)
(Below, right) Advertisement for Ethel Barrymore at Keith's Theatre, July, 1921 (HSP)

Broad Street Theatre
NEXT ATTRACTION—2 Weeks
BEGINNING JANUARY 21st
CHARLES FROHMAN PRESENTS
JOHN DREW

JOHN DREW
IN A. W. PINERO'S GREATEST SUCCESS
HIS HOUSE IN ORDER

B.F. **Keith's Theatre**
POCKET GUIDE FOR
COMING ATTRACTIONS

ETHEL BARRYMORE
America's Greatest Dramatic Star Here Next Week in
Sir J. M. Barrie's "The Twelve Pound Look"

AN ENGAGEMENT EXTRAORDINARY
So closely allied have become the tributaries of the theatre that the greatest stars of the stage step from the legitimate to the two-a-day and back again and vaudeville enjoys the same prestige and dignity as dramatic and operatic stages. The engagement of Ethel Barrymore for the week of July 18th at B. F. Keith's Theatre comes as the most important announcement of several seasons. Miss Barrymore is generally conceded to be America's greatest dramatic star. She is known, admired and loved wherever there is a theatre. For her short return to vaudeville she will present Sir J. M. Barrie's one-act play, "The Twelve Pound ($60) Look," supported by a selected cast, by special arrangement with Charles Frohman, Inc.

The waging of war required men, munitions, and money. Sympathy for the Allies, which had induced some Philadelphians to volunteer to beat the Kaiser even before war was declared, turned into an outpouring of fervor in April, 1917. The city's great factories and mills, such as Baldwin Locomotive Works and Midvale Steel, turned out cannon, naval guns, shells, and armor plate. The Navy Yard, Hog Island Shipyard, and Cramp's Shipyard launched warships of all sizes in prodigious numbers and built merchantmen to replace vessels lost to the German U-boats. In one month alone, April, 1918, the Navy placed half a billion dollars worth of orders for 382 ships in the Delaware River yards. The Frankford and Schuylkill arsenals were busy night and day producing guns and bullets for the use of the Army's "doughboys." In a very real sense the great industrial potential of the city was mobilized to make it, as it proclaimed itself to be, the "Arsenal of Democracy." The financial might of Philadelphia, too, was organized behind the leadership that insured success for the Liberty Loan drives. But if the war's excitement churned in factories, banks, and streets, peace brought an even more enthusiastic response. Happy crowds erupted everywhere on November 11th in anticipation of the time their boys would come marching home.

Philadelphia, although more fortunate than some other cities in matters of public health, had known yellow fever in 1793, cholera in 1832, and in the autumn of 1918 influenza. The first death from the 'flu was recorded in the city on September 18th. Within a week 1,400 cases were being reported daily and within two weeks over 4,000. Death claimed fifteen percent of those infected. Schools, churches, theaters, and all other places of congregation were closed. Mass funerals and mass burials at Second and Luzerne streets had to be organized to handle the shocking number of corpses. No medicine, no vaccine offered Philadelphians prospect of immunity; indeed the advice of Dr. David Riesman, one of the city's leading physicians, to drink as much whiskey as one could hold and stay home was not only the most pleasurable but also the most sensible prescription available.

(Facing, below) *In the Dry Dock*, lithograph by Joseph Pennell (HSP)
(Facing, above) Women Workers Camouflaging Wire Reels at the Brill Company, ca. 1918 (HSP)
(Facing, right) Armistice Day Crowd on South Penn Square, 1918 (HSP)
(Above) The Influenza Epidemic, *Public Ledger*, October 3-5, 1918 (Free Library of Philadelphia)
(Below) Taking 'Flu Victim into Hospital (Evening and Sunday *Bulletin*)

EPIDEMIC GROWS, DEATHS INCREASE, AS CITY ENFORCES CLOSING ORDERS

Krusen Stops All Sales and Deliveries by Liquor Dealers

City Health Board Prohibits All Sale or Delivery of Liquor

SOUTH PHILADELPHIA SECTION CLEANED BY VARE SHOWS HEAVIEST MORTALITY RATE IN THE CITY

Fourth of Whole Number in Area Where He Holds Contracts

RESIDENTS, DESPERATE, WILL APPEAL TO COURT

Eminent Italian Artist Enters Lists in Behalf of Countrymen

More than one-fourth of the 3234 deaths which occurred in Philadelphia for the week ending at noon yesterday were in the Third street-cleaning district, or that section of the city south of South street, between the Delaware and Schuylkill Rivers, for which State Senator Edwin H. Vare holds the contract.

Of the unprecedented toll of deaths, more than 80 per cent were due to epidemic influenza and resulting pneumonia, the wide and rapid spread of which, a score or more of the city's most prominent physicians and authorities on public health and sanitation have unqualifiedly declared, was largely due to the atmospheric circulation, of germ-laden dirt and filth that remained in the public highways. Particularly, said the foremost of them, did that condition prevail in the sections where Senator Vare held the lucrative contracts.

Eight hundred and eighteen deaths! In the nine wards below South street in one week have drawn, the deadly parallel between the disinterested statements of medical authorities and the denial of dirty streets by Senator Vare and the attempted backing up of that denial by Chief Hicks, of the Street Cleaning Bureau, whose sop to public opinion was a fine upon Vare of $645, a penalty so trivial as to cause a laugh throughout City Hall, where real conditions are known.

It required the authority and the action of Director Krusen, of the Department of Public Health and Charities, to force a clean-up of the streets by flushing, and the rather enigmatical statement made then by Senator Vare, that the streets were no dirtier than they always had been, stands in further contrast, in view of the indictment brought by disinterested medical authorities, with the fact that the largest number of deaths in any one ward in the city occurred in the Thirty-ninth, where Senator Vare

GIRL PLUCKILY ROUTS WRECKER GANG ON P. R. R.

Uniontown Operator Sets Signal as Bullets Graze Body

Special Telegram to Public Ledger

Uniontown, Pa., Oct. 12.—Barricading herself in the "HY" tower of the Pennsylvania Railroad at Gist passing, near here, after she had discovered and fired upon would-be train wreckers, Miss E. M. Vensel, tower operator, pluckily held her post. Despite a heavy revolver attack, she kept the gang at bay until the arrival of a freight train, the crew of which put the attackers to rout.

Tht young woman's pluck prevented the wrecking of at least one

By a Public Ledger Staff Photographer

The upper picture shows one of the streets in South Philadelphia where

Philadelphia's Sesqui-Centennial in 1926 was not a great success. The idea of celebrating the nation's 150th birthday was suggested by John Wanamaker in 1916. Plans were proposed, abandoned, revived, and eventually it was agreed to center an international fair on the muddy flats at the extreme southern end of the city, a site foisted upon Philadelphia by the Vares and Albert M. Greenfield for business and political reasons. Because his fellow Shriners were coming to town on that day, Mayor Kendrick insisted that the grand opening take place on May 31st. Many buildings were not yet finished and most had skimpy, if any, exhibits; all but the main throughways remained unpaved and were seas of mud when it rained. The Shriners were not impressed and poor reports from visitors held paid admissions to 6,408,829, representing fewer persons than had come to the Centennial. Only the colonial village erected and managed by the Women's Committee was outstandingly successful. The huge deficit was paid at Greenfield's urging from the city treasury. There was one surviving asset, the dramatic Delaware River Bridge, a masterpiece of the engineer Ralph Modjeski, and one white elephant, the Municipal Stadium, now used for the annual Army–Navy game and seldom otherwise.

(Above) Main Gate of the Sesqui-Centennial on Opening Day, 1926 (HSP)
(Facing, above) High Street in the Colonial Village at the Sesqui-Centennial Exhibition, 1926 (HSP)
(Facing, below) The Delaware River (now Benjamin Franklin) Bridge in the Course of Construction, 1925 (HSP)

UNEMPLOYED BUY APPLES 5¢ EACH

UNEMPLOYED BUY APPLES 5¢ EACH

UNEMPLOYED BUY APPLES 5¢ EACH

UNEMPLOYED BUY APPLES 5¢ EACH

UNEMPLOYED BUY APP

UNEMPLOYED BUY APPLES 5¢ EACH

1930-1945

The depression, the emergence of the Democratic Party, and World War II effectually changed the pattern of the city's ways. On the eve of the Wall street crash of 1929, Philadelphia banking and industry were tightly in the hands of men of old families by birth or by acceptance. Big businesses gradually ceased to be dominated by autocrats and came into the hands of corporate managers. Horace P. Liversidge was Philadelphia Electric; his successors were merely presidents of the company. Effingham B. Morris was Girard Trust and Joseph Wayne, Jr., Philadelphia National; those who followed them were but successful and competent employees. Instead of the man giving luster to the institution, it was the corporation which gave position to the man.

Nowhere was the change more clearly seen than in the legal profession, long the pride of Philadelphia and the reservoir whence many of its leaders came. Whereas George Wharton Pepper was recognized as the dean of the bar, Morris Wolf as the force behind the fastest growing office, and Robert T. McCracken as the most influential lawyer in town, it was firms made up of galaxies of specialists which emerged as important. As the period drew to a close no Morgan, Lewis, or Bockius was renowned as an individual, but the firm was the biggest, richest, and most active in the city.

As its light gray exterior was turned black by industrial soot, charges of graft, bribery, dishonesty, and malfeasance in office darkened City Hall and its Republican hangers-on. Significantly the building was cleaned by WPA help. In December, 1929, the United States Senate voted to exclude William S. Vare from membership for having spent excessively in winning the 1926 primary, but not for having cheated in the general election of that year. He had defeated Senator George Wharton Pepper and Governor Gifford Pinchot for the Republican nomination. It was reported that Pepper spent $1,800,000—chiefly from Mellon and Grundy interests—and Vare just under $800,-000—chiefly from contractors, real-estate developers, and office-holders. His customary efficiency in getting out the city vote won Boss Vare the election over Democratic William B. Wilson who carried the rest of the state. The validity of the election was challenged, and after years of investigation the Senate handed down its verdict. Bill Vare, broken physically and psychologically, had the reins of power wrenched from his hands.

(Facing) Broad Street looking North to City Hall during the Republican National Convention, 1940 (HSP)

The collapse of the Vares' unbridled political control opened the way for other men to succeed them. At almost the same time, the disenchantment nationally with the whistling-in-the-dark policies of Herbert Hoover and the smashing victory of Franklin D. Roosevelt in 1932 undermined the Republicans' ability to win every local election. It took some time for the Democrats to build a viable organization. The chairman of the city committee, John O'Donnell, had been little more than a very junior partner of the Vares. In 1934 on the wave of Roosevelt's popularity, John B. Kelly was elected in place of O'Donnell. The year before the Democrats had won all four municipal row offices and ten magistracies; in 1935 they carried the city for the first Democratic governor in forty-four years, wealthy, socially prominent George H. Earle, and their first senator since 1875, Joseph F. Guffey.

The change was neither complete nor permanent. Old habits were hard to change. Philadelphians continued to elect Republican mayors in spite of the widespread belief that, if not the men themselves, their supporters and underlings were corrupt. J. Hampton Moore was chosen for the second time in 1931, the erratic S. Davis Wilson in 1935, and Judge Robert E. Lamberton, a regular, in 1939. In May, 1938, a grand jury recommended the dismissal of a police inspector, a captain, and forty-seven policemen; in August a special grand jury charged conspiracy between gamblers, city officials, and police; and that same month another jury indicted Mayor Wilson for misbehavior in office. Nothing came of the charges. When Mayor Lamberton died in the summer of 1941, the president of the City Council, Bernard Samuel, was sworn in as acting mayor.

Roller-coaster election swings matched the weather in 1943. A chilling 3° on February 15th set a record for that day; it was a record 79° on March 31st, but 27° on April 15th. May was the wettest in ten years and June the hottest in eighteen years. The temperature dropped to 52° on July 1st. That year Samuel, a well-trained South Philadelphia politician, was elected mayor over the well-born New Dealer William C. Bullitt. A year later Philadelphia went Democratic to give Roosevelt a substantial majority and put Francis J. Myers in the Senate. The party took all six city congressional seats. In 1946 Samuel, who was permitted to succeed himself under a state bill pushed through in 1945, carried the city, trouncing Richardson Dilworth in his political debut. Patronage from the Federal government was balanced by that

(Above) William S. Vare Surrounded by Supporters at the End of his Career, 1930 (Philadelphia Inquirer)

of city and state, which returned to its Republican ways. Philadelphia had become politically schizophrenic.

Its status as a swing city was recognized by all the parties which chose Philadelphia as the site of their national conventions. In 1936 Roosevelt was nominated there. Four years later the Republicans came to town to choose their nominee, and it was the "We Want Willkie" chant of the galleries which persuaded the delegates to opt for Wendell Willkie. So hospitable was the city that in 1948 three national conventions were held in Philadelphia. The Republicans decided to put up Thomas E. Dewey in June; the Democrats were enthusiastic about Harry S. Truman in July; and at Shibe Park the left-leaning Progressive Party a week later entered Henry Wallace in the presidential race.

There was a feeling of optimism in the air. In the prewar period a survey showed that Philadelphia led the nation in petroleum refining, with tanks and the intricate lacework of the pipes and towers extending from the lower Schuylkill down the river to Marcus Hook where in August, 1943, the Big Inch pipeline finally arrived at tidewater. The city was also the largest producer of knit goods, refined sugar, cigars, carpets and rugs, cardboard products, dental supplies, streamlined trains, and autogiros. Once again when war came, Philadelphia's industries were ready and able to make what was needed. *Fortune*, writing in 1936, stated that its spendable annual income of $1,641,-000,000, of which $600,000,000 was plowed back locally, was larger than that of all but nine states.

As during World War I, there was an influx of blacks from the South attracted by the wartime labor shortage and consequent high wages. The population which had remained settled and stable in the depression years began to move again. From the fringes of the center city and cheap row housing first- and second-generation immigrants pushed farther away toward the suburbs and Negroes took over the expanding slum districts. At the same time a rising black middle class began to occupy handsome houses along Lincoln Drive and other parts of Germantown where already a substantial Negro community had developed in the poorer sections northeast of Germantown and Chelten avenues. Italian families started migrating farther and farther south and west from their earliest places of residence. In the new housing constructed by Erny and Nolen in West Oak Lane Irish Cath-

(Above) J. Hampton Moore being Sworn in as Mayor, 1932 (HSP)

olics first moved in. The old areas of settlement in West Philadelphia and Strawberry Mansion were abandoned to the growing need of blacks for housing as Oxford Circle became a new center of the Jewish population. The displacement of one group by another was a continuing process.

Meanwhile luxury apartment-house living, comparatively rare in Philadelphia, was adopted as a life-style by increasing numbers. City apartment buildings on Rittenhouse Square were the tentative beginnings of a trend given impetus when the large 2601 Parkway apartments were erected at the edge of Fairmount Park. The Alden Park complex near Wissahickon in Germantown had been a pioneering venture in bringing city-style living to a country atmosphere and the even larger Green Hill Farms across City Line at Lancaster Pike was the harbinger of more and bigger to come.

The move out to the suburbs was bringing the growth of the city population to an end; it was a shift which was to accelerate after World War II. The war itself, in spite of the rationing of gas, oil, and some foods, in spite of the dislocations caused by the absence of servicemen, was, as earlier wars had been, a unifying force. Some old prejudices were broken down. Catholics, Jews, and Protestants were able to come together to form the USO (United Services Organization). Men and women from all sections of the city and from all economic classes volunteered as air-raid wardens and auxiliary firemen and policemen. With the end of the war there was a feeling that the city could be made a better place. The homecoming veterans were determined that it would be.

(Facing) Wendell Willkie on Podium of Republican National Convention in June, 1940 (HSP)

The depression hurt Philadelphia less than it did most sections of the country; no one industry dominated its economy. But nonetheless the depression hurt. A committee for unemployment relief was set up under the chairmanship of Horatio G. Lloyd. Money was raised in a special campaign and a soup kitchen and dormitory opened for the homeless and jobless in the unused Baldwin Locomotive Works at Broad and Spring Garden streets. With a gallantry which reflected the concern of men like Cyrus H. K. Curtis who had wealth and were willing to give—Curtis' contribution was $300,000—the newly organized United Campaign, including the earlier separate Welfare Federation, Federation of Jewish Charities, and Lloyd Relief Committee drives, tried to stem the flow of misery which mass unemployment created. In the autumn of 1931 the citywide charity campaign raised $10,258,000, topping its goal by over a million dollars. It was the boy with his finger in the dike. Private philanthropy, even stimulated by the fear of revolution, could not contain the flood of poverty. It took state-financed welfare relief in massive amounts and the Roosevelt emergency programs, such as the WPA (Works Progress Administration), to provide the basic needed help. Apple-sellers were a common sight on the corners of busy intersections during the early 1930s.

(Above) Dormitory for Homeless Men in the Baldwin Locomotive Works at Eighteenth and Hamilton Streets, 1930 (Philadelphia Inquirer)
(Middle) WPA Writers Working on the *Philadelphia Guide*, 1937 (HSP)
(Below) Unemployed Receiving Boxes of Apples, photogravure (Free Library of Philadelphia)

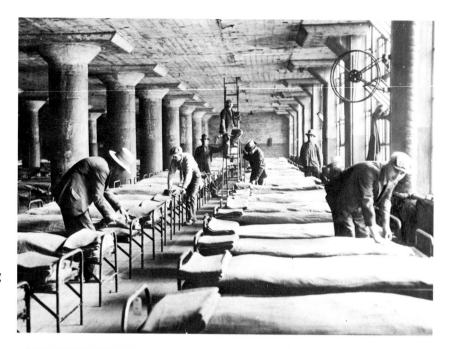

It all began in September, 1930, within the framework of the nation's financial crisis, when some people started worrying about the stability of Albert M. Greenfield's recently expanded Bankers' Trust Company. Depositors began a run on the bank. At first Joseph Wayne, Jr., of the Philadelphia National Bank and C. Stevenson Newhall of the Pennsylvania Company on behalf of the Clearing House tried to stem the tide with loans. Pressure in the form of withdrawals continued. The bankers decided they could offer no more support; just three days before Christmas the Bankers' Trust closed its doors. Greenfield was hurt financially but was far from ruined; his comeback was spectacular, his memory of the jettisoning ever green. Thereafter one other large bank, the Franklin Trust, went under and scores of small ones. The personality and determination of Wayne was the critical force in preventing more damage when every rumor started a run. President Roosevelt declared a bank holiday on March 4, 1933. For days there was no money, only scrip.

(Above) Run on the Erie National Bank, Sixth Street and Erie Avenue, 1931 (HSP)
(Below) Notebook of Herbert E. Amidon, Assistant Manager of the Philadelphia Clearing House Association (HSP)

Ideas and buildings, conceived in
the king-size bed of the boom, were
born on the bare floor of the depression.
In Robin Hood Dell, an outdoor concert amphitheater in Fairmount Park,
the annual free summer program for
music-lovers was begun just before the
bubble burst. The Rodin Museum, a
grace note on the Parkway bequeathed
to the city by Jules Mastbaum, was
dedicated just over a month after the
crash. And in sad and dreary 1931 the
city threw open the doors of its huge
Convention Hall, designed to bring—
and it did—gatherings, games, and
gawkers. The major architectural addition to the city was, however, the
striking, stark, glass-ribboned Philadelphia Saving Fund Society's building
at Twelfth and Market streets where
the William Penn Charter School had
stood. Designed by George Howe and
William Lescaze, it was praised by a
critic at the time as "the best multistory structure in America." It was
completed in the summer of 1932.

(Below) Philadelphia Saving Fund Society Building (Philadelphia Inquirer)
(Above) Robin Hood Dell (Philadelphia Inquirer)
(Middle) *The Rodin Museum*, pen-and-ink
drawing by Paul Cret and Jacques Gréber (HSP)
(Right) Convention Hall, 1945 (HSP)

Cornelius McGillicuddy provided good cheer in the years cheer was hard to come by. Better known as Connie Mack, he steered the Athletics, better known as the A's, to three successive World Championships in 1929, 1930, and 1931. The team was unbeatable with such great players as fast-ball pitcher Lefty Grove, knuckle-ball pitcher Eddie Rommel, the slugger Jimmy Foxx, a fine defensive infield, and a hard-hitting outfield. Basketball was kept alive and developed into a sport which would flower by Eddie Gottlieb's South Philadelphia Hebrew Association team, better known as the Spha's. It was only with the arrival of Steve Van Buren, the Eagles' finest running back, that professional football began attracting large crowds and citywide attention. When Penn played Franklin Field was filled with flask-toting enthusiasts; 80,000 came to see the Penn–Notre Dame game in 1932. From Penn came Barney Berlinger, a stalwart track star, who went on to represent the United States in the Olympics.

(Above) Connie Mack and Jimmy Foxx, 1935 (HSP)
(Below, left) "Lefty" Grove, 1931 (HSP)
(Below, right) Steve Van Buren (Philadelphia Inquirer)

Federal money for building started flowing into the city with the advent of the New Deal. Very shortly after the election of 1932 the contract for a new Custom House was awarded to McCloskey & Company. In two years it was completed. The huge structure at Second and Chestnut streets, which architecturally overpowered the historic area, housed many governmental agencies from the Cavalry Reserve to the National Labor Board. Paul Cret's handsome Federal Reserve Bank at Tenth and Chestnut streets rose at the same time. By 1935 the Post Office was completed to balance the new Thirtieth Street Station of the Pennsylvania Railroad; it was dedicated by Postmaster General Jim Farley. The most significant government contribution was, however, Public Works Administration Housing Project No. 1, the Carl Mackley Homes, at M and Bristol streets near Juniata Park, designed by Oskar Stonorov and built for hosiery workers—Mackley was killed in a strike—in 1933-34. Another complex of homes at Tasker Avenue followed.

(Below) The New Custom House at Second and Chestnut Streets, 1934 (HSP)
(Above) The Philadelphia Post Office, 1939 (Philadelphia Inquirer)
(Right) The Carl Mackley Homes (Philadelphia Inquirer)

Somebody had to be boss of the underworld when "Godfather" meant only the sponsor of an infant. In Philadelphia during the wide-open days of prohibition it was Max "Boo Boo" Hoff. He was the king of bootleggers, the biggest purveyor of illegal liquor, which was a very lucrative business indeed. He was well-known to some of the best people, who depended on him for "the real, imported stuff." To be sure, Hoff had sidelines in gambling and girls. After him the Lanzetti brothers held sway. At the end of February, 1931, the Philadelphia Club was subjected to a liquor raid. Although Philadelphia figured in stock jokes as the place where they rolled up the sidewalks on weekends, every neighborhood had its speakeasy. Elegant brownstone houses along once-fine residential streets in the center of town masked heady wine, women, and song. Bookies swarmed like industrious ants on Broad Street between Walnut and Locust, and numbers writers operated citywide.

(Below) Max "Boo Boo" Hoff Leaving the Federal Court Building, 1934 (HSP)
(Above) Police Burning Gambling Devices after Raids, 1929 (HSP)
(Middle) The Lanzetti Brothers in Court, 1933 (HSP)
(Below, right) The End of Prohibition, *Philadelphia Inquirer*, December 6, 1933 (Philadelphia Inquirer)

The Philadelphia Inquirer — LATE CITY EDITION

PROHIBITION'S 14-YEAR RULE ENDED; PRICES HIGH, SUPPLY LOW IN PHILA.

CITY 'DEAD,' REAL STUFF HARD TO GET

Liquor at $75 a Case, $6 a Pint and 50 Cents a Drink Scare off Patrons; Speaks Do Usual Business; Gin, Wines Plentiful, But Not in Great Demand

By JOHN M. McCULLOUGH

MERRILY WE TOSS 'EM DOWN, TOSS 'EM DOWN

ROOSEVELT ASKS U. S. TO GUARD LAW

President's Proclamation Declaring Repeal of 18th Amendment Calls on Nation to Cherish New Freedom; Utah's Ratification, as 36th State, Sounds Knell of Dry Era

It was a great day for the Irish, other
Democrats, and the overwhelming
majority of voters. The Union League
and the Rittenhouse and Philadelphia
clubs went into mourning or catalepsy.
Franklin Delano Roosevelt carried
the city big in November, 1936. He
had been nominated by acclaim in
the city's new Convention Hall a few
months earlier. As the old Republican
municipal façade shattered, handsome
Olympic oarsman and brick tycoon
John B. Kelly, the Democratic City
Chairman, emerged as a power to be
reckoned with. At his side was Matthew
B. McCloskey, contributor to and
fund-raiser for the party and a contractor whose business with the Federal
government increased greatly. Not far
behind them in the victory parade
were J. David Stern, editor of the city's
only Democratic newspaper, the Philadelphia Record, and his financial
backer, the entrepreneur sagacious,
Albert M. Greenfield, whose salesman-
ship brought the convention to town.

(Below) Democratic National Convention, 1936
(HSP)
(Above) John B. Kelly and Matthew B. McClos-
key, 1936 (HSP)
(Right) Ticket to the Democratic Convention
(HSP)

In 1936 Fortune *stated in an objective, if smart-alecky, look at Philadelphia that "wild horses are loose on
its streets." Two of those horses were
Mayor S. Davis Wilson and Albert
M. Greenfield. Both were changecoats;
Wilson, a Democrat, was elected as a
Republican, and Greenfield, a former
Republican councilman, became a
Democrat. Nobody could control the
individualistic Wilson, and Greenfield
was as elusive as a genie out of his
bottle. Wilson sought condemnation of
the transit system for the city; Greenfield wanted to control it. Wilson
appointed a woman, Georgiana Pope
Yeatman, city architect. In 1937 he
filed suit against the school board's
taxing power. He opposed the renewal
of the sales tax in 1937, and died
suddenly the summer of that year. The
new airport constructed at Hog Island
the mayor named the S. Davis Wilson
Airport; it no longer is. Greenfield
had a school named after him; it still is.*

(Above) Albert M. Greenfield and Mayor S.
Davis Wilson, 1937 (HSP)
(Below) The Municipal Airport, 1929 (HSP)

311   <1930-1945>

Except for a number of well-established trade and craft unions, Philadelphia was basically an open-shop town until the depression hit. Then, as a result of the National Recovery Act, unions, union membership, and union determination blossomed. Since old ways are hard to change, there were more, and eventually more violent, strikes than in many other cities. At the beginning of 1934 the taxi drivers were on strike; a bit later in a bitter election the workers at the Edward G. Budd Company voted in favor of the company union; in midsummer strikers were charged with planning to dynamite the Gulf refinery. The hard-fought Apex Hosiery strike was won by the union. However, it was a pyrrhic victory; the whole local hosiery industry, once the largest in the nation, moved south. When the court ordered the PTC to hire Negro conductors and motormen during the war in 1944, the transit employees walked out. The army was brought in to keep the trolleys on the tracks. There was a flurry of postwar strikes as CIO unions flexed their muscles. Within a period of several months in 1946 the PTC once again, General Electric, tugboat operators, Yale & Towne, Electric Storage Battery, and Reading Railroad all suffered work stoppages. More and more labor leaders grew in stature and influence, especially in the clothing, building, and transportation industries.

(Above) Strikers at the Apex Hosiery Mill, 1937 (HSP)
(Below) Soldiers Guarding Trolleys during the Transit Strike, 1944 (HSP)

Like it or not—and many did not—
the Pennsylvania Railroad continued
to make itself felt. Charles B. Hall, the
railroad's political tool, was the perennial president of City Council. By
building the Suburban Station at Sixteenth and Filbert streets where
commuters came and went and by
making the new Thirtieth Street
Station across the river the center-city
stop for through-trains, the Pennsy
changed the transportation pattern of
the city. Its powerful electric locomotive was put into regular service on
the Philadelphia–New York run in
1933, and with the help of the Public
Works Administration electrification
was extended to Washington two
years later. To meet the tremendous
added demand for power, Philadelphia
Electric installed a huge generator at
its Richmond Station. Vast movements
of troops and munitions flowed over
the tracks during the war. But the crack
Congressional Limited was responsible for the city's worst railroad
accident in modern times; eighty
persons were killed on September 6,
1943, when cars piled up and were
shattered at Frankford Junction. An
explosion of a beneficent kind was the
decision in 1946 to abandon Broad
Street Station and eliminate the
Chinese Wall whose grim brick length
kept development out of Market
Street West.

(Below) The New Electric Locomotive of the
Pennsylvania Railroad, 1933 (HSP)
(Above) *Philadelphia Electric Company's Generator at Richmond Station*, painting by Thorn-
ton Oakley (Philadelphia Electric Company)
(Right) The Wreck of the Congressional Limited
at Frankford Junction, 1943 (HSP)

In the city, as elsewhere during the war, shortages hit; gas, sugar, meat, and heating oil were rationed. In 1943 Sunday pleasure driving was banned; a year later lack of coal caused a brownout. There were some black markets and under-the-table payments for preferential treatment, but illegality was more notorious than widespread. Morale was high. The USO was brought into being as the first philanthropic collaboration by Protestant, Catholic, and Jewish organizations. A Stage Door Canteen for servicemen was opened in the basement of the Academy of Music. Frank Sinatra brought 80,000 persons to Convention Hall in November, 1944, to kick off the War Chest campaign. Volunteer Coast Guardsmen patrolled the waterfront night and day. A civilian defense organization of air-raid wardens and auxiliary firemen and policemen was quickly put together. Air Force Major (later General) Ellwood Quesada charmed dozens of women into manning an around-the-clock air-raid warning center at City Hall. And the Quakers, as in World War I, sent ambulances overseas and handled relief where it was needed. The Philadelphia-based American Friends Service Committee was awarded the Nobel Peace Prize in 1947.

(Above) Gertrude Lawrence in the Stage Door Canteen in the Basement of the Academy of Music, 1943 (HSP)
(Below) Quaker Relief Trucks of the American Friends Service Committee, 1947 (HSP)

While the "Day of Infamy," December 7, 1941, shocked the United States, the country was not unprepared for war. Lend-Lease for the Allies and military prudence had mobilized war industries and men. The draft became effective in October, 1940; almost a quarter of a million Philadelphians registered. When the Japanese attacked Pearl Harbor, recruiting records were broken. In 1940 alone the 35,000-ton battleship Washington was launched from the Navy Yard and the keel laid for the even larger New Jersey, while across the river at New York Ship seaplane tenders were completed and contracts received for cruisers. Baldwin's at Eddystone early in 1941 delivered its first 28-ton tank and was putting out 60-ton juggernauts by December. There were far more sophisticated tools of war needed than had been a generation earlier. Communications equipment was produced by Philco, plastic nose-cones for bombers by Rohm and Haas. Of even more far-reaching importance was the development and construction by J. Prosper Eckert and John W. Mauchly of the first computer, ENIAC, at the University of Pennsylvania's Moore School of Engineering.

(Below) The ENIAC Computer at the Moore School of Engineering, 1944 (University of Pennsylvania Archives)
(Above) Volunteers Crowding the Office of the Army Recruiting Service, 1941 (HSP)
(Right) Laying the Keel of the U. S. S. *Miami* at Cramp's Shipyard, 1941 (Philadelphia Inquirer)

Frequently unnoticed by the many and little touted by the few, the city's stature as an art center grew. The vast museum on the Parkway slowly filled. In 1933 the Orphans' Court, sometimes willing to break a will in the public interest, agreed that the superlative John G. Johnson collection of paintings, rich in early Flemish works, could be moved from his dingy, unsafe house near Broad and Lombard streets to the Philadelphia Museum. The successfully rude Fiske Kimball secured other important collections and attracted interested patrons, although his reverse blandishments did lose the Widener paintings to Washington and added fuel to the foul-mouthed antagonism of Albert C. Barnes. Entry to Barnes' vast assemblage of works by Cezanne, Renoir, and other Impressionists was denied the city's art pundits, but a select few reported on its greatness. Franklin C. Watkins was the Philadelphia "court-painter." Although he won his fame with imaginative subjects, he was most admired in town for his portraits. He was loved as a teacher at the excellent school of the Pennsylvania Academy of the Fine Arts.

(Below) Fiske Kimball, 1931 (Philadelphia Museum of Art)
(Above) *Sturgis [Ingersoll] and Prometheus on Spring Street*, painting by Franklin Watkins (Pennsylvania Academy of the Fine Arts)
(Right) Clothesline Exhibit in Rittenhouse Square, 1940 (HSP)

Never before nor since were central-city department stores so much a part of the life of the people. Even in the depression Wanamaker's, with the prime location in town, from Market to Chestnut streets and Juniper to Thirteenth, was doing $50,000,000 worth of business—at a profit. Old Philadelphians shopped there; hence not-so-old Philadelphians shopped there, too. The eagle in the Grand Court was a magnetic rendezvous. In 1934 in a burst of optimism the trustees of the Wanamaker estate began a skyscraper at the corner of Broad and Chestnut streets. The first two floors were occupied by what was hoped to be a prestigious men's store; it was not successful. Ellis A. Gimbel, one of the original Gimbel brothers, was the most colorful retailer in town. Natty, gregarious, he was known as "Uncle Ellis" to many, including the hundreds of orphans who came to his annual circus party and hundreds of thousands who watched Gimbel's Thanksgiving Day parade. The Strawbridges and Clothiers ran their store in a more Quakerly fashion, but they expanded, too. Lit's and Snellenburg's catered more to the masses. Market Street was, as it had been in the earliest days of the city, Philadelphia's marketplace.

(Above) The Eagle in Wanamaker's, 1937 (HSP)
(Below) Ellis Gimbel and Orphans at the Circus, 1934 (HSP)

1945-1976

"In the exciting decade of reform since the war," the sociologist E. Digby Baltzell wrote in his 1958 study, *Philadelphia Gentlemen,* "life in Philadelphia has changed, but it is still too soon for any objective assessment of the change." He saw the shifting of power from the traditional upper class, but he could not have seen the momentum of the shift which put Philadelphians Reverend Leon Sullivan on the board of directors of General Motors and William T. Coleman in the President's cabinet, and greatly increased the representation of all minority groups on the once exclusive boards of local banks, insurance companies, and cultural institutions. Even prestigious social clubs opened their doors part way.

The "Old Philadelphians" were a reticent lot who loved their city but thought boosterism undignified. Owen Wister described this attitude as the "instinct of disparagement." The "New Philadelphians," during the exciting early days of the urban renaissance, uncovered a reservoir of outspoken pride. Although the excitement has faded, principally through lack of leadership, the reservoir of pride remains. In the fall of 1974, to celebrate the Bicentennial of the First Continental Congress, a million Philadelphians descended upon "America's most historic square mile" to the utter amazement of the promoters of Olde City Sunday. The residents of rehabilitated Society Hill are proud of their neighborhood. So are the settlers farther south in Queen Village. So are the Polish–Americans in Manayunk and the Italian–Americans in deep South Philadelphia, the largely unhyphenated Americans in Chestnut Hill, and the Jews and Negroes in Wynnefield and Mount Airy fighting to maintain integrated communities. Community-based pride thrives. It requires only creative thinking and doing to turn these seeds of purely local enthusiasm into a flowering of citywide revitalization.

When World War II ended there was a feeling of both relief and rededication. Much that was old had been swept away in the cataclysm; the opportunity to build newer and better existed. In 1947 the first assault was launched against the begrimed, outdated structure of Philadelphia's dominant Republican organization. A coalition of labor leaders, some farsighted Democratic politicians, spokesmen for various minority groups, and a number of well-to-do Rooseveltian liberals began to build a political force under the umbrella of the local chapter of the Americans for Democratic Action. They were political ama-

(Facing) Society Hill Towers with Head House Square in Foreground, photograph by Geo. Adams Jones (Office of the City Representative, City of Philadelphia)

teurs, but they had intelligence and enthusiasm, qualities which the regulars of both parties sadly lacked. Richardson Dilworth ran for mayor that year with Joseph S. Clark as his campaign manager. Dilworth lost, but not by as much as Democrats usually did in local Philadelphia elections. It was the first time since the days of Boies Penrose that socially prominent gentlemen openly entered the political arena and stayed there. It was the first time in forty years that a reform movement made any headway.

In 1949 Dilworth was elected city treasurer and Clark city controller. The established pattern of Philadelphia municipal control was broken. Even the Republican City Council recognized the change. It authorized the writing of a new Home Rule City Charter. Largely the product of the able legal mind of Abraham L. Freedman, the instrument as framed gave the mayor, rather than as previously the Council, superior power in the municipal government, set up representative and competent nominating committees for various city boards, limited the political activity of some officeholders, and in general tried to create a framework which would result in decent, honest, and efficient administration.

"A new broom!" "Throw the bums out!" The citizens of Philadelphia approved the new charter in the fall of 1951. At the same time they elected Clark mayor by a plurality of 124,000, Dilworth district attorney, and a supporting slate of men and—precedent-setting—one woman to the City Council. The Clark administration was the closest

(Above) Joseph S. Clark and Richardson Dilworth, 1962 (Philadelphia Inquirer)

thing the city has seen to the virtue of the fabled Roman Republic which the Founding Fathers so hoped the nation would emulate. Graft was outlawed. The rehabilitation of the city was begun. Concern for education, recreation, and health became public policy. Appointments were made on the basis of competence. It seemed like the return of the Golden Age.

With the expert aid of handsome, white-haired James A. Finnegan, president of the City Council and chairman of the City Democratic Committee, Clark was able to sail through political channels without foundering on the rock of patronage. Finnegan understood and appreciated Clark's Sir Galahad policy: "My strength is as the strength of ten because my heart is pure." He was, however, not able to convince the not-so-pure Democratic ward leaders that what was good for Clark was good for the organization. The thin edge of hostility between the amateurs and the professionals widened. Eventually, Finnegan was persuaded by the pressure for patronage to resign as chairman of the party. The descent from the heights of integrity was gradual, but it began and within a decade accelerated.

In 1955, after Clark announced his candidacy for the United States Senate, Dilworth ran for and won the mayoralty by a substantial majority. During his administration the progressive drive of the reform movement continued. The old city around Independence Hall and on Society Hill began to emerge from the limbo of shabby neglect. The Chinese Wall came tumbling down and the Penn Center complex

(Above) Frank L. Rizzo as Police Commissioner, 1968 (Evening Bulletin)

started to rise. The much-needed Municipal Services Building was put up in Raeburn Plaza across from City Hall. Under the new charter a Board of Trade and Conventions came into being to hard-sell Philadelphia (unheard of!). Under its direction vast improvements were made to the old, dusty Commercial Museum and Convention Hall. These became the nucleus of the Civic Center with its great exhibition hall completed in 1967. Everywhere there was a feeling of onward and upward.

The momentum of physical progress carried on even after Dilworth resigned in 1962, half-way through his second term, to run unsuccessfully for governor. But the psyche of the city suffered a trauma. James H. J. Tate, the president of City Council, by law succeeded him. The *Philadelphia Inquirer* not long ago wrote concerning patronage: "Traditionally in Philadelphia a politician's ability to promise and deliver jobs on the public payroll furnishes important vote-getting leverage in the political wards." It was also important to see that friends and supporters were awarded lucrative municipal contracts or were given the benefit of advantageous zoning variances. Instead of the old Vare Republican machine, there was a Democratic steamroller kept well-oiled by contributions obtained by the party's treasurer, the trucking magnate James P. Clark, and his successors, and managed by astute chairmen such as Congressman William S. Green. In democratic America and Democratic Philadelphia Green was even able to hand down his Congress seat to his son. The city had become a Democratic stronghold. Bickering within the party changed the actors, not the scenario.

As evidence that both sides of the cloth had the same texture, Mayor Tate's police commissioner Frank L. Rizzo, duly anointed and elected as his successor, turned on his sponsor and later on the chairman of the City Democratic Committee. A maverick Democrat who supported Nixon, Rizzo campaigned as "a tough cop." He promised law and order, no increase in taxes, and a nonpolitical regime. Crime has not decreased; figures have been shown to be subject to manipulation. Taxes have not been increased across the board; services have been curtailed as a result. Politics is still the name of the game. There is a rough-hewn, unsophisticated charm about the former police officer—whose brother, incidentally, is fire commissioner—which has won the allegiance of municipal workers, the hard-hat unions, Italo-

Americans, and thousands who have confidence in the ability of brawn to accomplish what brains have not been able to. Rizzo soundly trounced the party's lack-luster nominee in the Democratic primary in May, 1975, and reigns supreme.

During the 1960s, Philadelphia, as did all other urban areas, underwent the travail of social and economic upheaval. There was an upperclass return to center city in Society Hill and in new high-rise apartments, including a cluster of architecturally mediocre buildings on both sides of the Parkway. There was, however, a far greater flight of the middle class to the suburbs. The black population pushed out from the old-time ghettos and spread north and west to the city limits where prices, zoning, and prejudice stopped them for the time being. Yet, the hope of the future lay with upward-mobile black families whose wage-earners were employed in banks, insurance companies, law offices, and government agencies at all levels, now settled in Wynnefield, Germantown, Mount Airy, Queen Village, and Fairmount.

In many of the federally funded housing developments and in blocks of decaying houses in North and West Philadelphia poverty still resides with crime, drugs, and gang warfare. During the hot summers of the late 1960s the Philadelphia ghettos may have seethed but a single destructive riot was contained along Columbia Avenue and the lid never blew off as it did in Watts and Newark. The problem of giving work, opportunity, and hope to those without them has not been solved, although the rise of a substantial well-to-do black community has been the result of only half a generation's effort.

As a result of shifting demography, more schools at all levels have become predominately or increasingly black. Interracial tension on the streets and gangs on their own turf have complicated the once direct art of educating children. Some strong-minded men, such as the late Marcus Foster at Gratz High School, were able to inspire their charges. Philadelphia led the nation in innovative experiments, like the out-of-the-school-building classes in the cultural institutions on the Parkway. Some rigid parents and teachers were hostile to change. The imaginative head of the school system, Mark Shedd, drew the fire of the mayor and conservative members of the school board and was forced out in spite of the support he received from the old crusader Richardson Dilworth, president of the board. Later another able

superintendent, Matthew Costanzo, ran into political difficulties but at first won out thanks to the support and active lobbying by interested parents. Eventually, politics felled him, too.

A dark cloud floats on the horizon. One of the main programs of the Catholic diocese during the three-decade era of Denis Cardinal Dougherty, from 1920, was the expansion of a parochial school system, which became the largest of its kind in the country. In recent years, with a diminishing supply of nuns and priests to teach at a nominal cost, the financial underpinning of the schools has become shaky and the exodus of white Catholic families from neighborhoods into which blacks have moved has reduced attendance. If the parochial schools cannot get government help, a sudden additional burden may be thrust upon the public schools already themselves on thin ice financially. In better shape are the suburban public schools and the prestigious private schools, many of them Quaker-founded, which serve the entire area. They, by virtue of their more privileged student body, offer better educational opportunities, but they have survived so far partly from the fear of city-street violence on the part of parents able to afford their high tuitions.

An area still with pride and less heralded problems is the vast Northeast, a post-World-War-II development of street after street of row houses, monotonous in the extreme, built chiefly by the Kormans and A. P. Orleans, where lives the city's largest concentration of Jewish families. In it on Cottman Street is one of the largest shopping centers in all of metropolitan Philadelphia. The growth of these centers has threatened the inner city, but the rebirth of the historic area and the creeping up-grading of the old mercantile Rialto, Market Street, west from Independence Mall will shift the balance of business. When Edmund Bacon's vision of Market Street East, with its new department stores, underground mall, and convenient connection of the lines of the Reading and Penn Central railroads, comes into being, a magnet will have been created to draw people back to the hub.

The taking over of local industries by national concerns and the flight of corporation headquarters from the city in the past quarter century did dampen Philadelphia's commercial spirits. The Chamber of Commerce was almost a silent mourner. Philco, a radio and television manufacturing company, was assimilated into the Ford Motor empire. The *Philadelphia Inquirer* became a link in the Knight newspaper chain, but, in this case, for the better. Even the prestigious erstwhile banking, now brokerage, house of Drexel is by merger the New York firm of Drexel Burnham & Co., with a branch office in town. One oil giant, Atlantic Richfield, turned its former main office on Broad Street over to the Philadelphia College of Art and moved to New York; another, the Pew's Sun Oil Company, transported its administrative heart out of the city to the Main Line. With N. W. Ayer's former president the Philadelphia booster Harry A. Batten removed from the scene, the largest advertising firm in town decamped.

The immediate past seems discouraging to many Philadelphians who thought that a share in the Pennsylvania Railroad was better than a government bond. Penn Central went under. Horn and Hardart, an Irish Catholic fiefdom, went into bankruptcy, but the nation's major dispenser of meals by hand and through machines, ARA, settled in town. Daroffs overexpanded and failed, but the promise of a center of the clothing industry in a redeveloped section north of Race Street is a creative effort which may yet challenge New York's suit-and-cloak primacy. The city's banks, long a drag on the city's progress, have become the bellwethers of aggressive promotion and have even expanded internationally. The Philadelphia Industrial Development Corporation, an arm of the municipal government, by making available attractive sites kept old industries from moving out of the city and brought new ones in. The diversity of Philadelphia's manufactures and commerce has been its strength and is still a powerful attraction.

In spite of the dismal failure of successive official Bicentennial corporations to get things moving, the city will attract millions of Americans in 1976. History, the cultural institutions, the beauty of the Schuylkill, and the relaxed ambiance of Philadelphia are trump cards in the tourist game. The annual Festival of the Greater Philadelphia Cultural Alliance, combining the resources of history, science, and the arts, is turning Quaker gray into rainbow hues. The head of a British corporation was recently quoted by the vigorous tabloid *Philadelphia Daily News* as saying, "I had expected to see a quaint old city living on its own past, but all those new buildings and so much construction! Philadelphia has a vitality like few cities I have seen in North America." He was charmed as are most visitors with the pace, scale, and livability of the town. "Have you people intentionally kept Philadelphia a secret? Very odd," he concluded.

The Philadelphia Renaissance
started in 1947 with a Better Philadelphia Exhibition. Huge maps and
models by Edmund Bacon, director of
the City Planning Commission, showed
what could be done to make the city
a more pleasant, more livable place.
Albert M. Greenfield, the chairman of
the Commission, got the necessary
political and financal backing. But it
took a congeries of governmental and
private agencies to get things moving.
In 1948 the Planning Commission
certified the rehabilitation of an area
which included the tract sold by Penn
to the Free Society of Traders and
which, greatly expanded, has become
known as Society Hill. The Redevelopment Authority, created two years
earlier, then took over to acquire land
and discover developers. In 1956
the Old Philadelphia Development
Corporation, a pressure and support
group of businessmen with Harry A.
Batten of the advertising firm of N. W.
Ayer as its chief promoter, came into
being to advise and to expedite. The
first extensive project was the demolition of the shabby Dock Street
markets and their reinstallation in
1959 in the new, modern Food Distribution Center in South Philadelphia.
Where the markets had been, town
houses and three multistory apartment
buildings, Society Hill Towers, designed by I. M. Pei rose in 1962-64.
By then, too, a start had been made by
private individuals to bring back
the charm and the dignity of the old
red-brick city.

More eighteenth-century houses and public buildings in Philadelphia have survived than anywhere else in the country. Until the 1950s they could hardly be recognized in the squalid and neglected neighborhood where they stood. The metamorphosis into elegance of court and alley slums, of boarding houses scarred with fire-escapes and of town dwellings defaced by incongruous store fronts took many years and millions of private and public dollars. The process is continuous and spreading. One by one old houses have been restored to their original appearance under the critical eyes of the Redevelopment Authority and the Historical Commission. Where no salvage was possible new colonial or attractive modern houses were put up. Trees have been planted, walkways cut through, and small parks dotted about. From Front Street to Seventh and from Locust to South a new residential section has been created. Restaurants and shops sprang up along Second Street south of Pine on either side of the handsome Head House with its sheds trailing behind it. On South Street bold young people revived derelict structures and brought a new community into being around a cluster of unusual stores. Newly married couples, emigrants from suburbia, and confirmed city-dwellers have turned an ugly urban duckling into an attractive residential area.

(Facing, below left) Albert M. Greenfield, Chairman of the Planning Commission, and James M. Symes, President of the Pennsylvania Railroad, at the Panorama of the Redevelopment Authority, photograph by Jules Schick, 1947 (Philadelphia City Planning Commission)
(Facing, above) View of the Old City from Sixth Street (Penn Mutual Life Insurance Company)
(Facing, middle) Dock Street Markets, 1920 (HSP)
(Facing, below right) Food Distribution Center, photograph by Lawrence S. Williams, Inc. (Philadelphia Redevelopment Authority)
(Above left) New House and Old House on Delancey Street (Philadelphia Redevelopment Authority)
(Above right) Shops on Head House Square, photograph by Geo. Adams Jones (Office of the City Representative, City of Philadelphia)
(Middle) Delancey Park, photograph by Lawrence S. Williams, Inc. (Philadelphia City Planning Commission)
(Below) Abercrombie House, 270 South Second Street before Restoration, 1963, and Restored as the Perelman Antique Toy Museum, 1968 (Philadelphia Redevelopment Authority)

Almost unnoticed in the churning of
the times, a wistful, nostalgic, almost
religious feeling had arisen for the
history of our nation. Millions of Americans came to Independence Hall
annually not only to see the Liberty
Bell but to touch it in a kind of tactile
return to past virtues. Judge Edwin
O. Lewis had long urged that something be done to enhance the setting
of the country's most historic building.
In 1951 Independence National Historical Park was established by the
National Park Service to restore Independence Hall and its satellite structures and to fashion a park with grass,
trees and restored or reconstructed
historic buildings. The Second Bank of
the United States is now a museum,
and the Merchants' Exchange, Bishop
White's house, the street-front of
Franklin Court and other sites redolent
with the past have been restored.
Land was ceded to the American Philosophical Society to build its library
on the Fifth Street site with the façade
of old Library Hall. The Pennsylvania
Horticultural Society was given quarters on Walnut Street and there has
planted an eighteenth-century garden.
Walkways tie in old churches and the
homes of Society Hill to the Independence Hall area giving the whole
a seductive ambiance of the old city.

(Above) Independence Hall from the Square
(Independence National Historical Park)
(Below) Colonial Garden of the Horticultural
Society on Walnut Street, photograph by Carole
Bell (Pennsylvania Horticultural Society)

Independence Mall has created a new urban focal point. To complement the national park which extended east and south of Independence Hall, the Commonwealth of Pennsylvania in 1953 began work on a mall. A welter of old buildings and lofts was cleared away. Trees, promenades, arcades, a large fountain, and an underground parking garage now run between Fifth and Sixth streets from Chestnut Street to the approaches of the Benjamin Franklin Bridge. Lining the parklike strip are the handsome modern buildings of Rohm and Haas, Group W Television, the Philadelphia National Bank, the United States Mint, and the Federal Court House. The Mall has become the place where crowds gather to listen to music, buy at a flea market, and celebrate such events as the Stanley Cup victory of the Flyers and the Olde City Sunday. The effects of the upgrading of the area have made themselves felt in new construction, particularly west on Market Street where a dramatic rebuilding of the city's great department store center is underway.

(Above) View North from Chestnut Street before Redevelopment, photograph by Lawrence S. Williams, Inc., 1952 (Philadelphia City Planning Commission)
(Below) View North from Chestnut with the Mall Completed (Penn Mutual Life Insurance Company)

It took dynamite to unhinge the
conservative arches of the Pennsylvania Railroad's Chinese Wall. Inside
the blind brick stretch between Market
and Filbert streets the Pennsy's tracks
ran to its main lines north, west, and
south to Broad Street Station. In the
days of sleeping cars it was a great,
if cavernous, train shed. But the
dynamite was like the breath of a genie.
Where the station and tracks had been
rose the towers of Penn Center, not
architecturally distinguished, but a vast
change for the better. A new clean
cluster of buildings on Market Street
and John F. Kennedy Boulevard pulled
the center of the city's business life
westward once again in Philadelphia's
history. From the twin-peaked First
Pennsylvania–Arco Building at 1500
Market Street, zigzagging through
the numbered Penn Center skyscrapers,
over to the Sheraton Hotel, coming
back to the IBM Building and west to
the Keystone Automobile–AAA, there
is a constant flow of people, an air of
something-doing.

(Below) Penn Center Esplanade View Toward
City Hall, photograph by Geo. Adams Jones
(Office of the City Representative)
(Above) View of the Pennsylvania Railroad
Tracks West from City Hall, photograph by
Lawrence S. Williams, Inc., 1950 (Philadelphia
City Planning Commission)
(Right) View West up Market Street from City
Hall, photograph by James Joern, 1974 (James
Joern)

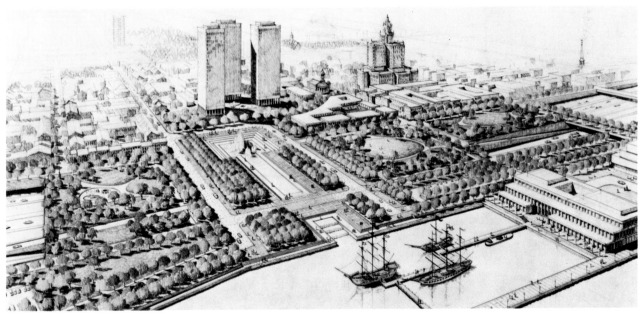

The Port of Philadelphia benefited from the postwar revitalization. Its development became a focal point of interstate cooperation through Penjerdel and the Delaware River Port Authority. As more Philadelphians moved back to the original city along the Delaware River or across it to the Cherry Hill development in New Jersey, their consciousness of bustling river traffic has grown. Freighters bring steel *down* from Morrisville; tankers unload oil at the biggest refinery complex on the East Coast; containerized cargos come by truck or train to the Packer Avenue Marine Terminal, and other bulk shipments are promised for the new Tioga facilities. As The Times of London noted, Philadelphia is, in terms of tonnage, "the third largest port grouping in the world." The recently opened Maritime Museum and the Penn's Landing project of restaurants, shops, offices, apartments, parks, marinas, and riverside promenades will bring more Philadelphians back to the sights and sounds of ships large and small.

(Above) Ships on the Delaware River North of the Benjamin Franklin Bridge, photograph by Joseph Nettis (Joseph Nettis)
(Below) Plan of the Delaware River Waterfront at Locust Street, photograph by Lawrence S. Williams, Inc. (Philadelphia City Planning Commission)

A city depends on its traffic flow as a heart depends on the circulation of blood. Few large cities in the United States have so easy, quick, and comparatively painless a network of roads, rails, and bus routes as those which bring people in and out, through and around Philadelphia. The scenic Schuylkill Expressway, which has regularly exceeded its planned capacity since its completion in 1959, has, nevertheless, brought the Main Line and other areas to the northwest within half an hour of center city, rush hours and accidents excepted. Apartment houses, office buildings, and shopping centers on both sides of City Line Avenue owe their existence to the Expressway, as does the huge business and industrial development at King of Prussia deep in Montgomery County. The local trains of the Penn Central, the subject of many Philadelphia jokes, and the Reading, both now part of the Southeastern Pennsylvania Transportation Authority (SEPTA), are among the most convenient commuter webs of any American urban area. Buses, subways, and a few remaining trolleys are also tied into the SEPTA system which is joined to a high-speed line across the Delaware serving the New Jersey satellite communities. Eventually the Delaware Expressway, the much-delayed Philadelphia link of I-95, will add a north–south strand. The airport, still in the process of improvement, is only twenty minutes by car from the center of town, one of the most convenient urban air terminals in the nation.

(Above, left) Schuylkill Expressway, photograph by Joseph Nettis (Joseph Nettis)
(Below, left) Development at King of Prussia Highway Interchange, 1970 (Philadelphia Inquirer)
(Right) Unfinished Delaware Expressway South from Market Street, photograph by Alexander McCaughey, 1970 (Philadelphia Inquirer)

A real-estate advertisement reads: "One of the finest estates on the Main Line; five acres of rolling lawns, stream and old trees surround a gracious residence half a century old." It could have been in Gladwyne or Gwynedd, Chestnut Hill or Bryn Mawr. The suburbs of Philadelphia, including the old suburbs within the city limits, are its crown jewels, and like some crown jewels, a number of them have been broken up and sold. No large American city, and few anywhere else in the world, have tree-lined roads and country living so close—less than an hour, and much less in some locations, by train or automobile—to center city.

After World War II many large estates were subdivided. Split-level ranch houses became common along the more accessible streets, and huge apartment buildings rose near railroad stations and along main arteries. Off the beaten track there was still green privacy and, in a sense, distinction. The hunt clubs still flourish in Chester County; golf clubs have edged their way farther and farther out as their acres became too valuable for mere sport. In the early spring when the dogwoods and azaleas are in bloom, the charm of the beyond-the-pavements Philadelphia is at its best.

(Above) House on Mill Road, Bryn Mawr (Roach Brothers, Realtors)
(Below) Mr. Stewart's Cheshire Foxhounds (A. James Purring)

His start in Philadelphia was not auspicious. In 1926 Louis I. Kahn was the chief of design for the ill-fated Sesqui-Centennial Exposition. It took some years until the world caught up with his architectural ideas, poetry and philosophy expressed in steel and stone. By midcentury Kahn was an internationally recognized master. The Richards Medical Buildings at the University of Pennsylvania, where he became professor of architecture in 1957, is his major local work, but his influence as a teacher was widespread. The Salk Institute at La Jolla, an art museum in Fort Worth, a government complex at Dacca, the Mellon Gallery at Yale, and a library at Phillips Exeter Academy made his reputation such that Louis Kahn may well have been the most famous Philadelphian of his day. He died on his way home from India in 1974.

(Above) Louis Kahn and the Richards Medical Research Buildings at the University of Pennsylvania, photograph by John Condax, 1973 (John Condax)

The Philadelphia Orchestra's invitation to tour the People's Republic of China merely underlined its stature, with Eugene Ormandy as conductor, as one of the finest symphony orchestras in the world. The city continues to live up to its rich heritage in the performing arts. The success of the summer concerts in Robin Hood Dell has stimulated the construction of a new, larger, and all-weather amphitheater. Long used by Broadway producers as a tryout town, Philadelphia, with the restoration and revival of the Walnut Street Theater, the aggressive showmanship of Moe Septee's Forum, the courage and dedication of a host of small nonprofit enterprises, has become a center of drama, dance, and innovative productions. In ten short years the **Pennsylvania Ballet** has become a corps of professionally recognized excellence, a tribute to the city's receptivity, as in turn the Ballet adds to the city's cultural reputation. And street theater is now regularly offered during the summer; historical vignettes in the area of Independence Hall and skits and interludes throughout the town are truly theater for the people. Philadelphians remember that from its streets came the incomparable Marian Anderson, Mario Lanza, and such popular entertainers as Fabian and Chubby Checker.

(Above) Eugene Ormandy and the Philadelphia Orchestra on the Chinese Wall, photograph by Kenneth Scutt, 1973 (Philadelphia Orchestra; color separation courtesy of *OnStage* Magazine)
(Below, left) Fabian on the Steps of His Home in South Philadelphia, 1959 (Philadelphia Inquirer)
(Below, middle) Marian Anderson at the Academy of Music, 1963 (Philadelphia Inquirer)
(Below, right) Street Theater (Frank C. P. McGlinn)

First there rose the Municipal Stadium, renamed for John F. Kennedy, where the Army–Navy game has been traditionally played, then the indoor Spectrum, and finally Veterans Stadium, the city's most expensive tribute to its citizens' love affair with sports. The Phillies play in the new stadium, as oldtimers recall the hit-rich bat of Richie Ashburn and the strong arm of Robin Roberts and the "Whiz Kids" of 1950 who won the National League pennant in now decayed Shibe Park. In the fall the Eagles cavort on the astroturf, attracting huge crowds to football's home games, although since the championship year of 1960 the team's owners have been more colorful than its players. One of the all-time "greats" of basketball, "Wilt the Stilt" Chamberlain, grew up in town—he really grew—and began his professional career with the 76ers, who in 1967 with the help of Wilt won the National Basketball Association's Eastern Division playoff. Still fresh is the saga of the local-boy-who-made-good, Joe Frazier, who won the heavyweight championship of the world by decisively beating Muhammed Ali in March, 1971. Nothing, however, in the history of Philadelphia sport has matched the excitement of the Flyers' Stanley Cup victories in 1974 and 1975. They were the roughest, toughest hockey players ever and their Philadelphia fans loved every bone-shaking crack they gave or took. When they won, the fans took over the city in a wild parade.

(Above) John F. Kennedy Stadium, Spectrum, and Veterans Stadium (Office of the City Representative, City of Philadelphia)

(Middle, left) Wilt Chamberlain after the 76ers Victory in the National Basketball Association's Eastern Division Playoff Series, 1967 (Philadelphia Inquirer)

(Middle, right) Joe Frazier Defeating Muhammed Ali, 1971 (UPI)

(Below) Crowds Celebrating the Flyers' Stanley Cup Victory in the Mall, 1974, photograph by Geo. Adams Jones (Office of the City Representative, City of Philadelphia)

In a crescendo from the time of the returned GIs of World War II, thousands of young men and women from all ways of life joined the privileged in college classrooms. As elsewhere in the nation, Philadelphia saw an expansion of the physical plants and academic faculties of its institutions of higher learning. The University of Pennsylvania shed many of its withered leaves of ivy and burgeoned under the administration of the physicist Gaylord Harnwell. In its area a whole University City came into being, encompassing Pennsylvania, Drexel, and an imaginative cluster of commercial research facilities, the Science Center. With the elevated tracks removed Market Street looks open, fresh, and attractive. Equally dramatic has been the transformation of Temple University from a little-esteemed institution into a major academic complex stretching north, south, and east from its hub at Broad Street and Montgomery Avenue with subsidiary facilities at Ambler and in center city. It is now one of Pennsylvania's state universities. Both Penn and Temple border black ghettos and have tried to walk the tightrope of expansion and neighborliness. As a kind of safety valve for the less academically inclined, the state in 1964 established a Community College in Philadelphia offering two-year courses, many with emphasis on skills.

(Above) View of the University of Pennsylvania, photograph by Elston Hillman, 1973 (News Bureau, University of Pennsylvania)
(Below) Bell Tower at Temple University, photograph by Bob Adler (Temple Times)

The availability of government funds which made possible the expansion of colleges and universities also enabled the many hospitals and the five medical schools of the city to grow. Philadelphia has one of the greatest concentrations of medical facilities in the world. At the University of Pennsylvania, the hospital and school were helped by the reputation of the surgeon I. S. Ravdin who conducted a well-publicized operation on President Eisenhower. More evident on the city scene has been the spread of the venerable Pennsylvania Hospital and the renamed Thomas Jefferson University and Hospttal which have razed old buildings from Walnut Street to Pine and from Eleventh to Seventh and erected new ones to meet their needs. A leading teacher and surgeon at Jefferson was Dr. John H. Gibbon, Jr., whose invention of the heart–lung machine permitted the life-saving advance of open heart surgery. The other schools, Temple, Hahnemann, and the Medical College of Pennsylvania, put up new hospital wings, staff residences, research buildings, and clinics. Philadelphia retains its traditional position as a center of medical science, and its major drug firms, Merck Sharpe and Dohme and SmithKline Corporation, still flourish. It is also a major medical publishing center which achieved notoriety when the staid firm of W. B. Saunders and Company found itself the embarrassed publisher of a bestseller, Dr. Alfred C. Kinsey's Sexual Behavior in the Human Male.

(Above) Dr. and Mrs. John H. Gibbon, Jr. and the Heart-Lung Machine, 1960 (Philadelphia Inquirer)

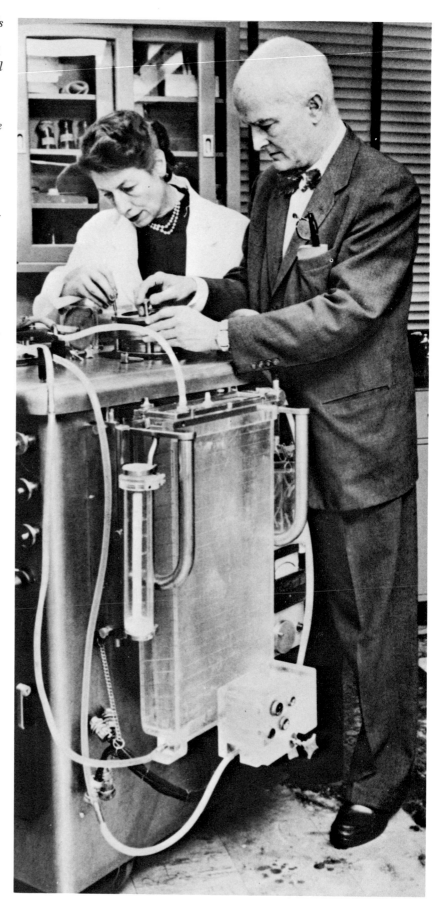

Art has moved out of the exhibition halls of museums. A bequest from Ellen Samuel has enlivened the banks of the Schuylkill with sculpture. In 1958 a city ordinance was passed requiring developers of Redevelopment Authority land to spend one percent of a project's total construction cost on sculpture, murals, fountains, or other forms of art. The result has been a blossoming of the unusual and sometimes the exciting in and around new buildings. Possibly the most dynamic of the outdoor productions is Leonard Baskin's stark, moving group in front of the Pei Towers, but the level of quality, judged by modernists, has been high. There have been conflicts of opinion. Mayor Rizzo did not like the free-form sculpture by Jacques Lipchitz destined for the Municipal Services Building; the late Sturgis Ingersoll did. It is not yet in place, but the more representational athletic figures of Joseph Brown at the Veterans Stadium are. Beyond the realm of "Fine Arts," painting has begun to brighten blank walls and streets. Perhaps, to the amazement of Philadelphians, the Renaissance, essentially a city-based movement, may be on its twentieth-century American way.

(Below) Copernicus Monument by Dudley Talcott, Gift of Polish Americans of Philadelphia, photograph by Bernie Cleff (Bernie Cleff)
(Above) Impala Fountain, sculpture by Henry Mitchell at the Philadelphia Zoo, photograph by Franklin Williamson (Zoological Society of Philadelphia)
(Right) Portraits over Graffiti, 544-554 South Fifty-third Street (Philadelphia Redevelopment Authority)

From the 1950s on, the balls of wreckers' cranes leveled thousands of substandard houses, chiefly in areas inhabited by poor blacks. Early in the history of federal-subsidized public housing Philadelphia learned that high-rise apartment buildings quickly became vertical slums. Some were built, but the preponderance of the construction for persons with low incomes has been two and three story homes which maintain the city's low-profile, residential appearance. Playgrounds, parking lots, and bits of greenery were created where solid rows of old houses had been, and at Broad and Master streets Progress Plaza, a black-managed shopping center, was carved out. The federal government, the city, private agencies, and churches have all contributed to redevelopment projects covering block after block west of Ninth Street between Diamond and Girard Avenue, in sections of Nicetown and Germantown and scattered through West Philadelphia. Elsewhere houses have been rehabilitated, and in 1973 a new Homestead Ordinance enabled those who would fix up dilapidated city-owned homes to buy them at bargain rates. Tens of thousands of persons still live in decaying neighborhoods. Progress in bettering their lot is slow, but it is continuous.

(Above) Houses at 3202-3218 Mantua Avenue before Redevelopment of Site, 1971 (Philadelphia Redevelopment Authority)
(Middle) Harrison Plaza at Tenth and Thompson Streets, 1967 (Philadelphia Redevelopment Authority)
(Below) Opening at Progress Plaza at Broad and Jefferson Streets, 1968 (Philadelphia Redevelopment Authority)

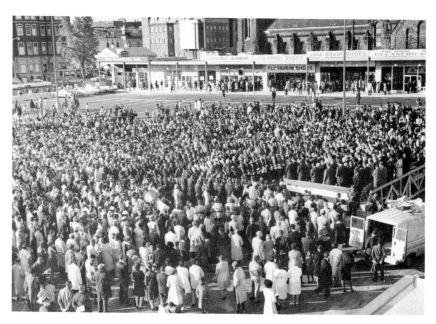

Although no Franklin has come along to become the new symbol of the city, other Philadelphians have in their diverse ways made their mark. Franklinian in his direct approach, physical build, humor, and ability to effect creative compromises was George W. Taylor, professor at the Wharton School and the most famous of American labor arbitrators. From the days of Franklin Roosevelt until his death in 1973, Taylor was called in to advise every president on labor matters and in many instances to resolve what no one else could. He brought to the bargaining board his unique acceptance by both industry and labor. Everybody loved Grace Kelly, too. When the classically beautiful daughter of the rowing hero, Democratic politician, and brickmaker John B. Kelly went to Hollywood, became a star, and won an Academy Award in 1954, Philadelphians were proud that one of theirs made it big. Two years later when Grace Kelly married Rainier III of Monaco and became a princess, a real-life Philadelphia fairy tale was made. For Walter H. Annenberg, former owner of the Philadelphia Inquirer, large contributor to the Republican Party and son of a Russian Jewish immigrant, to serve with honor, after a bad start, as the American ambassador at the Court of St. James was something of a fairy tale, too.

(Above) George W. Taylor Overseeing Election at United Pants and Overall Company, 1934 (HSP)
(Below) Grace Kelly on the Eve of her Marriage, 1956 (Philadelphia Inquirer)

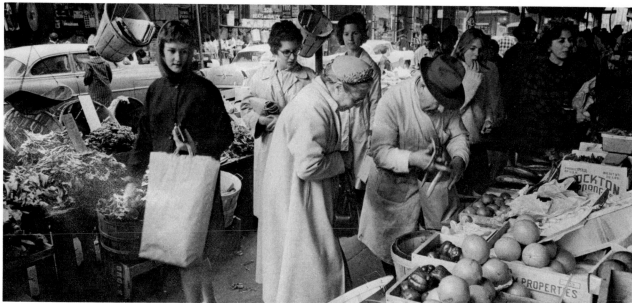

Good food was something Philadelphians ate privately in their homes and their clubs: pasta in South Philadelphia, roast beef and Yorkshire pudding on the Main Line, terrapin at the Philadelphia Club, and crab Lorenzo at the Locust Club. Food in the raw was always excellent. The Reading Terminal Market, now greatly contracted, still offers Margerum's meats, the best fresh fish and up-country sausages and apple butter. The Italian market along Ninth Street between Washington Avenue and Christian Street vividly displays fruits and vegetables, unusual herbs and cheeses. In Philadelphia, "the city of homes," eating out has not been a tradition. With the revival of center city, however, new restaurants have sprung up and prospered. The standard of gourmet dining has risen dramatically; the four-star restaurants, Le Bec Fin and La Panetière, are expensive and crowded. With all things Chinese in the ascendant, Tenth and Race streets has become a busy center where food is no longer Chinese–American but tangy Mandarin and spicy Szechwan. Philadelphia hoagies and hot pretzels with mustard are famous; its ice cream can't be beat.

(Above) Celebration of the Chinese New Year on Race Street near Ninth (Office of the City Representative, City of Philadelphia)
(Below) Italian Market on Ninth Street, photograph by Joseph Nettis (Joseph Nettis)

Whereas outpourings of people have always been caused by occasions such as armistices and strikes and demonstrations against war or for women, certain Philadelphia mass events have become regular and annual. Inaugurated in 1970, Super Sunday early in October has attracted hundreds of thousands to the institutions along the Parkway and the street fair around Logan Circle. The Mummers continue to parade up Broad Street, welcoming the New Year with fabulous costumes and string bands. Gimbel's Thanksgiving Day parade is as traditional as

turkey. There are parades celebrating Pulaski Day, St. Patrick's Day, Columbus Day, Martin Luther King Day, Puerto Rican Festival Week, and Israel Independence Day; they are expressions of ethnic pride and provide officials and candidates for political office a chance to be seen and heard. Appealing to all, the flower show of the Pennsylvania Horticultural Society, one of the finest in the world, fills the Civic Center with visitors and extraordinary blooms. The Academy Ball, instituted by Stuart H. Louchheim to repair and refurbish the century-old Academy of

Music, has become the city's most glittering gala for those eminent by birth, profession, or business, quite eclipsing the old, exclusive Assembly. Philadelphia hums with public parties.

(Above) Super Sunday at Logan Circle, photograph by Joseph Simon Studios, 1973 (Joseph Simon Studios)
(Overleaf) Philadelphia Mummers Preparing to Parade, photograph by James Joern (James Joern)

INDEX

347

SEAL OF PHILADELPHIA
COUNTY, 1683

Seal of Philadelphia
City, 1683